KING ARTHUR

Introduction

Britain and work forwards so that we can see all the contemporary evidence as it appears. It must be remembered that absence of evidence is not evidence of absence, but nor must we forget that there is not a single contemporary record, either from Britain or the Western Empire, that mention Arthur. Given the plethora of books and competing theories, the intention is to approach it in a new and hopefully useful way.

I will attempt to treat the material in a scientific way and conduct a proper historical investigation. A good example, given the subject of Arthur, is the saying 'there is no smoke without fire'; there is indeed plenty of smoke with this particular 'fire', especially from the Middle Ages, several hundred years after Arthur is supposed to have lived. Many point to all the legends and Welsh poems and claim there has to be something to it. However this approach is flawed historically and scientifically; therefore, I intend to be rigorous with the evidence and we may have to be brutal with speculation and hearsay. We will be focusing on original texts and contemporary evidence; later stories and legends written hundreds of years later cannot possibly have the same weight.

In a criminal investigation the police will collect evidence and then the CPS will decide whether to proceed on the basis that it is in the public interest and there is sufficient evidence. I would hope in our case there is still an interest. As to the evidence, I will attempt to present it in a slightly different way to some of the previous works. It will not start with a detailed investigation of stories written in the Middle Ages and then work backwards looking for links; rather, the evidence will be presented in a chronological order. This will mean it may take some time until we reach any references to Arthur at all. I would ask you to bear with this approach as the contemporary historical accounts are crucial in getting a clear picture of context.

Having discussed how we will go about the task, it would be useful to set out the order. A very brief outline of both the legend and the historical setting will be laid out below to aid understanding of what we are working towards and from where we should start our investigation. I will lay out the historical evidence starting from near the end of Roman Britain. That way one can see the body of evidence, or absence or evidence, as it builds. It also places the stories in their correct place: when they were written in the historical record, rather than placing them in the time about which they are written. As many of the stories come at the end of our chronology we will then investigate these legends. Finally we will then investigate

King Arthur: Man or Myth?

some of theories resulting from these legends and look at some specific proposals for the figure of Arthur. Hopefully, in conclusion, we may end with a list of things we can say are supported by the evidence, and on the other end of the spectrum theories, totally unsupported. In between these two extremes there may be suggestions as to what further evidence would be useful and areas worth prioritising in the search for truth.

Before we start we need very briefly to cover two important topics and list some of the major questions that require answering. First: what do we mean by King Arthur? Second: what is the historical setting and background both before and during the period in question? The historical references are quite sparse. What people imagine when they hear King Arthur is the legend created by mainly French authors in the Middle Ages, after an enormously successful book of that time by Geoffrey of Monmouth in 1138. However, what most people are unaware of is that a lot of the story we associate with Arthur, like the Round Table, were added after Geoffrey's book. In addition, a large part of that first story includes the invasion of the Continent and battles against the Romans. This important part is often ignored, but the connection with Gaul and the wider Roman Empire is vital in understanding this period.

Arthur is mentioned in none of the contemporary records at all. There are, however, the following tantalising references from later periods:

> Y Gododdin: a poem reportedly by the sixth-century poet Aneirin about a battle near Catraeth around AD 600 which mentions a warrior who, although brave, 'is no Arthur'. This only survives in a thirteenth-century manuscript.
>
> Poems attributed to Taliesin, who also from the sixth century but thought to be recorded in the eighth to twelfth centuries.
>
> AD 830 *Historia Brittonum* written by a Welsh monk Nennius, describing Arthur as a 'dux bellorum' (leader of battles, a general rather than a king) fighting with the kings of Britain against the Saxons. He records twelve battles, the last of which is Badon.
>
> 1138 Geoffrey of Monmouth's fantastical *Historia regum Britanniae* (*History of the Kings of Britain*) which describes an Arthur more in line with our modern tradition,

Introduction

but including invasions of various European countries culminating with a war against the Romans.

The lives of various saints written around from the eleventh century onwards often showing Arthur as needing to be brought to heel by a favoured heroic saint.

Welsh poems and stories found in manuscripts from the eleventh century onwards.

The Annales Cambriae (the Welsh Annals): A twelfth-century manuscript, presumed copy of a tenth-century one. It records two entries for Arthur, although dates in the annals are often unreliable and these entries could have be added later:

- Year 72 (c. AD 516) The Battle of Badon, in which Arthur carried the cross of our Lord Jesus Christ on his shoulders for three days and three nights and the Britons were victors.
- Year 93 (c. AD 537) The Strife of Camlann in which Arthur and Medraut (Mordred) fell and there was death in Britain and in Ireland.

Following the success of Geoffrey's *History of the Kings of Britain*, there followed an explosion of interest and further literature on the topic. Wace's Roman de Brut introduced the Round Table and Excalibur in 1155. Chretien de Troyes introduced Lancelot, Camelot and the Grail stories and added much of the chivalric code prevalent in his own time. *Le Morte d'Arthur* by Thomas Mallory in 1485 continued this tradition. You will notice much of this evidence, aside from Nennius, was written down 500 years and more after the supposed events. Geoffrey's book, it's fair to say, also contains a number of errors and mythical stories.

The Welsh legends and poems tend to show both a more mythical and, at times, a more down to earth figure, stealing and killing and generally behaving quite badly. The saints' lives often use this Arthur in their stories to show how godly their favoured saint is in bringing Arthur to submit to the church. We will look at all these stories as they appear in the historical record in chronological order; I think it is mistake to look at the legends first and then go back in time to find evidence, as this runs the risk of only seeing what we want to see and producing highly speculative

King Arthur: Man or Myth?

theories and tenuous links. It may disappoint the reader to learn that the chances of finding a chivalric knight riding out from a beautiful stone castle to protect the realm and any fair maidens found lying around in fifth- or sixth-century Britain are rather slim. Chivalry was as thin on the ground as stone-castle building in those same centuries.

The historical setting and background is much simpler to explain. Before the Romans, Britain was a patchwork of rival tribes. Four hundred years of Roman rule superimposed a political administration involving provinces and civitates. This was not a completely smooth, ordered time. Aside from tribal rebellions, the most famous being Boudica of the Iceni, there were times of civil war and revolt within the Empire. Britain broke away on more than one occasion and several times produced rival emperors who invaded the Continent from Britain. This is important to note because it demonstrates that, at the time, the end of Roman rule may not have been considered the end at all. It may have been thought of, or even hoped to be by some, a temporary transition. Towards the end of the Western Empire there were invasions and large tribal movements across the Western Empire, and Britain was no exception. There were 'barbarian' incursions from Irish, Picts and Saxons into Britain in the last years of Roman rule. The 'final' end is often seen as coming when Constantine declared himself emperor from his base in Britain in AD 407 and took the remaining troops to Gaul. Others date it to the rescript of Honorius in AD 410 when the emperor in Italy refused to aid the British and advised them to look to their own defences.

It is unlikely that the administrative structure of Britain fell apart the very next day, but certainly within 200 years it had broken into a patchwork of petty kings, and the Anglo-Saxons had taken a firm hold of much of the country. It is this 200-year period we will focus on. We have some contemporary sources from this time but only one from Britain: Gildas. None of them mention Arthur in any way. But we also have a plethora of material from Roman Britain and Anglo-Saxon England either side of this period. Any 'Arthur' existing in those times would be well documented.

As we work our way through the sources we will encounter evidence for the following tentative timeline, remembering the dates may be inaccurate and are often contradictory depending on the sources:

> In AD 407 Constantine declares himself emperor in Britain and crosses the channel with the last of the Roman legions and fights his way across Gaul before losing his head, quite

Introduction

literally, in AD 411. Sometime before Constantine's unfortunate ending the British had rebelled (again) against the officials left in charge, and in AD 410 were having so much difficulty from raiders that they sent a letter to the Emperor Honorius begging for help. Honorius, having enough trouble fighting both Constantine and the Visigoths, rejects this request and advises Britons to defend themselves. No Roman army ever returned.

However, two decades after the Romans leave there is still apparently a functioning administrative structure which is eventually led by a character possibly called Vortigern. The province is safe enough for Bishop Germanus to travel from Gaul to Britain in AD 429 to argue against the Pelagian heresy that had taken hold. Increased barbarian attacks cause the British to write again to Rome requesting help, possibly to General Aetius in the 440s. This is rejected. At some point, Saxon mercenaries are invited to help ward of Pictish and Irish raiders (AD 428 if one believes Nennius, AD 449 if Bede). They eventually turn on their employers, causing a period of turmoil and terror for the Romano-British. So much so that the *Gallic Chronicle* for AD 441 (a possibly inaccurate date) states the island has fallen to the power of the Saxons. Gildas, and later Bede, suggest this revolt was in the 450s. In these troubled times a significant emigration occurs during the fifth century from Britain to Amorica, present-day Brittany, bolstering an already established British community.

Out of this, one historical figure that we can be fairly sure existed appears. Ambrosius Aurelianus leads a counter attack which eventually culminates in the battle of Badon which, for the purposes of this introduction, we will place between AD 470 and AD 520. After this, in approximately AD 520–50, Gildas writes his famous tract castigating the many kings in Britain and bemoaning the land lost to the Saxons. It's from his work that we can be sure that both Ambrosius Aurelianus and the battle of Badon are not mere fables. By the mid-sixth century the first Anglo-Saxon kingdoms start to appear in the historical record.

Meanwhile, the Roman Empire had also been going through it's own interesting times on the Continent. Most relevant to our story are the following:

> Rome is sacked by the Visigoths in AD 410, having been preceded by years of unrest and migratory movements of

Germanic tribes. The last great Roman general, Aetius becomes the dominant force in the Western Empire from 430s to 450s (importantly for our evidence, he becomes consul for the third time in AD 446). Attila the Hun devastates Gaul in AD 451 to be repulsed at the battle of the Catalaunian Plains. Aetius received thanks for this service by being murdered by his emperor, personally, with a sword to the head in 454. The emperor may have regretted this in 455 when the Vandals sacked Rome. One of Aetius's lieutenants, Aegidus, becomes the last Magister Militum of Gaul at the same time as his allies the Franks rise in prominence under Childeric.

In AD 470–72, there is enough Roman strength left to fight to retain control of Gaul, and a request is made by the Romans to another possibly important character. Riothamus, king of the Britons, arrives by sea with 12,000 men to aid the Romans against the Visigoths, only to be defeated. Whether he comes from Britain or Brittany is a vital question in our investigation. Around this time there is evidence of Saxons in the Loire valley and Britons fighting against them. This may be relevant given the suggestion of Arthur fighting in Gaul.

A generation later in AD 487, Childeric's son, Clovis I becomes, at the age of 15, effectively the first king of what is now France by defeating and killing Aegidius's son Syagrius, the last Roman ruler of the last Roman enclave in Gaul. An interesting storyline given Geoffrey of Monmouth's story of Arthur being crowned at 15 and eventually fighting the Romans in Gaul. Clovis doesn't, however, succeed in a conquest of Brittany. By AD 476 Odoacer had already deposed the last western emperor and declared himself ruler of Italy before being deposed himself by Theodoric the Great, king of the Ostrogoths in 493. At the feast to celebrate the treaty, Theodoric killed him with a sword blow to the collar bone. Despite attempts by the Eastern Empire, especially under Justinian I in the sixth century, the Western Empire fragments into competing tribal areas that eventually form into the nations of the Middle Ages.

So, to summarise the historical situation from the middle of the fifth century: Britain, free of Roman rule, is busy fighting off Pictish and Irish raiders and resort to using Saxon Mercenaries. In Gaul the Romans are fighting Germanic tribes and then Attila the Hun, and cannot spare the

Introduction

troops to help Britain. Shortly after there is a Saxon revolt and large-scale devastation across Britain. A generation later Ambrosius Aurelianus has beaten back the Saxons in Britain, and in Roman Gaul the threat of the Huns has gone. Around the same time, Britons are fighting Saxons in the Loire valley in Gaul and Riothamus is helping the Romans fight the Visigoths in central Gaul in AD 472. Fifteen years later Clovis is turning against his former Roman ally and wiping out the last Roman ruler in Gaul. Meanwhile, the situation in Britain and Amorica appears to have improved for the Britons as they resist Saxon, and presumably Frankish, expansion. By 520 to 540, Gildas is describing the defeat of the Saxons forty-four years earlier at the battle of Badon, followed by several years of relative peace and prosperity, but lamenting the useless tyrants and general wickedness of the population that are going to send the country to hell in a handcart. Within a generation, from about 550, the Saxons begin again their relentless drive westwards that leads eventually to the Romano British being pushed into what is now Wales, Cornwall and Strathclyde.

All these strands of history are vital to our understanding if we are to place Arthur where the legends suggest. Most of the theories for Arthur place him in the period AD 450–550, but we will start our journey from the last days of the Western Empire. There are a number of important questions worth considering as we go through the evidence if we are looking for a war leader or king fighting battles across Britain and possibly in Gaul:

> In what way did the tribal structure and allegiances in Celtic Britain change during the Roman period?
>
> What was the political and administrative structure of Britain and the Western Roman Empire leading up to and after the end of Roman Britain?
>
> Who were the Saxons and what was the nature of invasion or political take over of parts of Britain?
>
> What does the archaeological and DNA record tell us about this period?
>
> What were the links between Britain and Armorica during this period?

King Arthur: Man or Myth?

What were the links, if any, between the Franks and other tribes with Britain?

What was occurring in the Western Empire in general during this period?

Is a localised Arthur restricted to one area of the country more likely than a national hero?

What was the nature of the Church in Britain and Gaul and how was this linked to the political situation?

Is the name Arthur Celtic, Roman, a nickname or a title?

How useful are the genealogies of Dark Age British kings?

Are there examples of mythical figures becoming historical characters and vice versa?

In addition to that, in the conclusion I hope to address two things that are often neglected. First, I will address the historical discrepancies concerning the Anglo-Saxon arrival. The lack of archaeological evidence for an invasion together with ambiguous genetic evidence contrasts with the literary sources. Within the literary sources there are contradictions between the *Gallic Chronicle* and Gildas, and later Bede, concerning the date of these alleged events. In particular an explanation for the apparent difference between the *Gallic Chronicle* and Bede will be offered. Second, I will attempt to put all the literary sources alongside each other and address the apparent contradictions and inconsistencies in the Arthurian stories. The timeline of events suggested in Gildas, Bede, Nennius, *Annales Cambriae*, *Anglo-Saxon Chronicles*, Welsh legends and saints' lives and Geoffrey of Monmouth's *History* will be laid out alongside each other and the differences explored.

The case for a historical Arthur would be as follows: Arthur is known to us down through the ages, from the time of Geoffrey of Monmouth in the twelfth century through the romance authors of the Middle Ages we have a picture of a nobler time and a golden age. A force for civilisation after the end of Roman Britain fighting against invading barbarians. For a time he held back that tide and after his victory at the battle of Badon at the start of the sixth century, there was a generation of peace. This lasted until his death and the steady advance of the Anglo-Saxons renewed

Introduction

again to consume what later became England. But this is not mere stories, for we have much older Welsh legends and poems to support this. In addition, you will see the historical and archaeological records all support this narrative and show there was indeed a gap between Roman Britain and the beginning of the Anglo-Saxon kingdoms. Within this period it is clear the advance of the Anglo-Saxons was halted and we must ask who halted them. The answer is Arthur.

On the other hand the case against would be this: we have historical records covering the whole of the Roman period and later the Anglo-Saxon kingdoms. While the records covering the period between the two are sparse, they are not non-existent. You will see that 'the Dark Ages' is an inaccurate term. A time of upheaval certainly, but not confined to Britain and not devoid of evidence. Aside from the archaeological evidence, there are written records and letters from across the Western Roman Empire. It is clear that in this whole period there is not one mention of an Arthur. This is for very good reason, he did not exist. It is not historians' place to provide evidence of imaginary figures. Extraordinary claims require extraordinary evidence. It will be demonstrated we do not have even ordinary evidence. The fact is, we do not need an Arthur. We have sufficient evidence to say much about the period and have no need to invent or supplant anything else. Otherwise where would one stop? There is no obligation to suggest reasons why this legend has come about, but other mythical characters have entered historical records and legends. It is likely that the figure we know today came from those myths and there is no evidence of a real historical basis.

We could start from the very first confirmed mention of Arthur. The *Historia Brittonum* in 830, possibly by the monk Nennius. However, it is quite clear from this he places Arthur sometime after the arrival of the Anglo-Saxons but before they gained dominance over much of what became England. In other words between AD 450–550. A more cautious approach would be to consider the wider time period AD 400-600. Plus there are theories that link Arthur to Roman times. With that in mind we shall start our investigation with Roman Britain.

Chapter 1

Roman Britain

Julius Caesar made two brief invasions into Britain in 54 BC and 55 BC. It is worth mentioning Caesar's description from his *Gallic Wars*. He describes the people of the interior as identifying themselves as 'aboriginal', but those of the coast being 'Belgic immigrants' come to plunder and later settle down. As we will see later, this could be quite important when it comes to language and ethnic identity. For the Belgae tribe, on the north coast of Gaul and south coast of Britain, were, according to Caesar, mostly Germanic in origin. It wasn't until AD 43 when the Romans, under Claudius, were able to succeed in gaining a large part of the island. The Romans were confronted with a patchwork of tribes ranging from friendly to hostile. Whether these tribal affiliations lasted 400 years will be covered later, but it is quite important when considering the political and cultural landscape Arthur would have lived in. In Augustus's reign two exiled British kings fled to Rome as supplicants, and later Caligula planned and cancelled an invasion in AD 40. The Catevellauni tribe in the home counties, north of what became London, were pressurising the Trinovantes centred on Camulodunum and the Atrebates (around Hampshire and Berkshire), ruled by descendants of Julius Caesar's former allies. The trigger for Claudius's invasion was supposedly to reinstate Verica as king of the Atrebates. After the invasion Caratacus continued a guerrilla war against the Romans before being captured by Queen Cartimandua of the Brigantes in Yorkshire around AD 51. This led to a Brigantian revolt from those unhappy with the Roman alliance. So we have a patchwork of relationships from friendly to openly hostile, not just between tribal areas but within regions as well.

What is known is that in AD 60 the Iceni rebellion led by Boudica succeeded in destroying Camulodunum, Londinium and Verulamium before being defeated by the governor and general, Gaius Suetonius Paulinus. The important thing about this is the rebellion wasn't about the Roman presence as such, but about very specific incidents. Boudica's husband Prasutagus had ruled as an ally of Rome and left his kingdom

Tribal areas first century.

jointly to his daughters and the protection of Rome. On his death this was ignored; his kingdom was taken, Boudica flogged and her daughters raped. What is less well known is that previously, Rome had encouraged influential Britons to take out loans and given donations. These loans were now called in and the donations confiscated. Leading Iceni men had their estates confiscated and this was mirrored by the behaviour of Romans in Camulodunum, at that time a Colonia, which meant it was settled by veterans. Nor did it help that a temple dedicated to Claudius had been constructed there and the expense forced on the Britons. At the same time, Paulinus was on campaign to destroy the seat of Druid power on Anglesey in North Wales, an act that would further alienate the Britons.

After the rebellion, much of blame was placed on the harsh behaviour of the former governor and procurator, who had fled to Gaul leaving London to its fate. The new procurator was Julius Classicianus and his policy of reconciliation eventually produced dividends. What is interesting about him is that he was Gaulish, the descendant of the very people Julius Caesar had subdued a century before. So here was a Gaul, with a Roman name, who had risen to high public office and would have considered himself part of the civilised Roman world. Given the Romanisation of Gaul, one wonders how the same process influenced Britain.

Indeed Tacitus, writing in AD 98, records a British client king, Tiberius Claudius Cogidubnus, as being loyal 'down to our times'. He ruled several civitates, or tribal areas, and was possibly seated at the Roman Villa found at Fishbourne near Chichester. Additionally he describes Agricola's governorship in AD 78–84. There seems to have been a policy of gradual Romanisation as temples, public squares and houses were built. They were introduced to Roman baths, arcades and towns. They started to mimic Roman dress and manners and encouraged their children to learn Latin. Tacitus goes on to describe their seduction by Roman civilisation as causing their 'enslavement'.

Each civitas required a capital to administer government. One settlement, though, was completely new and grew to overshadow them all. Built near the ford at which Caesar had crossed the Thames in 54 BC and Claudius a century later (although Claudius's troops failed to find the exact location). It started off as a fort on one of the three hills overlooking the surrounding marshland and the nearby ford near modern-day Westminster. Those hills are Cornhill, Ludgate Hill and Tower Hill. Opposite, on the South Bank, a further raised area allowed for occupation of modern day Southwark with the first bridge likely to be near to where London Bridge stands today. Being a new town in virgin territory, Londinium was home to Roman immigrants and quickly surpassed Camulodunum, becoming the centre of commerce and finance. We can see how much Roman Britain changed in a few decades by the expansion of London. The Basilica was the civic centre housing law courts and offices. First built in AD 70, it was replaced in the early first century by a building occupying 2 hectares, 300ft in length and three storeys high. It was the largest of its kind outside Rome, signifying the importance of London and Britain, and the extent to which the Roman way of life had embedded itself. The presence of two Roman bath houses and an amphitheatre further demonstrate this.

Two walls were built in the north of the province and are mentioned, inaccurately, in later evidence so I will include them here. Hadrian's wall was built in AD 122 and took six years to complete.[1] It was 73 miles long, 10ft wide and 12–15ft high. In front was a ditch. Behind was a rear earthwork, the Vallum, 20ft wide, 10ft deep and with a 20ft mound each side. There were 'mile castles' every Roman mile and a larger fort every 5 miles. There is evidence of decay and reconstruction until the end of Roman Britain. The Antonine wall between the Forth and Clyde in Scotland's central belt extended the frontier some 100 miles north of Hadrian's wall. It was a shorter construction of turf at 39 miles long, 10ft high and 16ft wide. Started in AD 142 it took twelve years to complete. There are nineteen forts every 2 miles. It is interesting to note that one of the forts north of the Antonine wall is called Camelon. Camboglanna, another possible derivation from Camelot, is on Hadrian's wall. There is, however, no evidence for this connection.

The provincial structure changed in AD 197 after a rebellion by Clodius Albinus. Albinus had been declared emperor by the legions in Britain and Gaul, but was defeated by Emperor Severus at the battle of Lugdunum in Gaul. Severus laid out the naked dead body of the unfortunate Albinus and reportedly rode his horse over it as a final act of humiliation. He then sent Albinus's severed head to the senate in Rome, some of whom had professed loyalty to Albinus. Having promised to protect his wife and sons, Severus soon changed his mind and beheaded them too. Just to make sure some future upstart wouldn't get similar ideas, he split Britain into two provinces: Britannia Superior in the south and Britannia Inferior in the north, as well as reorganising the military chain of command. Thus preventing one person from having a monopoly of power. This did not entirely work.

Around 260, a breakaway Gallic Empire including Britain survived for fourteen years before being recaptured by the Emperor Aurelian. Just thirteen years later in 286 another interesting figure, Carausius, appeared. Tasked with protecting the English Channel from pirates, he was found to be running a protection racket and sentenced to death. He responded by declaring himself emperor in Britain. He minted coins declaring himself *Restitutor Britanniae* (Restorer of Britain) and *Genius Britanniae* (Spirit of Britain), suggesting not just a flare for propaganda, but a possible disgruntled population willing to follow him. He was assassinated seven years later by his subordinate, Allectus, who was later killed in 296 when Constantius Chlorus invaded during the reign of Diocletian, after which the provinces were restructured again. Ten years later the son of Constantius, Constantine I, was declared emperor at York and went on to take the whole of the Empire under his control.

Fifty years later another breakaway emperor, Magnentius, proved to be popular in Britain, Gaul and Spain, mainly due to his tolerance of Christians and Pagans. His defeat in 353, three years after taking power, brought about two other interesting characters. The Emperor Constantius II sent an imperial notary to root out the usurper's supporters. Known as Paulus Catena, or Paul the Chain, for his cruel ways, he set to work across the province. The historian Ammianus Marcellinus records that Paulus soon started arresting people on false charges and engaging in all sorts of corrupt and cruel practices. This caused an unsung hero of British history to step forward and try to stop the injustices. Flavius Martinus, the Vicarius of Britain, received a false accusation of treason for his pains which caused him to try and kill Paulus, personally drawing his sword on him. Having failed, he committed suicide. Paulus carried on his murderous and torturous career in Egypt before being burned alive during the reign Emperor Julian the Apostate in 462.

So we already had a long history of usurpers and rebellions involving Britain before we get to a figure who crops up at the start of many of the narratives that concern the Arthurian legend. Magnus Maximus was declared emperor in 383 while serving in Britain and took control of the Western Empire. This figure comes up repeatedly in both later Welsh legends and and sources at the start of our period of interest. About twenty years after Maximus's death, Britain's 'last' emperor was Constantine III, who took the last legions to Gaul around 407. This is another figure sometimes connected to Arthur's story, although as we shall see later this may be someone with a similar name. What all this tells us is Britain had a rich history of rebellion, temporary periods of independence and usurping emperors. There was no particular reason for people living around 410 to think this was anything other than another upheaval in Rome's long history. It also demonstrates that we actually have a lot of good sources for the period prior to 410, and yet there is no hint of an Arthurian type figure or anything connected to the story. There is no indication of any warrior called Arthur, bear-gods, Sarmatian sword legends or any other related concepts being present.

King Arthur: Man or Myth?

Table 1

Year	Figure	Description	Comments
AD 193–197	Clodius Albinus	Declared emperor by troops in Britain and Gaul and crossed over from Britain in AD 196.	Defeated in AD 197. Britain divided into two provinces.
AD 259–274	Gallic Empire	Breakaway region of the Western Empire which included at its height: Brittania, Germania, Gaul and Hispania.	It was retaken by the Emperor Aurelian after the battle of Chalon in 274 AD.
AD 286–293	Carausius	Declared emperor in Britain and northern Gaul and called himself the 'Emperor of the North'.	Assassinated by his finance minister Alectus.
AD 293–296	Allectus	Constantius Chlorus (father of Constantine the Great) invaded Britain and defeated him.	Britain divided into four provinces.
AD 306	Constantine I (the Great)	Declared emperor in York after the death of his father.	The first emperor to convert to Christianity and stop persecutions.
AD 350–353	Magnentius	Defeated and committed suicide in Southern France.	Suppression of his followers in Britain led to further unrest.
AD 383–388	Magnus Maximus	Declared emperor in Wales and conquered much of Western Empire.	Defeated at the battle of Aquileia in Italy and being executed.
AD 406	Marcus	May have resulted from increased barbarian raids.	
AD 406/7	Gratian	Coincided with a huge barbarian raid in Gaul but refused to take army across channel.	Killed after four months.
AD 407	Constantine III	Invades Gaul taking much of remaining troops.	Defeated in AD 411.
AD 409	Briton's rebel against Constantine	Sent appeal to Emperor Honorius in Ravenna for help against raids.	AD 410 Rescript of Honorius instructs cities to look to their own defences.

Roman Britain

The provincial structure in the late fourth century involved four or five provinces, each with its own governor answerable to a Vicarius (meaning deputy) based in London, heading the diocese of the Britons, who in turn reported to a Praetorian Prefect of Gaul, overseeing Gaul, Hispania and Britannia.[2] There is some confusion as to whether Valentia was an additional province named for the Emperor Valentian after Theodosis recaptured the area between Hadrian's wall and The Antonine wall after the Barbarian conspiracy in AD 367, or whether it simply renamed an existing province in the emperor's honour. The provinces were as follows:[3]

- Britannia Prima covered the West Country and modern-day Wales with the provincial capital at Cirencester.
- Britannia Secunda covered the midlands and Lincolnshire.
- Flavia Caesariensis covered north of this line up to Hadrian's wall with the capital at York.
- Maxima Caesariensis covered the South East and East Anglia, with London being both the capital of the Province and the Diocese.
- Valentia referred to the renaming of Flavia Caesariensis or a new province (regained from earlier centuries) north of Hadrian's wall.

There is some debate about the exact position and boundaries of these provinces, but the important aspect is that the province was divided into administrative areas. Within each province were various civitates, so that over time more than thirty cities were created. *Coloniae* were created for veterans at Colchester, Lincoln and Gloucester, and there were three legionary fortresses at York, Chester and Caerleon.

The Magister Militum was created in the fourth century and took over the military functions of the Praetorian Prefect and, like him, was based in Gaul. Within Britain there were three commands:[4]

- Dux Britannarium controlled Limitanei (literally frontier troops) in the north including Hadrian's wall. Consisting of eight cavalry and twenty-nine infantry units.
- Comes Litoris Saxonici per Britanniam (Count of the Saxon shore) also utilised Limitanei across the forts along the southern and eastern coast. Consisted of two cavalry and seven infantry units.

King Arthur: Man or Myth?

- Comes Britanniarum who controlled the main field army consisting of four infantry units and six cavalry units suggesting a mobile force to combat raiders.

The Dux Britannarium was a casualty of the barbarian invasions of AD 367. Interestingly, one of our earliest references to Arthur is not as a king but as a 'Dux Bellorum', which may be a reference to this military title. The title *Comes Litoris Saxonici* is only known from a fifth-century military list, the *Notitia Dignitatum*, which might be dated to 425. Whether this was just a copy of previous titles in unknown. There is certainly no evidence concerning the fifth century from Britain. What it does show is the majority of the units were in the north. The location of

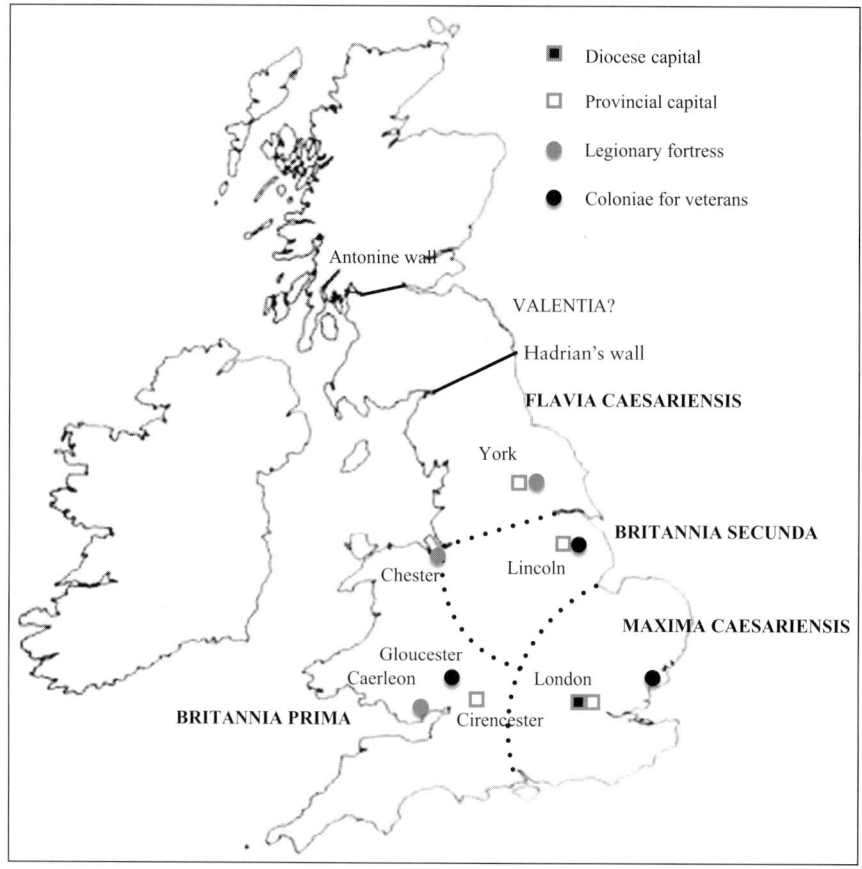

Provinces of Britain.

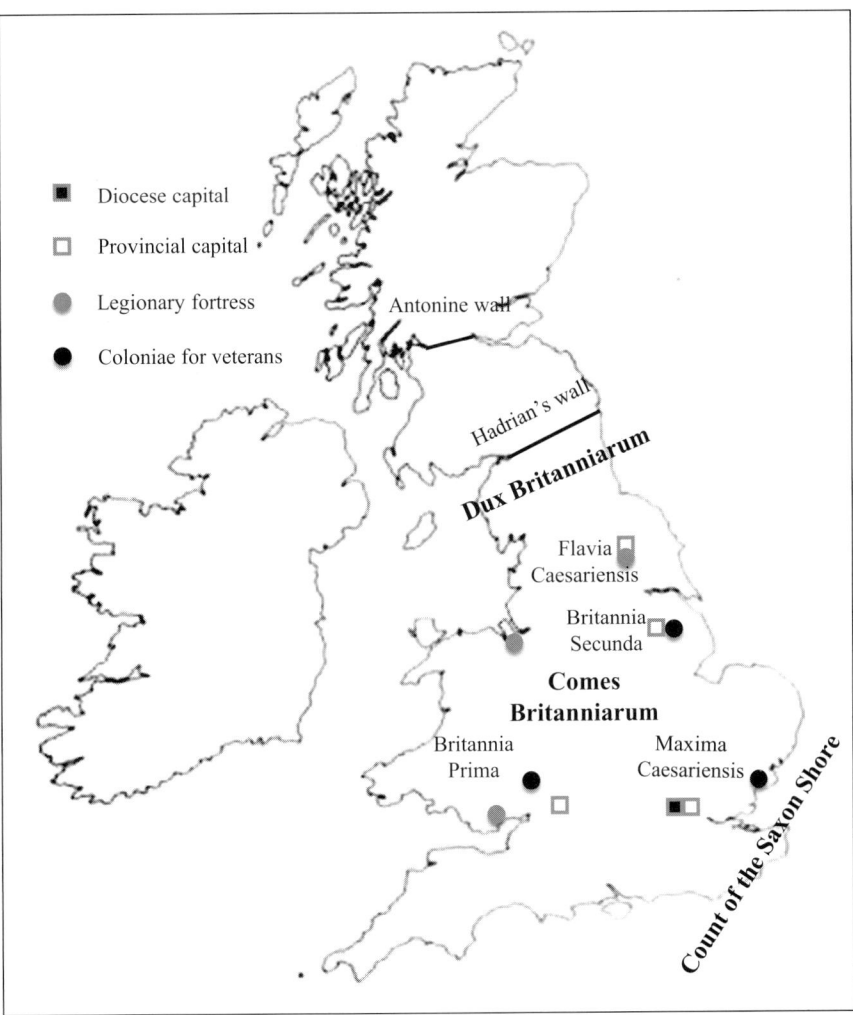

Military commands.

Coloniae, military fortresses and forces could indicate where rebellions might have taken place.

One might also assume that the Saxon Shore forts had something to do with Saxons. Yet nine out of the eleven forts were built two centuries earlier, and appear to be more related to trade than defence. They were part of a wider Gallic coastal system mirrored on the opposite side of the channel, likely built after the Gallic Empire. In fact there is no example of any Roman defensive system anywhere being named after an enemy,

King Arthur: Man or Myth?

but also no evidence to suggest allied Saxon troops were stationed there.[5] So I'm afraid we have no idea why the title 'Count of the Saxon Shore' came about. We could speculate about the presence of Saxons and what they were doing there, but it would be pure guesswork. However, later we will cover the *Gallic Chronicle* entry for 440, written in 452, which states Britain fell to the power of the Saxons. Given we know that Devon and Cornwall were not conquered for several centuries, it can only refer to the south east. It is likely this event affected the south-east province of Maxima Caesariensis, the diocese capital and major port, London, and the Saxon Shore.

At the end of Roman Britain the entire force is estimated at 20,000 troops, and possibly as low as 12,000 available at any one time, compared to a force of perhaps 50,000 in the second century.[6] There is some evidence that coinage ran out in the decades after the Romans left; there

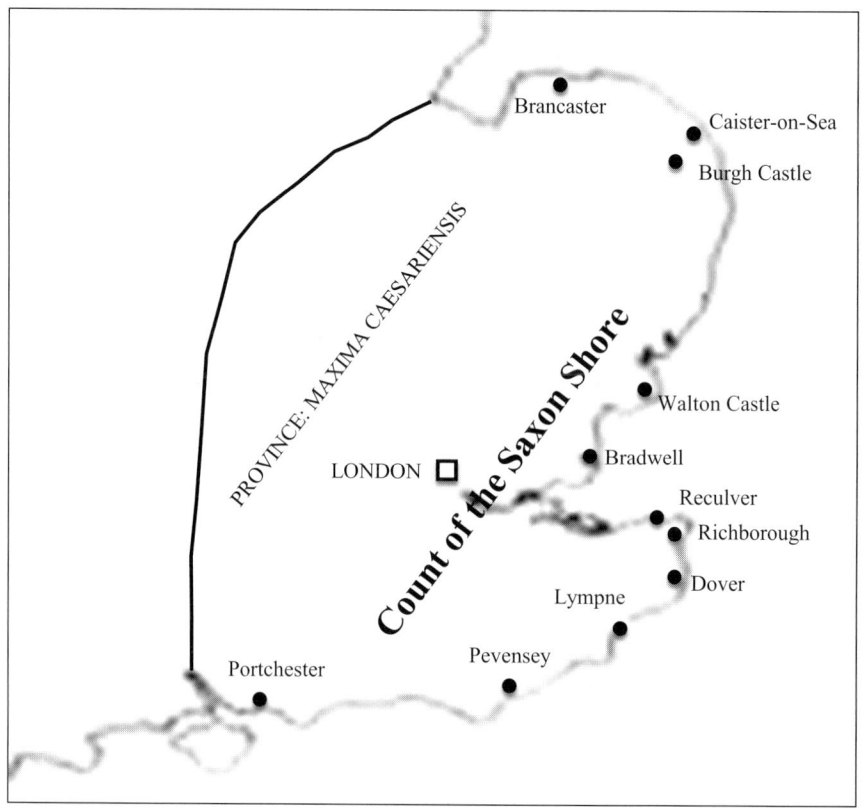

The Saxon Shore forts.

is certainly no evidence of new coins being minted. What this means for the payment of troops is unknown. There were a number of times when Britain rebelled, broke away, or invaded the Western Empire. Table 1 shows examples of periods of unrest which did not result in a permanent break, demonstrating that some continuity of Roman life may have been assumed by many after AD 410.

There were several occasions towards the end of the fourth century when barbarian raids were large enough to warrant a large-scale response. It may be worth remembering Table 2 below when we get to later evidence from Gildas and Bede:

Table 2

Year	Incursions	Comments
AD 360	Picts and Scots	Subdued by General Lupicinus
AD 364	Picts, Scots, Saxons and Attacotti	'constant raids' (Ammianus)
AD 367	Irish, Pict, Scots. Attacotti and Germanic tribes	The Great Barbarian Conspiracy. Widespread destruction including death of Dux Brittaniarum.
AD 382	Picts	Subdued by Magnus Maximus
AD 398	Picts	Defeated by General Stilicho
AD 408	Saxon raids	May have been reason for rebellion against Constantine and appeal to Honorius.

Picts were a collection of various tribes living north of the wall. The Scotti were originally from Northern Ireland and settled in the Western Isles of what is now Scotland towards the end of the fourth century, and the Attacotti were likely north of Hadrian's wall. 'Saxons' was a catch-all term for a number of Germanic tribes including Angles, Jutes, Friesians and Saxons.

We should also add that many of these tribes and others from across the Empire are listed as mercenary troops, although they were often posted far from their homeland. For example there are references to troops from the Attacotti presumably being co-opted into the army after their defeat by Theodosius in AD 368. There is evidence of extensive use of mercenaries from across the Empire stationed in Britain.[7] I would also emphasise the Sarmatian cavalry introduced in AD 175. Approximately

5,500 were posted to the north near Hadrian's wall after their defeat in the Sarmatian war of AD 170 in the Black Sea area. The Sarmatians, a nomadic steppe tribe, had perhaps relevant myths and legends, including standards with dragon heads (pen being the Welsh for head), swords being pulled from the ground and the hurling of swords into water. Plus they are connected to the only 'Arthur' recorded throughout Roman Britain, Lucius Artorius Castus.

Lucius Artorius Castus was a legion prefect in York and later a dux legionum (legion commander) leading troops to Amorica and Gaul towards the end of the second century. All we know about this Artorius comes from two inscriptions and there is nothing in the written historical record. This Artorius was a minor obscure figure, not even commanding a full legion. He ended his days as a Govenor of Liburnia in what is now Croatia. There are simply no records of him doing anything remotely connected to the Arthur legend in Britain or anywhere else. Most importantly, he is in completely the wrong time. In addition, it requires the legend to be carried forward several hundred years through a well documented time with no written record surviving.

By AD 350, Britain was a 'prosperous diocese'.[8] By the 360s, however, the towns were perhaps poorer and politically weaker, although by no means dead;[9] Britain's cities were 'strongly walled' in the fourth century and many of the most luxurious and largest villas were built in this time,[10] so we have a mixed picture. There is some archaeological evidence of a 'dark earth' layer at some sites in the late Roman period that may suggest dereliction or destruction. We should treat this with caution as it is inconsistent across both time and location and may indicate change of use or occupation rather than destruction. New coinage appears to have stopped reaching Britain by 402, but this doesn't mean money ceased to be used into the fifth century.

There is evidence to show a growing Christian community and the building of many churches in the fourth century. There is a record of three bishops from Britain in 359 attending the council of Arminium, modern-day Rimini in northern Italy, although their resources were such that they had to beg for funding. Having said that, evidence suggests that the number of bishoprics in late fourth-century Britain may have been in double figures and could number over twenty.[11] All major cities in the fourth century had built large churches and a majority of the urban and rural population was at least nominally Christian.[12]

Concerning post-Roman Britain, 'in the fifth and sixth centuries, neither the majority of Britons in the lowland half of Britannia, nor the Christian faith increasingly practised was expunged'.[13] Indeed St Patrick, of whom we shall hear more later, was a Romano-British Christian. Even the later Anglo-Saxon kingdoms, though pagan, may not have eradicated the religion; for example Pope Gregory's correspondence with Augustine who was sent to convert Anglo-Saxon Kent in AD 600 alludes to the 'bishops of the British'. So the evidence suggests a widespread Christian community, if not majority.

Later legends do portray Arthur and his knights as Christian and refer to him carrying the image of the Virgin Mary on his shield into battle. Additionally, the various *Lives of the Saints* paints a somewhat more Celtic, if not pagan, Arthur than the later medieval romances. It is possible for him to have been both pagan and Christian. For example Clovis I, king of the Franks, was born a pagan but later converted to Christianity around the same time period Arthur is said to have lived. However it's very likely a Romano-British leader would have been born Christian.

In a sixth-century version of the *Liber Pontificalis* by Bede, there is a record of a second-century British king, Lucius, for whom Pope Eleutherius received a request for baptism; it is further corroborated in Geoffrey of Monmouth's *History*. However, there is an acceptance that this is more likely a scribal error concerning 'Britium' in what is now Turkey. There is certainly no contemporary record of any British king either writing to a Pope, or being named Lucius. Like Artorius Castus, this figure often appears in Arthurian theories despite there being not a shred of evidence. For our purposes, it is enough to determine that Christianity was a well-founded and growing religion at the end of Roman Britain.

In summary, Roman Britain was a well established and prosperous province. Despite many rebellions, civil wars and barbarian incursions, especially in the late fourth century, it was not at all certain after 410 that the links had been severed forever. It may be that some of the incursions mentioned concerning Picts, Scots and Saxons are alluded to in later evidence from Gildas and Bede, as well as the subsequent military responses and repairs to defences such as Hadrian's wall. There was certainly a strong political and military structure. How long that structure lasted is open to speculation. What changes 350 years of Roman rule had on tribal affiliations is unknown. The effects of immigration and presence of federate troops is equally difficult to ascertain. As is the mix of ethnic, tribal, cultural, social and religious differences.

What we can be certain of is no contemporary record prior to the end of Roman Britain hints at any connection with the Arthurian legend. The only reason Lucius Artorius Castus is sometimes suggested as a theory is because he's the only Artorius recorded in Britain. This is an extremely poor reason to nominate someone. It would be like getting a tip-off for a murder but only getting a first name then arresting the first person one found with that name. It's worse than that, as it's being told that someone did something hundreds of years ago and going through the records pinning it on the only person of that name we can find. Artorius was a common name and there were, no doubt, scores of them throughout Roman Britain. We must therefore look for our Arthur after the fall of Roman Britain.

Chapter 2

The End of The West

Theodosius I was the last Roman Emperor to rule both west and east. On his death in AD 395 his sons Honorius and Arcadian split the Empire between them much of which was already home to a number of settled Germanic tribes including the Franks in Gaul and the Goths in the East. Around 400 there emerged the 'bacaudae', provincial rebels and slaves, who created significant civil unrest. Honorius, the western emperor, had sent General Stilicho to deal with barbarian incursions into Britain at the end of the fourth century. In around 402 Stilicho pulled troops, and much of the coinage, away from Britain and northern Gaul to deal with Visigoth rebellions.

In 406 there was a huge incursion of multiple tribes across a frozen Rhine into a relatively undefended northern Gaul which included Vandals, Burgundians, Alemanni, Alans, Saxons and Gepids. It was this incursion and Stilicho's apparent abandonment that caused the Britons to rebel, appointing three different leaders in quick succession, the last being Constantine III who invaded Gaul in 407. Without Constantine's army, and after Saxon attacks in 408, the Britons rebelled once more, this time against Constantine, and requested help direct from Honorius in 409, which we know was rejected in 410.

The Emperor Honorius, based at Ravenna, was still fighting against Constantine III and against Alaric, king of the Visigoths, who sacked Rome in that same year. He was unable to help and issued what is known as *The Rescript of Honorius*, where he urged the civitates to look to their own defences. Sent direct to the cities, the letter suggests that the Provincial apparatus had either broken down or could not be trusted by either the British civitates or Honorius. There is some contention that the reply from Honorius refers to Bruttium in Italy, but on balance it has been accepted to more likely refer to Britain. Much is made of this apparent ambiguity but for our purposes it is rather academic. The Romans never returned. What is important is what civil and military structures persisted in Britain after 410 and for how long?

General Stilicho was killed in 408 along with a large number of barbarian officers in the Roman army. In 410 Rome was sacked by the Visigoths who were eventually settled in south western Gaul. Constantine III was eventually defeated and killed along with his son Constans, a former monk, in 411. He did have another son, Julian, but there is no record of him being the father of Aurelianus Ambrosius or 'Uthr' Pendragon as claimed several hundred years later by Geoffrey of Monmouth, among others. Although it's not completely clear that this is the same Constantine, despite the inclusion in Geoffrey's twelfth-century book of Constans the monk as his other son.

The rest of the fifth century in Gaul can be seen in two halves. The first half is characterised by the attempts to control the Germanic tribes by giving them foederati status and using them to fight each other when one tribe rebelled. Franks in the north, Visigoths in south west, Burgundians in the south east and Alemanni in the east. The second half of the century sees a slow decline to eventual loss of control and then collapse of the Western Empire. Aetius was made Magister Militum in Gaul in 429, Consul for the third time in 446 and killed in 454. In the writing of Gildas, it is this Aetius to which the Britons appealed. What we do have at this point is one reference concerning Britain from a relatively contemporary source. The *Gallic Chronicle* written in 452 records that in 440, Britain fell to the power of the Saxons. What this means is open to conjecture. It is usually fairly accurate. Yet we know that parts of Britain did not come under Saxon control for several centuries. More of that will be discussed later.

As well as playing the different Germanic tribes off each other, Aetius had extensively used Hunnic and 'barbarian' mercenaries. The barbarians quickly adopted Roman behaviours and wished to be incorporated into the Empire rather than perhaps conquer it.[1] Thus, in general there seems to be a willingness, or even desire, to take over Roman concepts rather than replace them. The survival of villas and towns, for example, appears to be far less likely in Britain compared to Gaul.[2] While the barbarians were being Romanised, the Roman army and emperors were increasingly influenced by barbarians from Stilicho to Odoacer.[3] During this period the greatest single blow to the Western Empire may have been the loss of Africa to the Vandals starting from

429. Despite this, the Western Empire still held, and the situation in Britain was stable enough to allow Saint Germanus of Auxerre to travel from Gaul to Britain, visiting St Albans.

In 451 Attila the Hun invaded Gaul, which led to his defeat by Aetius and allied tribes (Visigoths, Franks, Burgundians, Saxons, Armoricans) at the battle of the Catalaunian plains. Attila made an abortive attempt at sacking Rome in 452, before dying in 453. The Huns soon ceased to be a viable threat. It is perhaps the murder of Aetius in 454 by Emperor Valentinian II which signals the beginning of the end for the Western Empire. There then follows a succession of nine emperors in twenty years, increasingly controlled by Germanic officers, first Ricimer and then Odoacer. It is telling that in the following year the Vandals, who had passed through Gaul, Italy and Spain before settling in North Africa, invaded Italy and sacked Rome.

We now get to roughly the time that may concern us about events in Britain. There is some debate and contradictory evidence concerning when the Saxons started to seize control and we will come to this later. There are already Saxons in the Loire valley, and General Odoacer uses Saxon mercenaries in fighting against the Goths in the 460s. In northern Gaul, around Soissons, a Roman administrative area survives headed by Aegidus, the last Roman Magister Militum of Gaul. He is succeeded in 464 by his son Syagrius, who become known as the 'Last king of the Romans' in the Roman rump state of the kingdom of Soissons in northern Gaul. In 476, with the removal of the last western emperor, this kingdom became effectively independent.

Around the 460s there is evidence of Saxons in the Loire and Saxon pirates on the coast.[4] In the sixth century, Gregory of Tours records that after Aegidius died in 464 the Bretons were expelled from Bourges, near the Loire river, by the Goths and many were killed in Bourg-de-Deol, central Gaul. At the same time a great war was occurring between Romans and Saxons, which the Saxons appear to have lost, being 'cut down and pursued' by the Romans and losing many of their islands, in the Loire, to the Franks.

In the middle of the sixth century, Jordanes, writing in *The Origin and Deeds of the Goths*, states the Emperor Anthemius (467–472) requests help from 'King Riotimus of the Brittones' to fight the Visigoth king Euric. He arrives with 12,000 men 'by way of the ocean'; as he disembarks, he is met by the Goths and is routed. He fled with his men to the neighbouring Burgundians in the East. Some have argued that this phrase 'by way of the ocean' surely means from Britain, and that 'Riotimus' is a Latinised translation of 'high king'. So we have a record of a British king able to muster 12,000 and travel to Gaul, presumably leaving his homeland defended. As Anthemius is soon recorded in the narrative as dead, one must conclude this battle was around 471. Additionally, the pressure on the Saxons in the Loire valley from 460 and the expansion of Frankish dominance of northern France does supply a reason, independent of British sources, for migration of Germanic peoples away from Gaul and towards Britain.[5]

However there are a number of problems with the theory Riothamus is the basis for Arthur. Firstly the phrase 'by way of the ocean' could easily mean from modern Brittany down the coast to the Loire river. The text says, 'to the state of the Bituriges', which is in exactly the area mentioned by both Gregory and Jordanes and accessible from the Loire. Plus we have the added difficulty in there is no record of this Riotimus either before or after, and no proof that this wasn't a Latinised version of his name rather than a title. Even if it was a title, and the force of 12,000 did come from Britain, then we would still be left to prove that he was called Arthur. Then there is the fact that the only record of him is a defeat by the Goths. There is simply no evidence of any connection to the legend.

Possible routes for army of Riothamus.

The End of The West

A Romanised administration persisted in Gaul in the fifth century,[6] and in 476 Odoacer deposed the last western emperor and sent the imperial regalia to Constantinople. Many date the fall of the Western Empire to this date. Clovis I became king of the Franks aged 15 in 481 and conquered Soissons, killing the 'last king of the Romans' in 487 before going on to defeat the Alemanni, Visigoths and Burgundians to control Gaul.

Clovis was then offered the consulship by the eastern emperor around 508. This means that Armorica, with it's many links to Britain, initially bordered the last Roman rump state in Gaul up to 487, and then subsequently a dominant Frankia. Given Geoffrey of Monmouth's narrative of Arthur being crowned at 15, invading Gaul and defeating the king of the Romans, this may be important. We will examine this in more detail later, but if there is any substance to it, then we have a few windows of opportunities for any significant military activity from Britain: The Romano-Saxon war of the 460s, Riothamus defeat by the Visigoths around 471, in the Frankish war with Soissons in 487 or in later border wars with the Franks from after that time.

In summary, a large influx of barbarian tribes together with civil war at the start of the fifth century caused major unrest in Gaul and the isolation of Britain from the Empire. The first half of the century

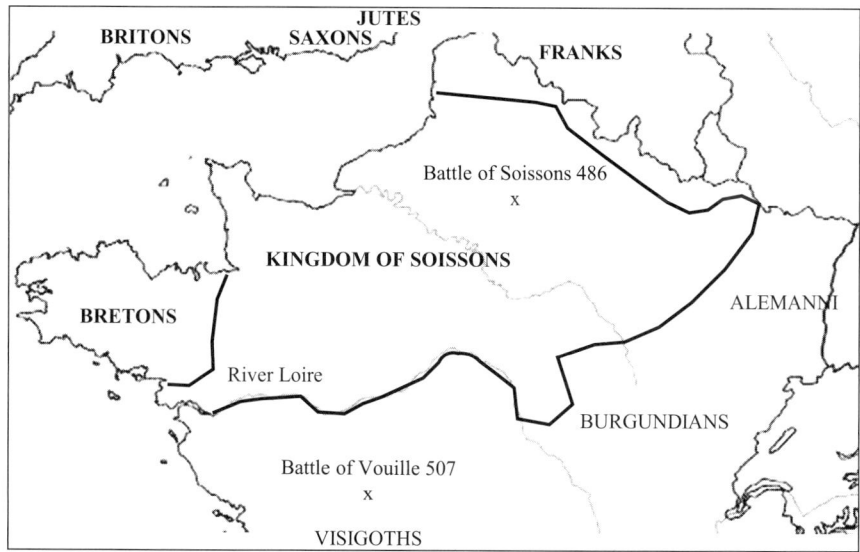

North western Gaul in the late fifth century.

19

involved Rome fighting against, and with, various tribes across Gaul and eventually resettling and making alliances. The second half of the century involved a rapid weakening of Roman power, and wars between Saxons, Bretons, Franks, Goths and Romans. The last Roman emperor was deposed in 476, but a rump Roman state survived until 488 as the Franks emerged as the dominant force in Gaul. During this time we have no evidence from Britain, except this tentative reference to a King Riotimus around 471. There is certainly no reference to anyone called Arthur. No letters from Popes, no Roman records, nothing from Gregory of Tours or Jordanes from the Franks or Goths.

We do have contemporary accounts referring to Britain, and also accounts *from* Britain. The first was written around 480 in Gaul concerning a visit by Germanus of Auxerre in 429, followed by a possible second visit a few years later. The second is the writings of St Patrick, whose floruit is debated with his death dated to either 462 or 493, although this tells us next to nothing about Britain. Lastly we have Gildas writing in approximately 540 who tells us quite a lot as we shall see. Frustratingly for the period we are interested in either side of 500, we have no contemporary sources about Britain. We do have a number of contemporary sources covering this period from other parts of the Roman world however, and it is on this we will focus next.

Chapter 3

Contemporary Sources

The first two chapters have painted a very brief picture of the events leading up to, and just after, the fall of Roman Britain. Below is a list of all the contemporary historical sources[1] that refer to Britain and the year in which they were written. It is worth noting that none mention any Arthur, any more than throughout Roman occupied Britain. Nor is there evidence of legends or myths from any source which even hint at the Arthurian legend at this point.

Table 3

List of contemporary sources referring to Britain:
393 AD Ammianus Marcellinus, (Res Gestae Divi Augustae): Describes a prosperous province supplying grain to Gaul in the 4th century. The incursion and subjugation of Picts and Scots in 360
402 AD Claudus Claudianus wrote a number of poems referring to the General Stilicho and his defeat of Scots, Picts and Saxons presumably in 396-8 AD
417 AD Orosius (Historium adversum paganos book vii) a native of Hispania, writing in North Africa. Referring to the barbarian incursion across the Rhine in 406 AD (Book VII, 40):   When the barbarians were overrunning Gaul in Britain Gratian, *'a citizen of the island, was made a usurper'* only to be killed. Then Constantine was elected, *'a man of the lowest military rank, on account of the hope alone which came from his name....'* Constantine then crossed over into Gaul.
390-425 AD the Notitia Dignitatum: A civil and military list of offices that may include updated or outdated posts with uncertain provenance and date. In summary it lists the following: *Provinciae, Britanniae V: Maxima Caesariensis, Valentia, Britannia prima, Britannia secunda, Flavia Caesariensis.*

(continued)

Table 3: (Continued)

> Consuls were responsible for the first two and 'presidents' for the other three with a Vicarius Britanniae overseeing all five.
>
> Militarily there were two counts: Comes Britanniarum and Comes Litoris Saxonici per Britanniam. Additionally one Duke (of the frontiers), Dux Britanniarum. There then follows a list of units.

425 AD Olympiodorus of Thebes referring to Stilicho leaving Britain and Gaul open to invasion:

> Records discontent in Britain, with the rule of the Stilicho, and *'with lack of attention his government paid to the defence of Britain against the Picts'*
>
> Constantine *was 'brought to power by a revolt of the soldiers....in the provinces of Britain.'*
>
> Then: *'in the provinces of Britain before the seventh consulship of Honorius in 407, they had stirred the army there to revolt, and proclaimed a certain Marcus as supreme ruler.'*
>
> Constantine is raised to *'supreme commander'* and crosses to Gaul with his troops gaining control *'as far as the Alps.'*

439 AD Sozomen originally from Gaza writing in Constantinople: Historia Ecclesiastica concerning the years 324-439. Regarding Britain after 406 AD gives more detail:

> *'The soldiers in Britain were the first to rise up in sedition.*
>
> First Mark was made 'tyrant' but then killed by the soldiers who had proclaimed him. This was followed by Gratian who they also killed four months later.
>
> Next came *Constantine* who they thought *'on account of his name... would be able to reduce the empire firmly under his authority.'*
>
> It describes Constantine nominating his son Constans Caesar then Emperor and sending him to Spain.
>
> After, Constantine with his other son Julian are *'waylaid and killed'* on their way to Italy.

450 AD The Narratio de imperatoribus domus Valentinianae et Theodosiane was an anonymous text concerning the emperors from Valentinian I to Honorius (364-423).

> It records in the reign of Honorius *'many heavy blows befell the state'* namely Gaula nd Spain were *'demolished and utterly destroyed by the barbarian nations of the Vandals, Sueves, and Alans'* and Rome was *'captured and overthrown'* by the Visigoth King Alaric.
>
> Most relevant though was: *'Britain was forever removed from the Roman name.'*

Contemporary Sources

452 AD The Gallic Chronicle (a)
The Britains were devastated by an incursion of the Saxons 409 AD

The Britains, which to this time had suffered from various disasters and misfortunes, are reduced to the power of the Saxons 441 AD

455 AD Prosper of Aquitaine later a notary of Pope Leo I wrote the Epitoma Chronicon.

Records that Agricola, *'son of the Pelagian bishop Severianus, corrupted the British churches'*. Then Palladius persuaded Pope Celestine to send Germanus, bishop of Auxerre, to Britain to combat the Pelagian heresy prompting Germanus's fisrts visit in 429 AD.

Then: *'Palladius was sent by Pope Celestine to the Scots who believed in Christ, and was ordained as their first bishop'.*

The Scotti being the Irish.

500 AD Zosimus, Historia Nova

Book VI.5.2-3

Records that the barbarians north of the Rhine *'reduced the inhabitants of Britain and some of the Celtic peoples to defecting from the Roman rule and living their own lives, independent from the Roman laws. The Britons therefore took up arms and, braving the danger on their own behalf, freed their cities from the barbarian threat.'*

Then Armorica and *'other Gallic provinces'* expelled the Roman officials.

Book VI.5-6

Gerontius in Spain rebelled against against Constantine. Then: *'the barbarians from beyond the Rhine overran everything at will and reduced the inhabitants of the British Island and some of the peoples in Gaul to the necessity of rebelling from the Roman empire'*

This defection occurred during *'Constantine's tyranny'* due to the *'carelessness in administration.'*

Book VI.10.2

Honorius writes to the cities of Britain, telling them to look to their own defences.

511 AD Gallic Chronicle (b) with reference to 440 AD
The Britains, lost to the Romans, yield to the power of the Saxons.

540 AD Procopius of Caesera (Palestine)

Concerning 407 AD:

Bellum Vandalicum 3.2.31

States the Britons revolted then the soldiers chose *'Constanti(us, a man of no mean station'. And* He gathered a *'fleet of ships and a formidable army and invaded both Spain and Gaul with a great force.'*

(continued)

Table 3: (Continued)

Concerning 411 AD
Bellum Vandalicum 3.2.38
Records the death of Alaric and the defeat and death of Constantine and his sons.
Then: 'the Romans never succeeded in recovering Britain, but it remained from that time on under tyrants.'

Concerning the middle of the 6th century
History of the Wars 8.20.6-10 (553 AD)
Three very populous nations inhabit the Island of Brittia, and one king is set over each of them. And the names of these nations are Angles, Frisians, and Britons who have the same name as the island. So great apparently is the multitude of these peoples that every year in large groups they migrate from there with their women and children and go to the Franks. And they [the Franks] *are settling them in what seems to be the more desolate part of their land, and as a result of this they say they are gaining possession of the island. So that not long ago the king of the Franks actually sent some of his friends to the Emperor Justinian in Byzantium, and despatched with them the men of the Angles, claiming that this island* [Britain], *too, is ruled by him. Such then are the matters concerning the island called Brittia.*

What all these sources tell us is that after Constantine III left Britain with the last legions around 407, the Romano-British were effectively on their own. The response by Honorius to their appeals for help in 410 confirmed this. It is only with hindsight that later sources pinpoint this as the moment that Britain broke away from Roman rule. In reality, the province may have continued regarding itself as part of the Roman world for some time.

It is worth taking particular note of the two *Gallic Chronicle* entries referring to 441 and Saxons gaining power over the Britons. They were written in 452 and 511 respectively in Gaul. These documents are usually reasonably accurate, yet this date does not fit into the narrative of either Gildas or Bede which we will hear later. It is also not accurate for the whole island given that Devon and Cornwall held out for hundreds of years, and Wales until the time of Edward I. So which part of the country fell and what 'yields to the power of the Saxons' means is open to debate. It is likely it refers to the South East as that is the closest to Gaul. This leads us to speculate about the province of Maxima Caesariensis, the Count of the Saxon Shore military command and the Diocese capital, London.

Contemporary Sources

It is worth pointing out that Nennius, in the ninth-century *Historia Brittonum*, does indicate a Saxon arrival in 428 and subsequent revolt which would tie in with this date, and it is this very source that first mentions Arthur. We need to compare this to Bede writing in the eighth century, who is more respected and yet posits a date of 449 for the Saxon arrival and a later date for their revolt. However it is true that the only contemporary source from the Continent does suggest an earlier date for any Saxon incursions. To focus on the *Gallic Chronicle* below are selected entries for the 440s:

Table 4: *Gallic Chronicle* entries

440	Deserted lands near the city of Valence were given to the Alans, ruled by Sambida.
441	The Britons, which to this time had suffered from various disasters and misfortunes, are reduced to the power of the Saxons.
443	The Alans ... subdued by warfare those who resisted them ... and obtained possession of the land by force.
444	Carthage, having been captured by the Vandals ... threw off the power of the Roman Empire.
445	Thrace is wounded by an incursion of the Huns.

A number of things to note:

After 446 the chronicle is accurate; before 446, the further away from Gaul the less accurate the record. So the entries for 444 and 445 are actually four or five years too late. What this means is that the entry for Britain for 441, being close to Gaul, is likely to be fairly accurate, but if not, could well be even earlier. The phrase 'reduced to the power of' is often used to mean a military take over. It could though mean something else such as a political change. This may be important when we come to later narratives. What this means for Gildas and Bede dating for the arrival of the Saxons is uncertain. Either they are are incorrect or they are talking about two separate events. We cannot equate this with Bede's date for the arrival of the Saxons for a couple of very good reasons. First, the Gallic entry most definitely does not relate to a simple arrival, but to a significant change in the balance of power either politically or militarily. Second, Bede makes it clear that the Saxon revolt occurred sometime after the arrival. So it's not simply a case of trying to bring the Gallic date of 441 forward to meet Bede's date for the arrival of 446 or 449, because Bede records the revolt as some time after that.

So in conclusion, the *Gallic Chronicle* is fairly reliable. It describes some sort of Saxon takeover in 441 which appears to contradict the timeline recorded elsewhere such as Gildas and Bede. But this date of 441 is vitally important in laying out a narrative that includes a historical Arthur. However, there is much debate in academic circles on this point and no clear consensus, certainly not for any precise dating.

The issue of the different timelines each of the sources offer is crucial in understanding this period. But we do have a contemporary source relating to a visit to Britain in AD 429, twenty years after the break from Roman authority. Constantius of Lyon, born in approximately 420, wrote *The Life of Saint Germanus* in around 480. In response to the rise of the Pelagian heresy, Bishop Germanus of Auxerre travels to Britain accompanied by Lupus. Pelagius is usually described as a British monk and subscribed to the idea that free will is more important than original sin. Anti-Pelagian legislation started to appear on the Continent in 418 and Prosper of Aquitaine relates that a Pelagian supporter, Agricola, fled to Britain where it appeared to be safe.[2]

Germanus is welcomed by crowds of people and later enters into some sort of debating contest with followers of Pelagius 'flaunting their wealth' in their 'dazzling robes', witnessed by a great crowd thus suggesting they come from a rich aristocracy. During this debate a tribune brings his blind daughter to the bishop who cures her in front of the crowd. The 'true church' wins the debate and Germanus visits St Albans just outside London. There then follows an incursion of Saxons and Picts, so possibly from the north. The British army retreats to a camp and requests help from Germanus. On arrival he baptises many of the soldiers and appoints himself Dux Proelii (leader for battle). He positions his army hidden in a steep valley between mountains which suggests Wales or the north, and on sighting the enemy they all shout 'Alleluia' repeatedly, scaring the enemy who run away, many drowning in a river. The 'most wealthy island' now secure, Germanus returns to Gaul

Some time later the Pelagian heresy returns and Germanus travels once more, this time with a man called Severus. Germanus meets bishops and a leading man of the province, Elafius, and cures his son's withered leg. The Pelagic heretics are banished from Britain and Germanus returns to Gaul to intervene in a dispute in Armorica before dying in Ravenna in Italy. So we have a picture of a Christian Britain, possibly with some form of Roman-like administration in the form of tribunes, leading men of the province and bishops. But there are also raids from Picts and interestingly, Saxons. Despite this, travel is possible both from outside of Britain and internally. There is some debate whether the second visit was in the 437, 442 or 448, with most scholars preferring the later date. However, it is important to consider this in conjunction with the *Gallic Chronicle*. A visit before 440 would explain why there is no reference to this Saxon power in the text. A later visit might explain where the author of the *Chronicle* got their information from.

In the past there was a consensus that he died in 448. This would make a visit in the 440s possible. There was some evidence he was involved in the deposition of Hiliary of Arles in 444. However, it is suspect if he was present. The *Vita Severi* describes the funeral procession of Germanus as passing through Vienne during the pontificate of Pascentius, who was dead by 441. We know his predecessor died on a Wednesday, 1 May, and that Germanus held the position for thirty years. Thus the three possible dates are: 407–37, 412–42 or 418–48. In the *Vita Germani*, he is said to have travelled to Revenna to settle a dispute in Armorica. We know from the *Gallic Chronicle* that this dispute occurred in 435–7.[3] Therefore we can say confidently that Germanus died in 437 and his likely second visit was indeed few years after the first in the mid-430s. It would make sense that this visit was before the event that caused the *Gallic Chronicle* to reference Britain falling to the power of the Saxons, because Germanus would surely have mentioned it; something as momentous would have been recorded, aside from the fact that Germanus seems to have encountered a Britain as reasonably stable as in 429.

The visit of Germanus suggests a number of things:

- Britain was stable enough to travel to and across.
- There were still links within the church between Britain and Gaul.
- The Pelagians are portrayed as being richly dressed and so might be aristocratic.
- The religious division between Pelagians and the church suggests a political divide too.
- In the first visit, the Pelagians are 'confounded', but in the second they are condemned and exiled, suggesting a shifting of power.

There are links between Bishop Germanus's visit and Vortigern, which I will cover later. However Constantius doesn't mention any Vortigern or even any king.

What this suggests is that Britain remained somewhat stable after the last legions left. Despite this, at least one incursion of Picts and Saxons occurred in 429. Links persisted with Gaul and the Western Empire, especially through the church. The island was largely Christian but there were schisms within Christian society. Whether the provincial structure held, or separate civitates operated independently is unknown. And lastly, around 440 something occurred to cause an observer in Gaul to regard part of Britain, at least, to have fallen to 'the power of the Saxons'.

Around the same time as the Germanus visit, we have Pope Celestine sending Palladius to Ireland to be bishop for an apparently established Christian community. Shortly after this we have records of St Patrick preaching in Ireland. There is no provable date for his activities,[4] although some traditions have his death in either the 460s or 490s. His mission to Ireland is thought to be in the 430s and there is a suggestion his letter to Coroticus may refer to a Strathclyde king around 450, but this is highly speculative. The dating is important because as we shall see the very first reference to Arthur places him after the death of St Patrick. Although it has to be said, the narrative and dating within the text is as open to criticism as the text itself. Having said that, a very credible theory suggests that St Patrick's arrival has been confused with Palladius and thus his floruit was a generation later, his death date being recorded in the *Annals of Ulster* as 493.[5]

Patrick wrote two works: the *Confessio* (a spiritual and personal autobiography) and *Epistola* (a letter written to the British king, complaining about the capturing and enslavement of Christians). From his *Confessio* we learn he was born in an unknown town of Bannavem Taburniae (*vico banavem* taburniae). He grew up on the country seat or small estate (villula). His father, Calpornius, was a decurio (member of town council) and a deacon in the church and son of Potitus, a priest.[6] This again suggests there were functioning town councils and an established Christian community in Britain at the beginning of the fifth century. At around 16 years old he was captured by Irish raiders. Six years later he escaped back to Britain and later travelled to Gaul, where he became a deacon and eventually a bishop. Later he went back to Ireland and became the 'apostle of the Irish', converting thousands and laying the foundation for a Christian Ireland.

His letter to King Coroticus suggests a number of things about the middle of the fifth century in Britain. There appear to be local kings at this point. Coroticus has been identified by some as from the Strathclyde area.[7] The community to which the letter is addressed is obviously Christian and there is still a connection with Roman citizenry. To be accused of being neither Christian nor a citizen is apparently an insult. He starts the letter by calling himself a sinner and a bishop in Ireland, although there is an element of pleading. He asks that the letter be read to the soldiers of Coroticus.

They are no longer 'fellow-citizens', or 'fellow-citizens of the saints of Rome'. He describes the scene of the newly baptised, still dressed in white robes, being attacked by the soldiers. Some are slain, others captured as slaves to be sold to their allies, the 'apostate Scots and Picts'. A letter sent the next day requesting the return of the captives is laughed at. There are some interesting clues here. The messenger is a priest he 'had taught from infancy', thus suggesting this incident occurred perhaps at least fifteen years since his arrival. Even taking the earliest date for his ministry, the very uncertain 432, this would suggest the raid, and thus his letter and Coroticus's reign, was near 450. The alliance with Picts and Scots suggest a location from Strathclyde to North Wales, although Ireland itself is not impossible.

He goes on to request that the people no longer offer food or drink to the miscreants until the captives are returned. Coroticus himself is described as 'evil-minded', betraying Christians into the hands of Scots and Picts. This appeal only makes sense if the intended audience, including Coroticus and his soldiers, are themselves Christian. Another interesting part is where he compares this behaviour with the Christians of Roman Gaul who negotiate with the Franks and other pagans to buy back captured Christians. He accuses Coroticus of killing them or selling them to 'foreign peoples'. The strong inference is that Coroticus and his soldiers are not foreign but British, and British Christians at that. He ends by asking for his letter to be read before all the people, but especially Coroticus himself.

St Patrick would have been a contemporary of St Germanus. Depending on the credibility of other sources he would also have been a contemporary of some of the figures connected to the Arthur legend.

Sadly, the surviving evidence sheds no light on this. It does suggest that in the mid-fifth century it was normal for a native Briton to consider himself Christian and still a citizen of the Roman world. To be accused of being neither appears to be an insult.[8] The fact he addresses his letter to a king with a British name may indicate the first beginnings of the breaking down of order. If his letter was to a provincial governor, or the Dux Brittanniarum, for example, we would have a completely different picture.

Absence of evidence is not evidence of absence, but it has to be stated that neither St Patrick nor Constantius writing about St Germanus refers to Arthur or any persons connected to the legend. Later we will come to the first mention of Arthur in the early ninth century, nearly 400 years after St Patrick. In that narrative Arthur is placed alongside, or just after, St Patrick. Unfortunately the sources are silent. In fact there are no contemporary sources from Britain until nearly 100 years after St Patrick's letter to Coroticus. That source is what we will cover next. It's from this person we can confirm the Battle of Badon took place, although he does not refer to Arthur. Unfortunately his purpose is not history, but to tell his fellow countrymen how thoroughly useless, lazy, cowardly and wicked they all are.

Chapter 4

Gildas, going to hell in a hand cart

Gildas was a sixth-century British monk who is believed to have lived between approximately 500–570. He wrote a scathing indictment of Britain around 540, titled *De Ecidio et Conquestu Britanniae* (*The Ruin of Britain*). We also know of his life through a hagiography (saint's life) written in Brittany in the ninth century and his death is recorded in the Irish annals. A further saint's life was written in the twelfth century by Caradoc of Llancarfan, who was a friend of Geoffrey of Monmouth. There is a consensus that he wrote the tract in the first half of the sixth century, but outside that neither the genealogical evidence or the annals contain reliable data for his life.[1] However, his denunciation of five kings, one of whom died around 547, leads scholars to believe the tract was written between 524 and 547.[2] This would tie in with his reported death in Irish annals in 570.

Additionally he refers to the Battle of Badon, which he seems to say was the year of his birth and that forty-four years have since passed. This is important because it places this battle sometime between 480 and 503. It is this battle that is later attributed to Arthur and thus the date is of great relevance in our investigation. There are other interpretations of this passage: Bede, writing 200 years later, appears to translate the forty-four years as being after the landing of the Saxons, rather than before the birth of Gildas writing in *De Ecidio*. The key passage[3] concerns the Saxon revolt and British recovery, which involves the emergence of a British leader, Ambrosius Aurelianus. It describes a period of victories and defeats which led,

> up to the siege of Badon Hill, pretty well the last defeat of the villains and certainly not the least. That was the year of my birth; ... one month of the forty-fourth year since then has already past.

There have been some scholars that have translated it as Bede did, but there is a general consensus that it is the year of Gildas's birth. In addition Gildas also lambasts the grandchildren of Ambrosius, who is mentioned as leading the British, which would tie in with the writing being forty-four years after both the time of Ambrosius and Badon. However there are other interpretations. It really isn't clear if the forty-four years start from the coming of the Saxons, the fight back by Ambrosius, or the battle of Badon. Nor is it clear if the end of the forty-four years is the Battle of Badon, or the time of writing. If we take a literal translation, without attempts by modern translators at punctuation, it would be even less clear:[4]

> ... now citizens now the enemies were victorious ... up to the year of the siege of Mount Badon almost the last defeat of the rascals and by no means the least one month of the forty fourth year as I know having passed which was of my birth.

That reads to me, as a lay person, forty-four years from the 'that time' has passed. So, from the time of the fight back to the time of writing. Which means Badon was at some unspecified time between those two dates. Gildas also talks about a time of peace, at least from 'foreign wars', which suggests a generation or more has passed since Badon. Gildas only names Ambrosius in this part of the history, and even then the text is not clear about whether he led the Britons at Badon, only that he led the fight back after the initial revolt.

The whole document is, in layman's terms, a sermon in three parts. The first part is a historical narrative covering the arrival of the Saxons and subsequent wars which culminated in the battle of Badon. The second part is a denunciation of five tyrants, and the third part concerns the church. He intimates he is now writing at a time of relative peace, but if they don't mend their ways they will soon succumb to the same turmoil that occurred two generations previous.

So Gildas is saying: we've suffered all these past calamities due to our wickedness, and if we don't change we are all going to hell in a handcart. He uses the examples of the wicked tyrants and priests to emphasise this. It's important to note his purpose is not to relate accurate historical information. He has an agenda; it is a religious message, not an attempt

Gildas, going to hell in a hand cart

at history. Although he makes some historical errors, as he gets nearer to describing his own time he naturally becomes more accurate and what he says in passing, so to speak, can help the historian.

He inaccurately portrays Hadrian's wall as being built at the end of Roman Britain, but he is writing 150 years after the Romans left and 400 years after the wall was built. He obviously believes this to be the case but is wrong, which means he is likely to have lived a considerable time after the end of Roman rule. Not only that, he is likely to be living at a time when even the oldest person known to Gildas was born beyond living memory of the end of Roman Britain. This is another indication he is writing in the sixth rather than the fifth century. The last generation with experience of Roman Britain would have largely died out by around 470, the next generation may have had some fairly accurate information passed on. However, by the third or fourth generation their knowledge would have been as accurate as the average person today about the Crimean War 150 years ago. Remembering, of course, there was limited literacy and Gildas himself stated that all the records had been lost. Perhaps he has mistaken stories of repairs undertaken in that period handed down through a couple of generations. But the Battle of Badon would have been in living memory, so is likely to be accurate.

Perhaps the most revealing line is near the beginning where he refers to 'the unhappy partition with the barbarians', with the implication it affects the whole of Britain.[5] He laments the fact 'our citizens' can no longer visit the graves of the holy martyrs and he names two locations: St Alban of *Verulam*, and the martyrs Aaron and Julius. Some translations record this as Caerleon, or Carlisle. However, the language is quite vague and a more accurate translation is simply 'city of the legions'. This could be Chester, York or possibly even Lincoln. We know the original city of London was abandoned by around 500 and that significant Saxon settlement had already appeared outside the city and across the home counties. He seems to be saying that the barbarians are in St Albans and other areas, preventing the British from visiting various shrines. Or it could be that their presence in other areas prevents travel across Britain, and of course we don't know where he is writing from, other than he is likely to be located in Britain, Ireland or Gaul.[6] We can speculate about the precise nature of this partition, but it included at least parts of the South East.

The five kings he denounces all appear to be in the west of the island, but the tract as a whole makes clear in several places that he is referring

King Arthur: Man or Myth?

to the whole island and not just one part. The most likely explanation is that the partition refers to the eastern side of Britain, involving the South East, East Anglia, Lincolnshire, Yorkshire and the North East up to Hadrian's wall. This would then make access to Canterbury, London, Colchester, Lincoln and York difficult and would fit in with later archaeological evidence, later historical evidence, and literary sources, but it has to be admitted that we simply don't know what Gildas meant.

There is an implication the Romano British still control a large part of the province. In fact, later sources record the British in the north pushing the Angles back to be besieged at Lindisfarne on the north-east coast as late as the 570s. The *Anglo-Saxon Chronicles* describe later expansion down the Thames valley, and Welsh sources record seventh-century expansion into the midlands reducing the kingdom of Powys. All this suggests that at the time Gildas was writing the British were still a force to be reckoned with. While he talks of many kings and a love for civil wars, he also states Britain has governors which suggests some sort of provincial structure survived. His audience does seem to be the whole of the Romano British, which suggests a single unitary political body in theory if not in practice.

Additionally he is writing in a style of Latin that suggests he has had training and is the product of a late Roman school.[7] It shows that in 520–40 Latin is still a living language and there is an audience who would be expected to understand it. It is also felt that Gildas benefited from training in grammar and rhetoric, which suggests a form of Romano-British government or administration in early sixth-century Britain. It is possible that much more of the fabric of Roman civilisation was visible much later than has been imagined.[8]

The last contemporary account of Britain was Germanus in 429 where there is a sense of an 'intact' province. To quickly recap from the previous chapters: at the end of fourth century, Roman Britain has possibly five provinces each with a governor and a Vicarius in London; plus the three military commands. In 407 there is a succession of revolts that finally produces Constantine III, who moves his army to Gaul and eventually dies in the ensuing civil war. Meanwhile the British have again revolted and request help from Honorius. How much of this structure survived is unknown, but in 429 Germanus is able to travel to Britain, St Albans in particular, and then somewhere else to fight a battle. His biographer refers to a 'tribune' and 'leading man of the province', plus an established church.

Gildas, going to hell in a hand cart

St Patrick is little help because he refers only to Ireland, other than a letter to a presumed British king which tells us nothing about the wider political or military situation. The Continental sources are confined to the enigmatic *Gallic Chronicle* entry for 440 which tells us Britain fell to the power of the Saxons, which we know from history cannot be true for the whole country. Now, over 100 years later, Gildas is living in relative peace after a time of war. Some Romanised life has survived but the island has been 'partitioned', although by how much or where we know not. But now 'Britain has kings, but they are tyrants; she has judges, but they are wicked', and later 'Britain has priests but they are fools; very many ministers but they are shameless'.

It is possible to suggest that at some point between 429 and 540 the provincial structure broke down and kingdoms emerged based on previous civitates, tribal areas or other power bases such as cities and towns. Also, this was either caused by, or allowed, the influx of Anglo-Saxon invaders which caused enough disruption from before 440s to cause a Gallic chronicler to view Britain as lost to the Saxons by that date.

I will skip over his general history and start from the point where Maximus 'had his evil head cut off at Aquileia', which refers to the battle where Magnus Maximus died in 388. Gildas himself doesn't mention a date, but we know this from a variety of other sources. He then describes how the Britons 'groaned aghast for many years', due to 'two exceedingly savage and over-seas nations', meaning the Scots and the Picts (the 'Scots' at that time meant the Irish). Envoys are sent seeking help and a legion is despatched to deal with it. Having done so, a turf wall is built linking the seas. This is probably Gildas wrongly attributing the building of the Antonine wall to that time.

There is then a second incursion and a second request for help which again is answered and results in another wall, this time of stone. This appears to be Gildas again misunderstanding when and why Hadrian's wall was built. This could be a reference to rebuilding either by Stilicho in 398 or sometime after. There is evidence of rebuilding and maintenance at the beginning of the fifth century. In any case, after this second incursion the Romans tell the British that they 'should stand alone'; leaving them 'manuals for weapons' and placing towers overlooking the sea at intervals on the south coast, 'they say goodbye, meaning never to return'.

The Picts and Scots then return, the wall and towns are abandoned and the barbarians seize the 'whole of the extreme north of the island right up to the wall'. There is no mention of Constantine III and no way of knowing when these three incursions took place. They may be confused references to several barbarian invasions in 360, 367, 382, 398 or 407. Alternatively they could be unknown incursions in the 420–30s. The Romans saying goodbye could reference the Honorius rescript of AD 410, which puts the last incursion after the end of Roman Britain. But in truth we just don't know what exactly Gildas meant.

But the next important event can possibly be dated. He describes how the survivors, the 'miserable remnants', sent a letter to the Romans begging for help, demonstrating that some at least in Briton still saw

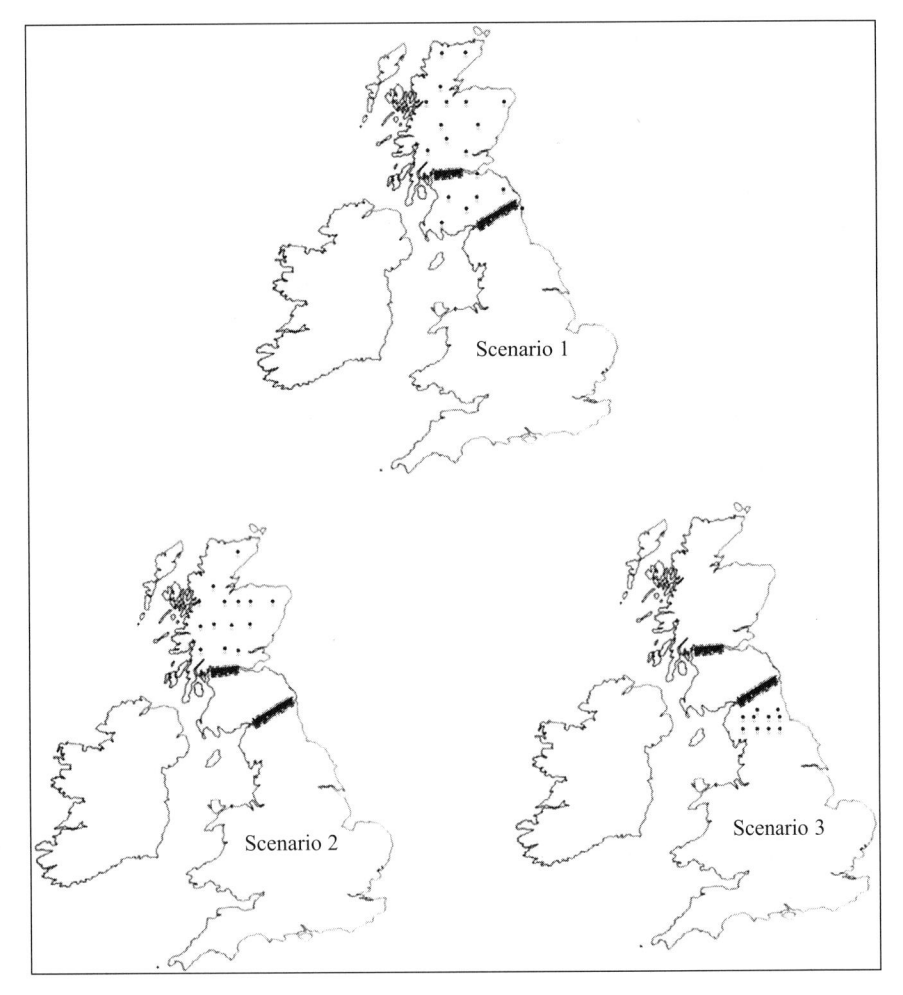

'Barbarians seize ... up to the wall.'

themselves as part of the Roman world. Gildas seems quite clear in saying this appeal is in response to Picts and Scots invading the north. He doesn't at this point mention Saxons or any part of Britain 'falling to their power'. Given his misunderstanding of history beyond his lifetime it is quite possible he is as mistaken about this as when or why Hadrian's wall was built:

> To Aetius, thrice consul: The groans of the British.

Further on came this complaint:

> The barbarians push us back to the sea, the sea pushes us back to the barbarians; between these two kinds of death, we are either drowned or slaughtered.

Gildas then makes it clear that no help came. We know Aetius became Consul for the third time in 446 and died in 454, so we have a date there from which we can fix the narrative. There is an obvious discrepancy with the *Gallic Chronicle* entry for 441 in which Britain 'fell to the power of the Saxons'. We know parts of Britain did not fall to the Saxons for hundreds of years. There's evidence of continuing trade and other links between the West Country, Wales and Europe. Perhaps the chronicler is referring to the fall of one part, say the south east. Or an increase in piracy in the Channel cut Britain off, giving the impression it was lost. Or the wars involving Saxons, Britons, Romans, Visigoths and Franks in the fifth century did indeed cut Rome or Gaul off from Brittany and Britain.

Either the *Chronicle* or Gildas is wrong, or mistaken, or refers to something we don't fully understand yet. It is assumed when Gildas wrote 'To Aetius, thrice consul', this dates the appeal to 446–54. However, Aetius became Magister Militum of Gaul in 423. Later evidence will attempt to bring what is known as the 'Adventus Saxonum' forward about twenty years to 428 and not 449. This would tie in exactly with a revolt, Bishop Germanus's visit and subsequent battle, and the *Gallic Chronicle* entry for 441. How we explain these apparent contradictions will be crucial in forming a coherent timeline.

The name Gildas used is actually 'Agitius', and there are other possibilities for who he could be referring to, Aegidius is just one example. Even if this is to be translated as Aetius, then it is possible the letter was sent, but much earlier, say in 430s, and Gildas added 'thrice consul' as a qualifier or epithet. But there is a consensus that Gildas is quoting from a known source and does mean Aetius.[9] So the most likely explanation is that it does refer to Aetius in the period 446–54.

Gildas's overall framework is rather confused and scholars don't rely on the accuracy of the chronology he puts forward.[10] He states the appeal was in response to raids by Picts and Scots, not Saxons, although one must note Roman writers often mislabelled Germanic raiders as Saxons. We recall Germanus responds to a raid by Picts *and* Saxons. It must also be remembered Gildas is writing in the sixth century and his references to events from fifty years in the past get more disjointed the further back in time he goes. Additionally his main concern is to drive home a message rather than to be historically accurate.

The table below summarises the main events with an estimate of when the events occurred. Some have estimated the arrival of the Saxons to around 480, and then twenty years of war leading up to Badon. On the other hand Bede and the *Anglo-Saxon Chronicles* place the Adventus Saxonum much earlier around 450. Nennius places it in 428 and from the *Gallic Chronicle* we can imply a date prior to 440.

Table 5

Chapter from Gildas	Year	Contents of chapter
13	383	Revolt of Magnus Maximus.
13	388	Death of Maximus.
14		Despoiled of army, military resources, governors and youth.
		Attacks by Picts and Scots for 'many years'.
15		Envoys sent. First appeal for help. Legion despatched. Turf wall built. (Antonine wall?)
16		Legion leaves. Picts and Scots return.
17		Envoys sent again. Second appeal. Romans send help again.
18	Honorius Rescript of 410?	Romans say they can no longer help. Build wall (Hadrians?), towers (Saxon Shore forts?) and left 'training manuals'.
19		Scots and Picts return. Seize part of far North. Towns and 'high wall' abandoned.

Gildas, going to hell in a hand cart

20	446–54	Appeal to Aetius. Denied.
		Britons fight back and for the 'first time ... inflicted a massacre on them' (Picts and Scots).
21		Irish return home. Picts settle in northern part (Scotland?).
		Partial truce.
		Famine followed by 'period of abundance' and luxury.
		Kings anointed.
22		Rumour of return of Picts and Scots. A council is convened.
23		All the members of the council together with the 'Proud tyrant' invite the Saxons to fight for them. Three keels (warships) arrive and are settled in the 'eastern side of the island'.
		Second, larger group of Saxons join the first.
		Supplies granted to them 'for a long time'. Saxons revolt.
24		'Fire from sea to sea burned nearly the whole island', all major towns laid low.
25		Many killed, some enslaved, some emigrated over seas.
		Saxons return home 'after a time'. Ambrosius Aurelianus leads fight back and initial victory
		His grandchildren, 'greatly inferior', are alive today.
26	Approximately 500	From then on (see previous chapter) victory went back and forth up to the battle of Badon Hill neither the last or least defeat.
		This was 'the year of my birth' forty-four years ago.
		Cities still not populated as they once were.
		External wars have stopped but civil wars persist.
		New generation has only experienced calm and are turning away from 'truth and justice'.

King Arthur: Man or Myth?

The only correct, verifiable date in this chronology is the death of Maximus in 388, all the other suggested dates are tentative estimates. The appeal to Aetius around 450 can be regarded as a strong possibility based on the balance of probabilities. Given the mistakes concerning the building of the wall, no mention of Constantine III and confused chronology, it would be true to say the three invasions by Picts and Scots could refer to any of the raids before or after Maximus, or after 410.

If this date for Aetius is accepted then we can place the arrival of the Saxons just after, with the rest of the narrative leading up to Badon in the second half of the fifth century, with the battle being fought around 500 and Gildas writing forty-four years later. However, we shall see from later evidence that it is not that simple. There are some who have argued that Gildas didn't mean Aetius at all. Others accept that he is referring to Aetius, but that the appeal may have been earlier and the title 'thrice consul' may have been added by Gildas, not the original letter writer. If these points are credible this could pull the whole narrative away from 450 as the date of the appeal, the Adventus Saxonum and subsequent war leading up to Badon.

The problem with this is some sources will try to drag these events twenty years back in time to fit in with Nennius and the *Gallic Chronicles*. Others will try to pull them forward to fit in with the *Welsh Chronicles*, which place Badon in 516 and Camlann in 537. They cannot all be true as we cannot have known figures such as Ambrosius, or indeed Arthur, fighting battles in both the 430s and in the 530s, leaving us to explain how this was possible in a time when people often didn't reach 50 years of age.

To summarise so far, Gildas was a monk writing around 540 (although it could be between 520 and 550). His intention is a sermon rather than historical accuracy. For our purposes we can start his chronology from the death of Maximus in 388. The next important date is the appeal to Agitius which is likely to be Aetius after 446, but this is not certain. He describes the coming of the Saxons and subsequent rebellion after this appeal. Eventually there is resistance led by Ambrosius Aurelianus, whose grandchildren are alive when Gildas writes. This puts Ambrosius around 470–500 which ties in

Gildas, going to hell in a hand cart

with the assumption about Aetius in 446. In addition he mentions the battle of Badon as the culmination of this fight-back and seems to date this at the time of his birth forty-four years previously in the 490s. At the time of writing there is a partition of the island between the Britons and Saxons, although they are now in a time of relative peace. This line of partition is likely to contain the south east at least but possibly further north.

There is further clues for dating Gildas as he goes on to describe five kings in less than complimentary language, one of which we can be fairly certain reigned from 534 to his death around 549. We can see these five kings below.

The partition of the island.

Table 6

King	Description	Sins	Possible identification	Possible location
Constantine	'whelp of the filthy lioness of Damnoniae'	In the 'habit of a holy abbot' killed 'two royal youth and their two guardians' while unarmed in church. Adultery, put away lawful wife.	Unknown	Either Dumnonia in modern Devon/ Somerset or Damnonia in modern Strathclyde.
Aurelius Caninus	'lion-whelp'	Parricide (killing of a parent or other near relative). Adulteries and fornications. 'Unjust thirst for civil wars'.	Unknown. (Cynan)	Unknown. (Powys)
Vortipor	'Bad son of a good king', 'leopard ... spotted with wickedness', Tyrant of Demetae.	Rape of shameless daughter. Removal and death of wife.	Guortepir (old Welsh) or Uortiporius.	Dyfed in South West Wales.
Cuneglasus	'Bear', 'Driver of the chariot of the bear's stronghold', 'Red butcher', 'with arms special to yourself'.	Wage civil war. Rejected wife. Took her sister from holy orders.	Unknown. (Cynlas)	Unknown. (Rhos – eastern Gwynedd)
Maglocunnus	'Dragon of the island', 'last in my list but first in evil'.	'Killed the king your uncle' in his youth. Broke vow to be monk.	Maelgwn King of Gwynedd circa 534–49.	Gwynedd, North West Wales.

Gildas, going to hell in a hand cart

These are kings that were ruling at the time of Gildas, and a generation or two after Ambrosius and the Battle of Badon. There are some tentative suggestions that I have included in brackets, but these are highly speculative. Maglocunnus has been identified as Maelgwn, King of Gwynedd whose death is dated in annals as 547–9. One such annal, *The Annales Cambriae*, is a tenth-century adaption of Irish annals of uncertain date. The Welsh pedigrees are of equally uncertain validity.[11] Thus in neither the annalistic, nor the genealogy evidence, have we sufficiently early or reliable data to identify, date or locate Gildas's five kings.[12]

We should make a note of Cuneglasus, described as a bear and linked to the 'bear's stronghold'. The name Arthur, if Celtic in origin, derives from 'Arth' – the bear, so this might be significant. Additionally Aurelius Caninus may well be derived from Ambrosius Aurelianus. Gildas does mention his descendants not being as illustrious as the grandfather. Gildas states: 'Certainly his parents, who had worn the purple, were slain in it.' This could mean senatorial rank or even imperial family. Bede, in the eighth century, describes him as having a 'royal or famous name'. In the ninth century, Nennius names him as the son of a consul. Geoffrey of Monmouth in the twelfth century has him being from Brittany and the brother of Uther Pendragon and son of Constantine. Whether this is Constantine III or some other Constantine is not clear. The most likely explanation is that his parents were of the ruling class in Britain at the time of the revolt and died in the warfare.

There are records of Roman Consuls with similar names from that time: Quintus Aurelius Symmachus was Western Consul in 446, the same year Aetius was awarded consul for the third time. There was a similar-sounding figure in 485 and either of these two historical figures could be contemporary with Ambrosius Aurelianus. There was also an Aurelius Ambrosius, or St Ambrose, who was a Bishop of Milan 340–97. A connection with the Aurelii Symmachi family is possible therefore, although it must be admitted this is purely speculative.

Other than Gildas identifying Vortipor as being king of the Dematae, even identifying Maglocunnus as Maelgwn isn't certain. There is a stone in the church of Nevern, Pembrokeshire, with an inscription, both in Latin and Ogham. The Latin reads MAGLOCUNI FILI CLUTORI, while the Ogham reads 'maglicunas maqi clutari', translated as '[the stone] of Maglicu, son of Clutarias'. The stone is apparently dated to

King Arthur: Man or Myth?

the fifth or sixth century. The translation of Gildas actually names this 'dragon of the island' Maglocuni. I am not suggesting this 'Maglocuni' has anything to do with it, but it does raise the possibility that the identification with Maelgwn is purely an educated guess. Deduced from the narrative and the likely time span of his life, plus the identification of Vortipor as king of the Dematae.

So, the only contemporary British source for this period outlines a historical narrative that is somewhat confused and inaccurate. It's purpose is a sermon. It may well be exaggerated. It does, however, corroborate the coming of the Saxons, a civil war, a 'partition' of the island, the fight-back led by Ambrosius Aurelianus and the Battle of

Possible locations for kings mentioned by Gildas.

Badon. It doesn't mention, or hint at, any person called Arthur. There is a much later explanation for this absence. Gerald of Wales, writing in the twelfth century, records that Gildas was angered at Arthur for killing his brother Hueil. This caused Gildas to throw into the sea a number of books he had written in praise of Arthur. Needless to say there is not a shred of evidence for this and, being 700 years after the events, can hold no weight. Some theories make much of this explanation, but it's one thing to claim you've lost your evidence so to speak, quite another to claim someone threw it into the sea hundreds of years ago.

We should also note that he does not mention Vortigern, and any attempts to claim 'proud tyrant' to justify this connection lack validity. Two hundred years later Bede borrows much from Gildas and names this leader as Vortigern, but we shall address that in the next chapter. The only person he names in the first section is Ambrosius Aurelianus who, in some translations, could be interpreted as being the victor at Badon. This could mean that Ambrosius Artorius Aurelianus is our man, but we have nothing on which to base that. Indeed, all the later stories seem to make clear he is not. In the later legends there seems to be a consensus that Arthur is the generation after Ambrosius. It would not be impossible for Badon to be the culmination of Ambrosius's career and the start of Arthur's. We must also bear in mind the five kings, like Gildas, are contemporaries, or the sons and grandsons of those who fought at Badon and so might be directly connected to Arthur in some way.

Concerning the location of Badon; later it is identified as Bath in other sources, but there are a number of problems with that. Firstly 'Montis' generally means mountain rather than hill. This would tend to favour a more northern or westerly location. Secondly 'Badonici' would tend to indicate Badon's mountain, or a mountain connected with Badon, whether Badon is a place or person is unknown. The problem with Bath is the Romans knew it as Aqua Sulis and there's no clue as to what it was called in the Brythonic tongue other than something similar to 'Sulis', which the Romans utilised. Later, the first written record in an Anglo-Saxon charter in 675 records 'Hat Bathu', or 'Hot Baths', for Bath. 'Badum', 'Badon' or 'Badan' are all derivatives of that with the 'd' sounding like a 'th'. Badanceaster from the *Anglo-Saxon Chronicles* means literally 'City of Badan'.

The problem is, Gildas was writing before 550 and the Anglo-Saxons didn't conquer the area until a generation later, after the battle

King Arthur: Man or Myth?

of Dyrham in 577. There's no Roman Badon recorded anywhere, so one would assume Gildas has Latinised a Brythonic name of which we have no record. Also, it is the Brythonic '-dd- sound that creates a '-th' as in Gwynedd. Nor is there any indication who is besieging whom. With the Belgae tribal area in the south and Germanic mercenaries stationed near the Saxon Shore forts and elsewhere in Britain, it is possible Bath was known as 'Badan' much earlier than is thought. We will revisit the possible location of Badon when we come to Arthur's twelve battles listed in the *Historia Brittonum*. First we will cover the next contemporary Britain writing nearly 200 years after Gildas, the Venerable Bede.

Chapter 5

The Venerable Bede

So far we have had no hint of an Arthur figure in any of the historical sources. We will now cover someone known as the 'Father of English History', Bede, a monk writing in the eighth century in the north east. He is writing 200 years after Gildas and is writing in the Anglo-Saxon kingdom of Northumbria. He was born near Jarrow around 673, admitted into the monasteries of Wearmouth and Jarrow aged 7 and was ordained aged 29. His most famous work, *The Ecclesiastical History of the English People*, was written around 731, four years before his death in 735 – dates we can be fairly confident about. His methods are respected even today and he was the first person to date events from the birth of Christ, a method adopted by later writers which is of great help to modern historians.

He had access to an enormous library at the monastery which contained many of the sources we've already mentioned: Orosius, Eusebius, Gregory of Tours, Constantius's *Life of St Germanus* and Gildas to mention just a few. He also lists those who helped him to compile the recent history of the Anglo-Saxon kingdoms: Abbott Albinus from the Kentish church; Nothhelm, a priest from London; Daniel the bishop of the West Saxons; the brethren of the monastery of Lastingham in Mercia; Bishop Cyneberht of Lindsey; and his own knowledge and connections in Northumbria. So he appears to have collected an extensive body of evidence.

By 731 the Anglo-Saxon kingdoms had expanded further westwards from Gildas's day. Many of the British enclaves and small kingdoms had been swallowed up. We will cover briefly the expansion of Anglo-Saxon kingdoms a little later and will now concentrate on the actual text concerning the period in question. The first few chapters are a description of Britain and history leading up to the end of Roman Britain. A short summary of the relevant chapters can be seen below.

Table 7

Chapter 11	407 Gratian set up as dictator in Britain and killed. Two years before the Goths sacked Rome (actually sack of Rome was 410). Constantine elected in Britain and crossed to Gaul. Soon after he was killed with his son Constans. After this the Romans ceased to rule in Britain.
Chapter 12	Bede seems to copy Gildas in relating three different invasions of Picts and Irish, the first two being crushed by Roman legions responding to cries for help. Bede copies Gildas's mistake of attributing the building of the Hadrian's and the Antonine wall to this period. The Romans vow never to return and leave plans for weapons and lookout towers. The Irish and Picts return capturing the whole northern part up to the wall, cities left deserted, people massacred and whole land left without food.
Chapter 13	In 423 Theodosius becomes emperor. 431 Palladius sent to the Irish by Pope Celestinus. 446 Appeal to Aetius (no confusion from Bede about to whom the appeal is made). Aetius unable to help because of struggle with Blaedla (died around 446/7) and Attila of the Huns. At the same time there was famine in Constantinople (verified by other sources in 446).
Chapter 14	Chapter 14 follows Gildas's narrative aside from Bede naming Vortigern as the leader of the council. Famine in Britain. British fight back causing severe loses to the enemy. Irish return home. Picts settle in northern-most part. Time of abundance, affluence and luxury followed by vice and 'every kind of foul crime'. Plague in Britain so there was 'not enough people to bury the dead'. King Vortigern agreed to call for help of Saxons to fight Irish and Picts.
Chapter 15	'In the year of our Lord 449 Marcian, forty-sixth from Augustus became emperor with Valentinian and ruled for seven years. At that time the race of Angles or Saxons, invited by Vortigern, came to Britain in three warships' and given 'settlement in the eastern part of the island.'

	Their numbers increase, the treaty is broken, there is rebellion and they 'lay waste to every part of the island'.
	Bede is the first to detail the origins of kingdoms present in his day as coming from three powerful Germanic tribes:
	The Jutes settled in Kent and Isle of Wight.
	Saxons in Essex, Sussex and Wessex.
	Angulus in East Anglia, Northumbria and Mercia.
	He also named Hengist and Horsa as their leaders.
Chapter 16	Saxons return 'home' (to eastern part of island?).
	Britons fight back and win victory under Ambrosius Aurelianus.
	From that time each side wins victories up to the siege of Mount Badon when the Britons slaughter 'no small number'.
	This was forty-four years after the Saxons arrival (493 although this is a possible misunderstanding of Gildas).
	Bede finishes this part of the history with: 'But more of this hereafter.' But frustratingly he does not return to the subject.
Chapter 17–21	A repetition of Constantius's *Life of St Germanus*
Chapter 22	He returns to the narrative in Britain and appears to repeat Gildas.
	'Britain had a rest for a time from foreign though not from civil wars'.
	Cities remained banned, enemy remained in Britain.
	A generation that kept to it's bounds was replaced by one who forgot the 'calamity' and lesson.
	Quotes Gildas as describing many crimes but the worst being not preaching the faith to the Angles and Saxons.
Chapter 23	Bede jumps to the year 582 and leads up to St Augustine's mission to Kent in 597.

It is quite similar to Gildas's narrative in parts and it is clear that he has used that material. Yet it does add something to our understanding in terms of dates and names. Having said that, if Bede relied on Gildas too much then he may have assumed Agitius meant Aetius and filled in the blanks. As we don't have all his sources we can't know. One of the problems is many later sources quote, and rely upon, much earlier sources, but if they are all based on one source and that is incorrect then we are building our knowledge on sand.

Nevertheless, he used a number of sources and is well respected as a historian and his purpose for writing this work was as a historical piece, as apposed to Gildas's sermon. He dedicates it to King Ceowulf of Northumbria and, for it's time, it is a detailed and professional historical work. Not only does he corroborate Gildas, but he also has a body of other sources that do likewise. Despite the fact we don't know all his sources we know his intention and reliability and the finished work is the result of those sources. There are things that Bede adds to the narrative. We now have a name for Gildas's Superbus Tyrannus (Proud Tyrant), Vortigern. We also have a different interpretation or translation of the Mount Badon passage which puts the battle forty-four years after the arrival of the Saxons, rather than before Gildas is writing.

This could be a mistake on Bede's part, or perhaps our modern translations are in error. I should add that in various parts he gives conflicting dates for the arrival of the Saxons. In two chapters (1.15 and 2.14) he gives 446 and in another two (1.15 and 5.24) he suggests within a range of 449–55. It is possible both Gildas and Bede are correct, although it would be a coincidence if Badon was forty-four years before Gildas was writing *and* forty-four years after the arrival of the Saxons. Given that Bede is obviously using Gildas, it seems more likely it is a misunderstanding. Whether Bede's or ours is difficult to say. There is a consensus among historians today that Gildas meant forty-four years before the time of his writing, so this places the battle around 500.

This dating of Badon is crucial in placing Arthur so it's worth looking at the options more closely. The starting point of this forty-four year period could be either the coming of the Saxons, the rebellion, the first victory of Ambrosius, or the battle of Badon. The end point of this 44 forty-four could be the battle of Badon or the time of writing. So the alternative interpretations are as follows:

1. Bede states the two dates are from the arrival of the Saxons to the battle, which would be in the early 490s by Bede's dates but as early as 472 from later sources.
2. Many others translate it as between the battle up to the time of writing, which assume Gildas was written in the time of Maelgwn, 534–47 and thus put the battle between 490–503.

3. It could be from the time of Ambrosius to the battle. We will see elsewhere that Bede places Ambrosius in the time of Zeno 474–91. This could be from where the *Annales Cambriae* and later Welsh sources get a date of 516–20 for the battle.
4. Lastly, the forty-four years could be from the time of Ambrosius to the time of writing, which would tie in with the comment about degenerate grandchildren. Badon would be sometime between these dates, allowing for a period of peace.

It has to be accepted Bede has access to other sources which hasn't prevented him from dating their arrival to 449. I would also add that Bede gives a clue in another of his works, the *Chronica Majora*, written in 725. He places Ambrosius in the reign of the eastern emperor Zeno, 474–91. Whether this is an assumption from an interpretation of Gildas or he had other sources is uncertain.

In summary, sometime between the Romans leaving in 410 and Gildas writing before 550, there was a British/Saxon war that culminated in a Battle at Mount Badon. On the balance of probability it's possible to accept the appeal was to Aetius and that this appeal occurred around 446. We then have to decide what to make of the *Gallic Chronicle* entry on 441 and how this fits with Bede's assertion that the Saxons arrived in 449. It would appear Bede understood that Ambrosius began his fight back in the 470s. Lastly, we will have to decide what, if anything, can help us determine a date for the Battle of Mount Badon as this will be central for any dating of a historical Arthur. We can be fairly confident of a date between 470–520, perhaps less so for Bede's implied date in the 490s.

Concerning the *Gallic Chronicle*, there's no way of interpreting Bede to arrive at a revolt in 440. However, it might be important that he describes three distinct groups and areas: Angles in the East, Jutes in Kent and Isle of Wight and Saxons in the South. The implication of his narrative is the Angles and Jutes are more likely to be involved in the arrival he describes and subsequent revolt. So the *Gallic* entry for 440 and Bede's reference to 449 might be describing two separate events. Either that or one of the sources is inaccurate. We will come back to this conflict later.

If we can take Bede's dating of Ambrosius as accurate, then the discrepancy in the sources concerning the Saxon arrival and revolts become academic because Arthur comes in the generation after

Bede's locations for Angles, Saxons and Jutes.

Ambrosius, who in turn follows Vortigern and Hengist. Once more there is no reference, hint or mention of anyone in the text or any of Bede's writings called Arthur, king or otherwise. Nor is there any reference of any aspect of the later legend. History at this point is silent. We must keep repeating absence of evidence is not evidence of absence – yet we still require some evidence. The next chapter gives us just that. It's at least 300 years late and turns up to our witness box unshaven and slightly drunk, but he's all we have up to this point.

Chapter 6

The *Historia Brittonum*

We now come to the first historical record of Arthur. There are some who will claim the Welsh poem *Y Gododdin* has this title. However, the dating for that is not without controversy and the surviving copies are from the Middle Ages, so we will address that source later. The *Historia Brittonum* is a ninth-century text written possibly by Nennius, a monk in modern Wales. The earliest full text is dated to 828 but the date of the first edition is unlikely to be before 800. It was written in Gwynedd in north-west Wales in 'the fourth year of King Merfyn circa 828'.[1] Nennius is described as a disciple of 'holy Elvodug' who died in 809. He bemoans the lack of records claims:

> I have therefore made a heap of all that I have found, both from the Annals of the Romans and from the Chronicles of the Holy Fathers, and from the writings of the Irish and the English, and out of the tradition of our elders.

Some scholars have concluded the preface was not part of the original text but added much later, and the preface is absent for all manuscripts earlier than 1164.[2] Some copies name Mark the Anchorite as author, and one destroyed during the Second World War has Rhun, son of Urien, as the author. If true this would place it much earlier in the seventh century and also give it a northern provenance.

It has a list of contents which includes the following for chapter fifty-six:

> King Arthur the warrior; the twelve battles that he fought against the English; the image of Saint Mary in which he triumphed; and how many of his enemies he laid low in a single attack.

There is a consensus that the preface is valid, despite being absent in the earliest manuscripts. The actual text is consistent across the surviving copies and is split into a number of sections with the fourth, the *Kentish Chronicles* being the most important concerning Arthur. The first section describes the ages of the world. The next section concerns British and Irish origins. He describes the Irish as coming from Spain, the Picts arrived first in the Orkneys, and he gives two alternative stories for the British. One is the tale repeated by Geoffrey of Monmouth 300 years later describing Aeneas escaping the fall of Troy and settling in Italy. His grandson Britto (Brutus in Geoffrey's work), kills his father and is banished. After many adventures he lands in Britain giving the land his name.

The next section describes the coming of the Romans and makes a number of errors concerning Caesar's campaign and the number of emperors. He does, however, mention Maximus and correctly describes three Roman 'generals' being killed by the British before the end of Roman rule and the subsequent appeal for help. The fourth section is termed the *Kentish Chronicle* and starts as follows:

> It came to pass that after this war between the British and the Romans, when their generals were killed, and after the killing of the tyrant Maximus and the end of the Roman Empire in Britain, the British went in fear for 40 years. Vortigern ruled in Britain, and during his rule in Britain he was under pressure, from the fear of the Picts and Irish, and of Roman invasion, and, not least, from the dread of Ambrosius. Then came three keels, driven into exile from Germany. In them were the brothers Horsa and Hangest, sons of Wichtgils … Vortigern welcomed them, and handed over to them the island that in their language is called Tanet, in British Ruoihm.

Tanet may refer to Thanet in Kent. Although there is also a river Tanat near Ruthin in North Wales. Interestingly, there is a connection with Ruthin and Gildas. There is a monument in St Peter's Square called Maen Huail. It is here that Arthur is recorded in a sixteenth-century chronicle (Elis Gruffydd) as executing Huail, the brother of Gildas. We will recall this being the cause of Gildas refusing to name Arthur. Yet the Life of St Gildas records this unlikely event as occurring on the Isle of Man. In any case, Gildas is quite clear that the first arrivals 'fixed their dreadful claws on the

The Historia Brittonum

east side of the island', and this source is equally clear they are given an island to reside in. So Thanet in Kent is the most likely location.

As to the date, there are a number of contradictory statements within the text concerning the arrival of the Saxons:

Table 8

Chapter and page	Text (known dates in brackets)	Date of coming of Saxons
Chapter 16	From the year when the Saxons first came, to the fourth year of King Mervyn, 429 years are reckoned.	399
Chapter 31	From above: 'the British went in fear for 40 years.' Not clear if this is forty years from the death of Maximus (388), killing of the 'generals' (407), or end of Roman Britain (410).	428 447 450 depending on interpretation.
Chapter 31	When Gratian ruled for the second time with Equitius (375), the Saxons were received by Vortigern, 347 years after the Passion of Christ.	375 380? Passion of Christ.
Chapter 66	Vortigern, however, held empire in Britain in the consulship (emperors of East and West?) of Theodosius and Valentinian and in the fourth year of his reign (428) the English came to Britain, in the consulship of Felix and Taurus (428), in the 400th year from the the Passion of our Lord Jesus Christ.	428
Chapter 66	From the year when the English came to Britain and were welcomed by Vortigern to Decius and Valerian are sxty-nine years.	Unknown. No record.
Chapter 66	From the reign of Vortigern to the quarrel between Vitalinus and Ambrosius are twelve years, that is Guoloppum, the battle of Guoloppum (possibly Wallop in Hampshire).	N/A but places battle, and thus Ambrosius, in 437.

There's no real consensus from historians; however, many theories focus on the 425 date for Vortigern's reign and the 428 dating of the Adventus Saxonum, which would tie in with the *Gallic Chronicle* entry for 440. The evidence for Bede and the Anglo-Saxon chronicles would all favour the later date of 449, which in turn ties in with a subsequent Ambrosius living two generations before Gildas. The other dates are all conveniently ignored, but there's no logical reason to favour one above another.

The following chapters, 32 to 35, are a retelling of the visit by St Germanus which we know was in 429. Here, though, he introduces an unknown 'miracle'. Germanus confronts a wicked king called Benlli 'a great tyrant'. His fortress was burned with fire from heaven, with Benlli and all his men perishing. His servant, Cadell, was made king by Germanus, and his descendants ruled Powys from that time on. This is at odds with later Welsh genealogies which will be looked at later. Below is a brief outline of the chapter contents.

Table 9

Chapter 31	425	Vortigern ruled in Britain.
Chapter 31 (and 66)	428	Three keels arrive led by Hengist and Horsa (chapter 31). English came to Britain in consulship of Felix and Taurus (chapter 66).
Chapter 32–35	429	Life of St Germanus part 1 concerning King Benlli and kings of Powys.
Chapter 36		English encamped in Tanet. Numbers increase. British can no longer supply them and tell them to leave. Saxons take counsel to break peace.
Chapter 37		Hengist negotiates with the 'British King' and envoys sent across the sea. Sixteen more keels arrive, along with Hengist's daughter. Vortigern falls in love and gives Hengist Kent in return for her hand.
Chapter 38		Hengist persuades Vortigern to invite his sons, Octha and Ebissa with forty keels to fight the Irish and settle them near the wall (Hadrian's). They wasted the Orkneys and districts to the borders of the Picts. More keels arrive leaving their homeland empty and they came to the city of the Kentishmen.

The Historia Brittonum

Chapter 39	A continuation of the life of St Germanus.
	Germanus confronts Vortigern for taking 'his daughter to wife'.
	Vortigern is condemned by 'the whole council' and flees.
Chapter 40–42	Tale of Emrys Ambrosius:
	A legend of two dragons, one white, one red, causing Vortigern's new fortress near Mount Snowden to collapse. This is later attributed by Geoffrey of Monmouth to Merlin.
	Vortigern grants Ambrosius (identified as son of a Roman consul) the fortress and 'all the kingdoms of the western part of Britain'.
	Vortigern 'went to the northern part' and came to the region called 'Gwynessi' and built a city called 'Caer Gwrtheyrn' (identified in South West Wales).
Chapter 43	Vortigern's son, Vortimer, fights against Hengist and Horsa and drives them back to Tanet. Attacking them three times.
	Hengist summons more men then fights against British, 'sometimes victorious. … sometimes defeated and expelled'.
Chapter 44	Vortimer fought four battles:
	Derguentid (Darenth in Kent?)
	Episford (Aylesford in Kent?) in which Horsa and Vortigern's son Catigern fell.
	Third battle in open country by the inscribed stope on the shore of the Gallic Sea.
	Vortimer 'soon after' died.
Chapter 45	Saxons return, Hengist asks for peace, Vortigern persuades council to accept.
Chapter 46	At peace conference Saxons treacherously kill 300 British nobles and capture Vortigern who cedes Essex, Sussex and Middlesex to save his life.
Chapter 47	Vortigern flees eventually to country of Demetians (Dyfed) to the fortress of Vortigern on the river Teifi (SW Wales), followed by St Germanus. Vortigern and his fortress is destroyed by fire from Heaven.

(continued)

Table 9: (Continued)

Chapter 48	This includes an alternative ending for Vortigern.
	Vorttigern's four sons described.
	Vortimer who fought the Saxons.
	Catigern (died in battle).
	Pascent, who ruled Builth and Gwerthrynion after his father by permission of Ambrosius who was the 'Great King' among all the kings of Britain.
	Faustus born of incest, cared for by St Germanus, became Bishop of Riez in France.
Chapter 49	Genealogy of Vortigern.
Chapters 50–55	After his (Vortigern's) death St Germanus returns to his own country.
	Details of Life of St Patrick.

So we have some similarities with Gildas and Bede except there are far more details. While many of the dates provided are wildly contradictory, there are indications that it happened much earlier than in Gildas's account because the author places all these events before Germanus returning to Gaul. We begin to see two slightly different timelines emerging. One places the arrival of the Saxons around 428 and a rebellion in 440, the other a generation later with the arrival in 449 and the revolt in the 450s. This difference is important because Arthur always appears in the tale a generation after Ambrosius leads the fight back against the invaders. The earliest Arthur would have lived according to this narrative is in the 450s and the latest, before 550. We will attempt to narrow this 'window' as we proceed.

It is also worth noting Vortimer, Vortigern's son. This is the first recorded source for this figure who, similarly to Arthur, has been regarded as fictitious by many academics. Vortimer's battles, recorded in Nennius and Hengist's battles in the *Anglo-Saxon Chronicles* are located in Kent. Both these sources record Hengist's brother Horsa as dying at the battle of Aylesbury. The *Historia Brittonum* adds that Vortigern's son Catigern also died. So there is a tradition that appears to cross cultural differences.

We then have the most important section and the very first reference to Arthur in any historical source. Nennius states the English increased their numbers and after Hengist died, his son Octha came from the north of Britain to the kingdom of Kent and all the kings of Kent came from him.

The Historia Brittonum

Dinas Emrys: Location of pool with 2 dragons
Caer Gwrtheyrn: Vortigern's castle
Gwerthrynion and Builth: Ceded to Pascent
Glywysing: Boyhood home of Emrys Ambrosius

Thanet: Arrival place of Hengist and Horsa.
Kent: Ceded to Saxons and location of Vortimer's battles.
Gwynessi: Connected to Vortigern.
Essex, Middlesex and Sussex ceded to Hengist

Locations in *Historia Brittonum*.

Chapter 56:
Then Arthur fought against them in those days, together with the kings of the British; but he was their dux bellorum [leader in battle].

The first thing one notices is that he is not titled king. Of course, nor does it state that he wasn't. There is no alternative title given, although the epithet 'dux bellorum' has sometimes been used to justify an interpretation of a Roman title such as Dux Brittaniarum, there's no evidence for that here however. Indeed, it is very similar to a biblical reference of Joshua. The suspicion is that he is using the references to St Patrick followed

King Arthur: Man or Myth?

by the soldier, Arthur, as a nod to the book of Deuteronomy which has Joshua following Moses. The phrase 'together with the kings of Britain' has not only been used to suggest he wasn't a king, but also that he wasn't British at all. Again there is no way of knowing.

More interestingly is the preceding phrase, 'At that time', for the previous chapter refers to the time of St Patrick. He doesn't date St Patrick and frustratingly there is a debate elsewhere whether his death was 462 or 493, although as we have seen the latter is more likely. Nor does he clarify whether 'at that time' refers to St Patrick's life, or after his death; once again we are left with a large 'window'. Another clue is in the text, 'On Hengist's death', later evidence in the *Anglo-Saxon Chronicles* date Hengist's death to 488, so we begin to see a theory emerging which places Arthur after the death of Hengist and St Patrick, which all ties in with the consensus for Badon in the 490s.

It isn't that easy of course. First, the dates in the *Anglo-Saxon Chronicle* for that time cannot be trusted. Second, it's not accepted that the figure of Hengist was anything more than fictional, as we shall discover in later chapters. One also has to wonder how likely it would be that a Hengist who arrived fighting-fit in 428 would have lived into the latter part of the century, which is what this source suggests. There are also contradictions from later sources concerning whether Octha is his son or grandson, even if their existence could be proven, which it can't. But what does seem to be clear from this source is that Arthur is associated with at least one generation after Hengist.

Twelve battles are then attributed to him:

> The first battle was at the mouth of the river Glein. The second, third, fourth and fifth were on another river, called the Douglas which is in the country of Lindsey. The sixth battle was on the river called Bassas. The seventh battle was in the Celyddon forest, that is the battle of Celyddon Coed. The eighth battle was in Guinnion fort, and in it Arthur carried the image of the holy Mary, the everlasting virgin, on his shoulders and the heathen were put to flight on that day, and there was a great slaughter upon them. The ninth battle was fought in the city of the legion. The tenth battle was fought on the bank of the river called Tryfrwyd. the eleventh battle was on the hill called Agned. The twelfth

The Historia Brittonum

battle was on Badon hill and in it 960 men fell in one day, from a single charge of Arthur's, and no-one laid them low save him alone; and he was victorious in all his campaigns.

It has proven difficult to locate any of these battles. The phrase 'Then Arthur fought against them' comes just after a reference to Kent, but none of the possibilities appear to point in that direction.

Table 10

Battle	Translation	Possible locations
Glein	Mouth of the river Glein.	Glein derives from the Celtic 'glan' meaning pure or clean so could refer to any number of rivers. There are two river Glens in Britain, in Lincolnshire and Northumberland.
Dubglas, Linnuis	On the river Douglas in the country of Lindsey.	Four battles at the same site. Dubglas may derive from 'blackwater' or 'black green/blue water', of which there are many. Linnuis is usually taken to mean Lincoln, but also referred to Lennox in Scotland. Additionally, the Lininius referred to Hampshire and Lindinis to Ilchester.
Bassas	On the river Bassas.	Several Bas- suffixes usually referring to Anglo-Saxon names. There is also a Baschurch in Shropshire connected to Powys.
Celidonis (or) Cat Coit Celidon	Celyddon Forest.	Usually assumed to mean the Caledonian forest, but could also refer to the forest of Celyddon located possibly in Gwent; Celyddon is a Welsh name and is referred to in later poems. There are also links to Kit Coit, the burial place of Catigern after the battle in Kent, mentioned in both Nennius and the *Anglo-Saxon Chronicles* where Horsa died.
Castello Guinnion	In Guinnion fort.	Winchester was called Caer Guinn and Vinovium near Durham, Gwinnouion. There are several Gwynion-type names that could have been given to a fort. The image on his shoulders could be a mistranslation of the Welsh word for shield.

(continued)

Table 10: (Continued)

Battle	Translation	Possible locations
Urbe Legionnis	In the city of the legion.	Caerleon, Chester or York most likely, but any town or city where the army was based at that time.
Tribuit	Bank of the river Tryfrwyd.	Some people identify it's location as the river Frew at Stirling; others, the river Ribble in Lancashire, the Severn at Gloucester or the Eden at Carlisle. It's mentioned in the Welsh poem *Pa Gur as Trywruid*.
Agned (or Breguoin in other copies.)	Mount Agned.	Geoffrey of Monmouth sites *Monte Agned* at Edinburgh. A tenth-century version of Nennius's *History* gives this battle the alternative name of Breguoin. This could be Bravonium in Herefordshire or Bremenium, High Rochester in Northumberland.
Monte Badonis	Badon Hill.	Nennius mentions the baths of Badon as one of the wonders of Britain and implies it is Bath. Badon or Baddon was the British for bath, but there were other 'baths' or hot springs in Britain. Plus Bath was known as Aquae Sulis in Gildas's time. It wasn't known as Badon, Badan or Badum until after the Saxon conquest in 577. Perhaps more importantly Monte, or mons in Gildas, usually means mountain or very large hill, which doesn't describe the area in the South of the country. British Din Badon would be translated into Baddanbryg in Anglo-Saxon and there are a variety of Bad- suffixes across the country. Alternatively Caer Faddon is mentioned in the Dream of Rhonabwy and is located on the Severn near Welshpool. Mynydd Baidan is another possibility in South wales. Buxton also has a spring and Roman baths and a Roman Road called Bathamgate and is in a more mountainous area.

The Historia Brittonum

There is a case for locating these battles in various areas of the country and these may give clues as to whom he was fighting and whether he travelled over the whole country or was more localised. There are a number of different theories which have been used to locate all twelve battles either in Wales, the South, the North or the East depending on your preference.[3] There is evidence the list may contain the 'resonance

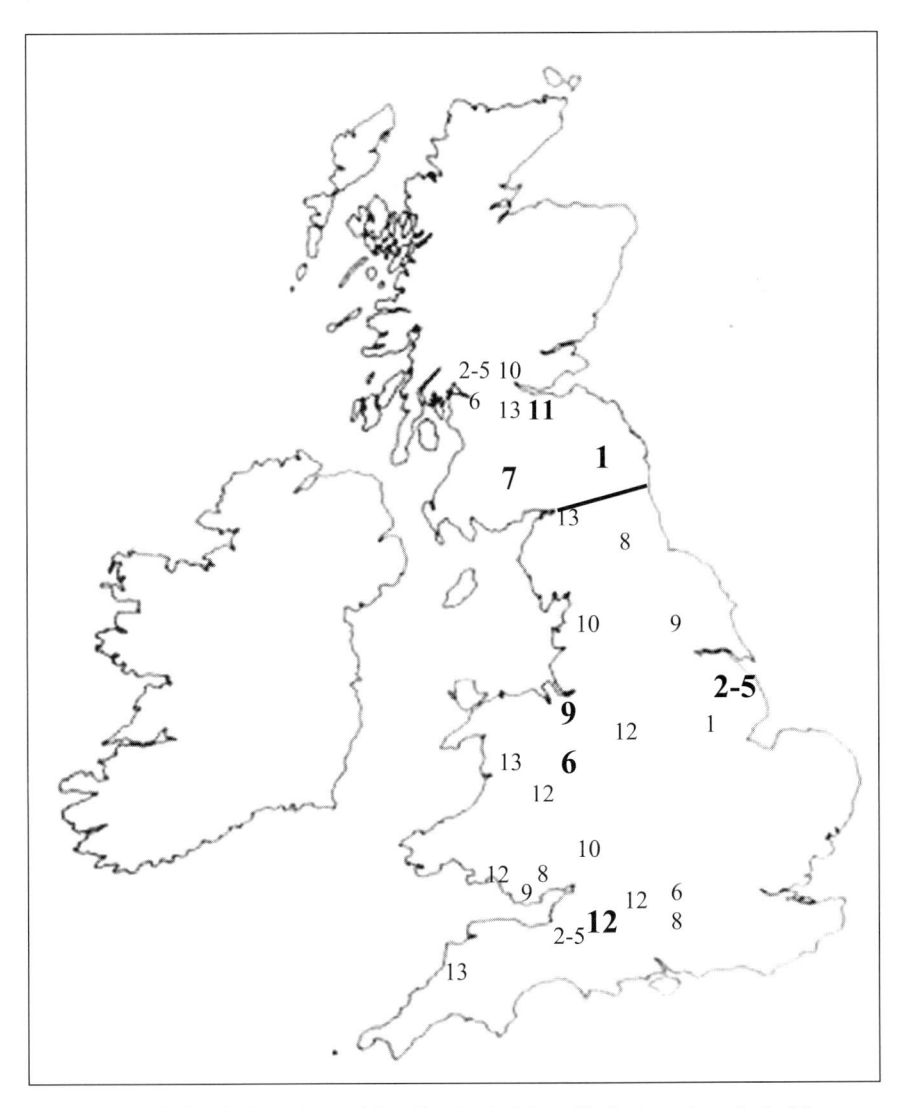

Some possible battle locations (13 = Camlan). Most likely locations in bold.

of Old Welsh poetic structure',[4] basically a battle song or poem. While some scholars think one or two locations can be identified,[5] others, such as Higham, find the battle list is one 'which our author largely compiled himself',[6] and Padel finds 'safe identification is impossible'.[7]

I might also add that some have identified other battles not connected to this time at all. The Battle of Celyddon Forest may refer to The Battle of Arfderydd in 573, fought in Strathcylde and traditionally has Myrddin turning mad and fleeing to the Caledonian Forest. The Battle in the City of the Legion may refer to the Battle of Chester in 616. It has even been suggested that the Battle of Badon was simply attributed to Arthur falsely to enhance his prestige. The text suggests he was fighting against 'them', by which it implies saxons. Specifically Hengist's son, who moved from the north to Kent, but it's difficult to come up with any locations from Kent that might be relevant.

If we could locate Badon, for example, this might help us understand the political and military situation. Battles confined to one area, or spread out across the whole island, would indicate if Arthur was a local ruler or operated across the whole country. Unfortunately no one has ever actually proved the location of any of these. Even those where there might have been a consensus, such as Celyddon or Badon, there is none.

The most we can say is that Celidonis is likely to be the Caledonian Forest and Linnuis is likely to mean Lincoln, given the location of Angle settlement and likely areas of contention. Aside from that I wouldn't be confident about any of the locations. Bede mentions a river Glen near Yeavering Bell in Northumberland. He's referring to King Edwin of Bernicia around 627, and of course is writing 100 years later. It may well be significant given that Nennius refers to a battle by a river of the same name. If Glein is likely to be Northumberland, Celidonis the Caledonian Forest, and the four battles of Linnuis, Lincoln, then we have a northern Arthur fighting the Angles on the east coast from above Hadrian's Wall to the Wash. Given also that 'Mons' means mountain, there is a distinctly northern flavour to many of the battles.

One theory suggests Artur Mac Aedan of Dalriada from around 600 as the basis of the legend. Many of the locations in that area have been connected to these battles, but also many sites from the legend itself. Going against this is the fact we have reasonable sources covering that period and there's no hint that this is the Arthur of legend, or anything in his life connected to the legend. We will discuss this theory among others much later, but it's possible Nennius found a battle list of this Artur, Arthwys of the Pennines, or some other Arth-like name and assumed it was Arthur. Even that would still leave us with an Arthur located by Nennius as being sometime before or after the turn of the century.

The important point is that this is the first text to mention Arthur anywhere in history, albeit 300 years or more after the events. We must accept that we cannot identify the dates or locations – or even veracity of any of these battles save Badon, which Gildas mentions. The important question remains: can the text of the *Historia Brittonum* concerning Arthur fighting the Saxons be regarded as accurate? Even if the battles were appropriated from someone else or simply made up, we are still left with a claim that sometime after Hengist and St Partick but before Ida of Northumbria, Arthur 'fought against them'. I would suggest there are five main options:

- He is a complete fabrication of the author.
- He is a mythical figure the author knowingly uses.
- The author erroneously believes him to be a historical figure.
- Arthur is a historical figure but the author misplaces him in the chronology.
- Arthur is a historical figure and the author correctly places him around 500.

We must look at the intention of the author. The text itself says far more about the ninth century than the fifth or sixth.[8] Although some have argued it is no less historical than other major histories of the early Middle Ages.[9] It is written for the political situation at the time, but also in some ways as a counter to Bede's 'English version', which the author appears to know well.[10] Some of the content suggests he is contrasting two dynastic foundations' tales, Gwynedd and Powys.[11] So it could be argued he is writing for King Merfyn and thus showing Gwynedd in a good light while Powys and other areas less so. The text contradicts and undermines many of the dynastic positions of contemporary British kings elsewhere in Wales.[12] Additionally, he is placing much of the blame on Vortigern rather than the British as a race.

It thus has a political purpose, so when he introduces Ambrosius, this time it's a very different character from the Romano-British warrior of Gildas and Bede. Here we meet him as a small orphan boy called

King Arthur: Man or Myth?

Emrys Ambrosius, and there is a legend of two 'worms' fighting, often retold as a red and white dragon. Three times they fight until the white (representing the Saxons) is finally defeated by the red (the Britons). Nennius is the first person to mention Vortimer and Arthur in history. The purpose could be to demonstrate that Merfyn will be the third successful British ruler to drive the Saxons out.

This seems to contradict his comment in the preface of 'made a heap of all I have found'. The evidence suggests this is not a committed historian collecting various bits of evidence, some contradictory, and attempting to write an accurate account.[13] Rather it is a purposeful synchronising history and the text should be viewed as a whole, a narrative with a purpose. Many texts in the early Middle Ages combine the history of a people with a history of the church and the text is constructed to form a narrative. That doesn't necessarily mean the contents aren't true, but one must remember the content and style has a purpose.

The Saxons are portrayed, unsurprisingly, in a bad light; succeeding through treachery, murder and poisoning. The fault on the British side is laid squarely at Vortigern's feet. Vortimer is there to show that the British were not the weak cowards portrayed by Gildas and Bede. Later he introduces St Patrick and Arthur, both British, one clerical and one martial. This is to demonstrate the spiritual and military prowess of the British. Arthur's construction is similar to the Book of Deuteronomy, where Joshua follows Moses in the same way Arthur follows St Patrick.[14] Joshua is also called a 'leader of battle'. It positions the Britons as the new Israelites overcoming their enemies and re-occupying the promised land.

Straight after the battle list the text describes how the English continued to increase their numbers despite their defeats and brought their kings from Germany to rule over them until the time when Ida reigned. It records him as the son of Eobba and titles him the first King of Bernicia, also known as Berneich. The interesting thing about Berneich, or Bryneich, is it has a Brythonic etymology and so implies a former British area taken over by Angle settlers. Bernicia was the northern part of the later kingdom of Northumbria, although at that time it was likely confined to the eastern coastal area. Arthur's time was before Ida, who we know from other sources was king in that part of Northumbria from around 547. Thus if we were to trust the accuracy and chronology of the text Arthur is militarily active from the time of St Patrick (died 461 or 493), after Hengist (died 488) to some time before the reign of Ida (547). In other words, we have a tentative timeframe of 450s–550 if we can trust the dates. Indeed, the text suggests some time passed between Arthur's victories and the time of Ida. If we trust the more likely later date for St Patrick's death, then we could tentatively suggest an orbit of 490–520 for Arthur being militarily active. Sadly it is not that simple as we can't be certain, and definitive support is lacking.

It is true to say there are a number of known historical characters in the text. It's difficult to be certain if any of the others are knowingly fictitious. The early part concerning Brutus appears completely unhistorical and is not supported by any evidence, archaeological or otherwise. The magical elements of the *Wonders of Britain* and the tale of Emrys Ambrosius also detract from it as a historical source. First, where it impinges on history the text is either demonstrably wrong, or evidence has been distorted. Second, the weaving together of different strands of stories such as St Germanus and Vortigern, then Vortigern and Hengist, and Ambrosius and the two dragons, suggests the author is manipulating sources and legends for a purpose; but still we cannot prove that for the key passages there are fictitious persons.

The author then goes on to list various genealogies, the cities of Britain and the wonders of Britain. In the latter he lists two wonders concerning Arthur.

The first is in the country of 'Builth', modern Wales, and describes a heap of stones with the footprint of Cafal, Arthur's dog. When he hunted a great Boar (Twych Trwyth, also found in the later legend of Culhwch and Olwen) Cafal, the warrior-Arthur's hound impressed his footprint on the stone, and Arthur later brought together the pile of stones called Carn Cafal. Men can come and take the stone for a day and a night, but on the next day it is miraculously found back on the stone pile.

The second is the tomb of Arthur's son, Amr, in the country of Ergyng, South Wales. Arthur himself is said to have killed and buried him there though the circumstances are not recorded. It is claimed it's length changes every time someone measures it and the writer himself has tested this.

So in this section we have a purely mythical Arthur, and some have suggested it negates the whole text. It certainly detracts from the validity of the source overall. What it does show is there were legends of Arthur circulating as early as 830. How much these legends changed over 300 years from Arthur's time is lost to us, but we can say that by the ninth century there was already a mythical Arthur as well as a historical one in people's minds. There are plenty of examples in history of mythical persons being made real in stories and legends. Historians require proof and one account 300 years later is not proof enough on it's own.

In summary, we have a ninth-century text that could be drawing on earlier sources.

Concerning this document we have two opposing Arthurs. One is portrayed as a historical figure fighting the Saxons at a particular time in history, but that portrayal is slightly misleading because it is clear from Bede and later archaeological evidence that these aren't Saxons at all. If he fought those who had came from the north as the text claims, then he fought Angles, not Saxons. And if he fought the Kentish men it is likely they were Jutes. In fact, as we will see from later DNA and archaeological evidence, it is debatable what percentage of the population was Germanic at all, and how much of the original Romano-British population stayed where they were. We will see later this could be anything from 50 to 90 per cent. The other Arthur is a mythical figure with magical stones and tombs embedded in a narrative which includes the story of Emrys and the magic pool containing two worms or dragons. There is no good reason to pick one and dismiss the other. The source is neither contemporary nor regarded as valid by historians in general. But we can't dismiss it completely – and not just because it's the first reference of Arthur in any known source. Despite it's magical elements and possible propaganda purpose, it was written for an audience who understood who or what Arthur represented.

Chapter 7

The Welsh Annals

We will now move on to the Welsh Chronicles, *The Annales Cambriae*, the earliest copy of which is found with a copy of the *Historia Brittonum* discussed previously. They are a number of Welsh-Latin chronicles thought to derive from St David's in Dyfed, south-west Wales. The *Annales* would have had a number of different authors using sources from three main areas: *Irish Chronicles*, northern sources, and from Dyfed. The earliest text is a twelfth-century copy of a mid-tenth-century text. They include events from across the British Isles. It was likely written in 954–5,[1] around a century-and-a-quarter after the *Historia Brittonum*. However, others have argued the earliest date of composition of some parts could be in the late eighth century, although the Arthurian entries are likely to be mid-tenth century.[2] The political situation was rather different compared to the *Historia Brittonum*. The Annals were compiled in the middle of the Viking age, the Mercian threat is reduced and there is less antagonism towards the Saxons as a result. It is also written in Dyfed rather than Gwynedd, so the target audience is different. It contains the first attempt at dating the Battle of Badon.

The earliest source is found attached to a copy of the *Historia Brittonum* held in the British Library and was written around 1100. The annal starts in 445 and ends in 954. I have used the translation from Morris that we used with the evidence for Nennius. The first few entries are provided below; the relevant years and the two entries relating directly to Arthur are in bold:

Table 11

Year	Entry
447	Days as dark as night.
453	Easter altered on the Lord's day by Pope Leo, Bishop of Rome.
454	St Brigid is born.
457	St Patrick goes to the Lord.

(continued)

Table 11: (Continued)

Year	Entry
458	St David is born in the thirtieth year after Patrick left Menevia.
468	Death of Bishop Benignus.
501	Bishop Ebur rests in Christ he was 350 years old.
516	**The battle of Badon, in which Arthur carried the Cross of our Lord Jesus Christ for three days and three nights on his shoulders and the Britons were the victors.**
521	St Columba is born. The death of St Brigid.
537	**The battle of Camlann, in which Arthur and Medraut fell: and there was play in Britain and Ireland.**
544	The sleep of Ciaran.
547	A great death in which Maelgwn, King of Gwynedd died. Thus they say 'The long sleep of Maelgwyn in the court of Rhos'. Then was the yellow plague.
558	The death of Gabran, son of Dungart.
562	Columba went to Britain.
565	The voyage of Gildas to Ireland.
569	The 'Synod of Victory' was held between the Britons.
570	Gildas wisest of the Britons dies.
573	The battle of Arfderydd between the sons of Eliffer and Gwenddolau son of Ceidio; in which Gwenddolau fell; Merlin went mad.

The 573 entry concerning the battle of Arfderydd may well be the battle of the Caledonian Forest listed as one of Arthur's battles. A further entry in 613 lists the Battle of Caer Legion referencing a known battle at Chester, which also could have been misappropriated. There is also the interesting reference to Merlin, which would date him decades after Arthur. You will note there is no reference to Vortigern, Ambrosius, or the coming of the Saxons. This could be because the Author dated these events prior to 445 when the Annals begin.

There appears to be some similarity in wording concerning Badon and the battle of Guinnion fort in the *Historia Brittonum*. The Annals state:

> The battle of Badon, in which Arthur carried the Cross of our Lord Jesus Christ for three days and three nights on his shoulders and the Britons were the victors.

The Welsh Annals

Whereas the Historia states:

> The eighth battle was in Guinnion fort, and in it Arthur carried the image of the holy Mary, the everlasting virgin, on his shoulders and the heathen were put to flight on that day, and there was a great slaughter upon them...

> The twelfth battle was on Badon hill and in it 960 men fell in one day, from a single charge of Arthur's, and no-one laid them low save him alone; and he was victorious in all his campaigns.

The Badon entry may have derived from the *Historia Brittonum*, but the discrepancies between the texts are significant.[3] The carrying of a cross rather than the image of Mary, and the reference to the duration make it difficult to draw any conclusions. It could be poetic licence, or the three days and nights might be a biblical reference. Alternatively, there is a later entry in the *Historia Brittonum* relating to Urien of Rheged besieging Lindisfarne in the Saxon kingdom of Bernicia for three days and nights before being poisoned by Morcant. Urien, and his son Owain (Gwain), have often been linked to the Arthur legend in later literary works. The Christian image carried into battle is also similar to Constantine the Great ordering his army to paint the Christian chi-rho symbol on their shields before the battle of the Milvian Bridge in AD 312.

Concerning Badon, there has been debate over the source for this entry; whether it was from a distinct northern source, or from the *Chronicles of Ireland*.[4] The date of the battle appears, on the face of things, at odds with the narrative of either *Historia* or Bede, which place the Adventus Saxonum in either 428 or 449. There is a second battle of Badon recorded in the Annals for 665 alongside the first celebration of Easter by the Saxons. If we take these to be connected, then at this time Bath would indeed have been within the land of the West Saxons and known as Badon, but that wouldn't explain why Gildas, a sixth-century writer in Britain, would Latinise a later Saxon word for a town that was in British territory at the time of writing. Bede does mention the conversion of the South Saxons and the Anglo-Saxon Chronicles dates this to AD 661. For the same year there is a record of the Mercian king, Wulfhere, campaigning 'as far as Ashdown' (possibly in Sussex) which would cover many of the suggestions for a southern Badon.

The entry for AD 675 mentions a battle at Biedan Heafde between the Mercians and West Saxons, but neither of these references mention any British involvement. So the location of the second battle of Badon becomes as mysterious as the first.

Regarding the Camlann entry, this is the first reference to this battle and it is impossible to confirm the source or historicity of it. The entry is unverifiable and possibly 'entirely unhistorical'.[5] The two Arthurian entries are thus suspect and could easily be later erroneous insertions. Interestingly, Medraut is seen as a virtuous and valorous figure in his earlier appearances in Welsh legends and seems to be on the same side as Arthur. He did not begin his long slide into villainy until Geoffrey's twelfth-century work portrayed him as Arthur's nephew and cause of his ruin. It may be worth noting there is no mention of anyone knowingly fictitious in the Annals.[6]

The Arthur of the *Annales Cambriae* should be seen in a southwest-Wales context. The Arthur of the *Historia* was, therefore, being used to support the political agenda of King Owain (of Deheubarth) in the mid-tenth century. This Arthur is intended as a Demetian ancestor figure. There is indeed an Arthur mentioned in the genealogies: Arthur map Petr (son of Peter), thirteen generations before Owain, but he appears too late and there is no evidence connecting him to the legend. Both the *Annales* and *Historia* are non-contemporary politically biased tracts. The *Annales* therefore lacks credibility for anything other than the time in which it was constructed. This is not to dismiss the *Annales* completely. There is a possibility that it reflects a now-lost northern, or even Irish, source that contained information on both Badon and Camlann, drawn upon by the author. Similarly to the *Historia Brittonum*, the *Annales* is generally regarded with scepticism among academics; in terms of trying to construct a historical Arthur, they are viewed as valueless.[7] However, they were written to be read and, presumably, believed.

In summary then, we have two pieces of evidence so far, neither of which are generally considered credible sources by the majority of academics. However, they suggest that a ninth- and tenth-century audience would have read and understood the entries; the implication is that they were believed to be true. This doesn't of course make it true. People today may well believe all sorts of erroneous things about events in the 1600s, books and films may contain all sorts of factual errors and fictional characters, even when intended to be accurate. But if taken at

The Welsh Annals

face value, both sources point to an Arthur fighting sometime between 490 and 537. Even if we accept a historical Arthur, it is unlikely he was militarily active for fifty years, although there are generals throughout history who campaigned late in life. If his association with Badon is accurate, we also now have a range of dates for that battle. From an implied 493–500 in Bede, 490–503 in Gildas, after Hengist (488?) and St Patrick (493?) in the *Historia*, and now a definite date of 516 in the *Annales Cambriae*. On face value this latter date seems like an outlier, but there is one interpretation that could reconcile it with the others which we will cover later.

Chapter 8

The Anglo-Saxons

The *Anglo-Saxon Chronicles* had their origins towards the end of the ninth century, possibly commissioned by King Alfred of Wessex.[1] They were most likely written in the south west as they appear more knowledgeable about that part of the country. The year, rather than the event, is the primary significance;[2] it is the first continuous history of any western people in their own language. There are a number of surviving manuscripts, the oldest being the Winchester Manuscript written around 891. It begins with a genealogy of the Wessex kings from Cerdic to King Alfred. It proceeds from the time of Julius Caesar and goes up to just after the Norman conquest in 1066, although other manuscripts go a little further.

I will begin with the entries from the end of Roman Britain to the appeal to the Romans:

Table 12

Year	Entry
409	Here the Goths destroyed the stronghold of Rome, and afterwards the Romans never ruled in Britain; that was eleven hundred and ten years after it was built. In all they had ruled there four hundred and seventy years after Julius Caesar first sought out the country.
418	Here the Romans assembled all the gold-hoards which were in Britain and hid some in the earth so that no one afterwards could find them, and took some with them into Gaul.
423	Here Theodosius the younger succeeded to the kingdom [Western Empire].
430	Here the Bishop Palladius was sent from Pope Celestine to the Scots [Irish] in order to strengthen their faith.
443	Here the Britons sent to Rome and asked them for help against the Picts, but they had none there because they were campaigning against Attila, king of the Huns; and then they sent to the Angles and made the same request to the princes of the Angle race.

The Anglo-Saxons

So this deviates from some of the other evidence. There is Palladius's mission, but nothing about St Germanus or St Patrick. The appeal is dated as 443, a little earlier than in Bede. There is no reference to explain the *Gallic Chronicle* entry of 441 which stated Britain fell to the 'power of the Saxons'. The entry for 449 does however appear to have been influenced by Bede.

It notes Mauricius and Valentinian succeeded to the kingdom (i.e. the Roman Empire) and ruled for seven years. Then 'in their days', Hengist and Horsa arrive, invited by Vortigern, who is titled king of the Britons. They land at Ebba's Creek (Ebbsfleet, East Kent). At first they assisted the Britons winning victories over the Picts in the north. They then 'sent to Angeln' requesting more help, implying they are Angles, although next it states: 'these men came from three tribes of Germany: from the Old Saxons, from the Angles, from the Jutes.' It then confirms much of what Bede says listing the the tribal areas:

- Jutes: Kent, Isle of Wight, parts of Wessex still called 'the race of the Jutes' (likely the New Forest area).
- Old Saxons: East Saxons (Essex), South Saxons (Sussex) and West Saxons (Wessex).
- Angles: East Angles (East Anglia), Middle Angles (Mercia) and Northumbrians.

It names Hengist and Horsa and lists their genealogy: Wihtgils, Witta, Wecta and Woden, thus claiming Woden originated the Wessex royal family and 'that of the Southumbrians too'. It may be worth noting that Hengist and Horsa mean 'stallion' and 'horse' respectively, and some have thus suggested there is poetic licence or mythology at play here. There is also the reference to Woden in the genealogy tree which is similar to founding myths in other tribal societies. There is archaeological evidence concerning areas of north-west Europe being left uninhabited around this time, however, so that part of the narrative at least has some corroborative evidence.

We then have a list of four battles involving Hengist, one of which seems to replicate some of Vortimer's battles in the *Historia Brittonum*. They all appear to be in Kent.

Table 13

Date	Text
455	Here Hengist and Horsa fought against Vortigern the king in the place which is called Aylesford, and his brother Horsa was killed. And after that Hengist and Aesc his son succeeded to the kingdom.
457	Here Hengist and Aesc fought against the Britons in the place which is called Crayford, and there killed four thousand men; and the Britons then abandoned the land of Kent and in great terror fled to the stronghold of London
465	Here Hengist and Aesc fought against the Welsh near Wipped's Creek, and there killed 12 Welsh chieftains and one of their thanes, whose name was Wipped, was killed there.
473	Here Hengist and Aesc fought against the Welsh and seized countless war-loot and the Britons fled from the English like fire.

In 488 there is an entry recording Aesc as succeeding to the kingdom of Kent for twenty-four years, so presumably Hengist dies in that year. However other traditions name Oisc as the founder of the Kentish royal house.[3] We recall the *Historia Brittonum* has Octha succeeding Hengist and then 'Arthur fought against them'. Shortly after Hengist's battles in Kent, there are several battles by Aelle recorded. These all appear to be in Sussex on the south coast. At that time the Weald separated Kent from Sussex and so it would have be difficult for armies to move from Kent to Sussex, or from Sussex north towards London. If these dates are in any way accurate, then it is interesting to compare them with the military activity of Ambrosius Aurelianus in 'the time of Zeno' (474–91) as described by Bede.

Table 14

Date	Text
477	Here Aelle and his 3 sons, Cymen and Wlencing and Cissa, came to the land of Britain with 3 ships at a place which is named Cymen's shore [probably Selsy Bill, West Sussex], and there killed many Welsh and drove them into the wood which is named the Weald.
485	Here Aelle fought against the Welsh near the margin of Mearcred's Burn.
491	Here Aelle and Cissa besieged Anderitum [Roman fort at Pevensey], and killed all who lived in there; there was not even one Briton left there.

The Anglo-Saxons

The last table concerns the foundation of the West Saxons:

Table 15

Year	Entry
495	Here two chieftains; Cerdic and Cynric his son, came to Britain with 5 ships at the place which is called Cardic's Shore (probably Charford in Hampshire) and the same day fought against the Welsh.
501	Here Port and his 2 sons, Bieda and Maegla, came with 2 ships to Britain at the place which is called Portsmouth, and killed a certain young British man – a very noble man.
508	Here Cerdic and Cynric killed a certain British king whose name was Natanleod, and 5 thousand men with him – after whom the land as far as Charford was named Netley [probably Hampshire]
514	Here the West Saxons, Stuf and Wihtgar, came to Britain with 3 ships in the place which is called Cerdic's Shore [same location as Cerdic and Cynric] and fought against the Britons and put them to flight.
519	Here Cerdic and Cynric succeeded to the kingdom of the West Saxons and the same year they fought against the Britons at the place they now name Cerdic's Ford [probably Charford in Hampshire]. And the royal family of the West Saxons ruled from that day on [last line added by later annalist].
527	Here Cerdic and Cynric fought against the Britons at the place which is called Cerdic's Wood.
530	Here Cerdic and Cynric took the Isle of Wight and killed a few men at Wihtgar's stronghold.
534	Here Cerdic passed away, and his son Cynric continued to rule 26 years. And they gave all Wight to their two nephew's Stuf and Wihtgar.
544	Here Wihtgar passed away and they buried him at Wihtgar's stronghold.

You will note there are three separate tables as the entries, though continuous, appear to concern three distinct geographical areas and individuals. So, we have three sets of foundations stories and battle lists. Hengist in Kent between 455 and 473, Aelle in Sussex between 477 and 491 and then Cerdic, among others, in The New Forest area of Hampshire from 495 onwards.

The question of whether we can trust these dates arises. For example, there are two entries of eclipses for 1 March in 538 and 20 June 540. While it is recognised the dating is not exact, there were indeed eclipses on 15 February 538 and 20 June 540.[4] There is then an entry for 547 in which Ida succeeds to the kingdom of the Northumbrians, which begs the question what was the political and military situation prior to that? The entry then lists Ida's genealogy back to Woden, thus linking him to Hengist. A later entry for Cynric also links his Genealogy back to Woden. Hengist is mentioned as a character in the epic poem Beowulf, so the name would already be familiar.

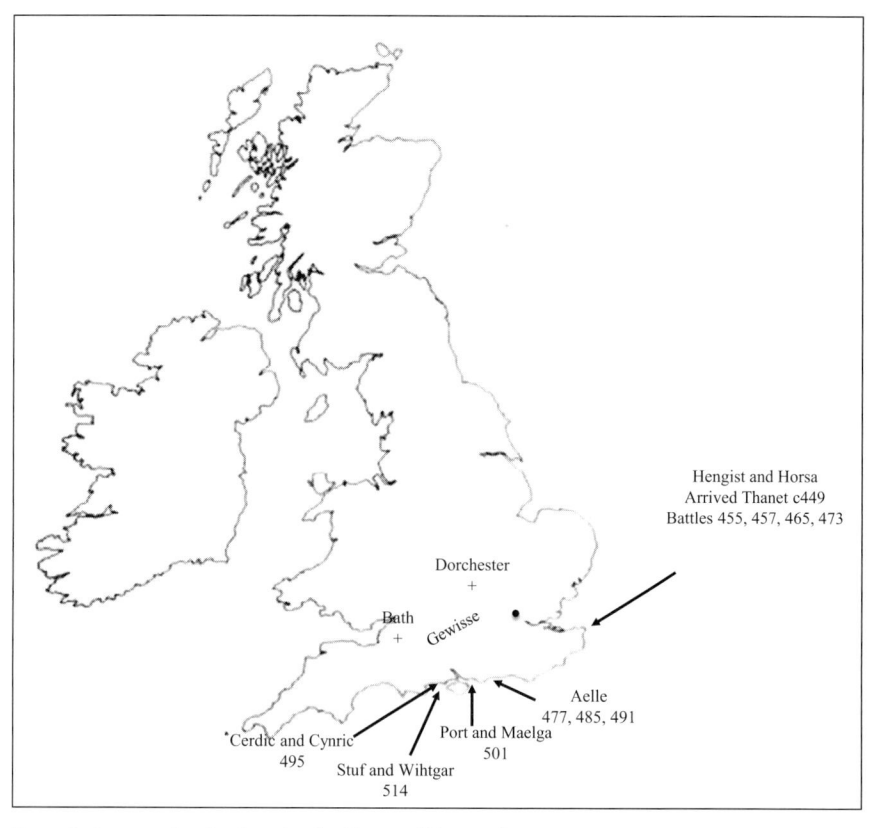

Foundation stories in the *Anglo-Saxon Chronicles*.

Victories for the West Saxons in 552 at Salisbury and in 556 at Bera's stronghold (Barbury in Wiltshire) then follow. They are powerful enough to defeat Aethelbert of Kent in 568. There is then a further expansion:

> 571 Battle at Bedcanford and taking of settlements of Limbury, Aylesbury, Benson and Eynsham
>
> 577 Battle of Dyrham against three British kings and taking of three cities: Gloucester, Cirencester and Bath.

So we have activity in Kent involving Vortigern, Hengist and later Aesc between 455 and 473. We then have activity in Sussex by Aelle 477–91. Lastly, there are incursions by various people in the New Forest and Portsmouth areas from 495. The *Chronicles* list two as victories in 508 and 514, but are ambiguous about other battles. We then have a lull in military activity which ties in with Gildas referring to an end of 'external wars'.

For Cerdic and Cynric the reference and likely location of the later battles do suggest a more defensive situation. There does seem to be a double entry for the arrival of Cerdic however: first they are said to arrive in 495 and take the kingdom six years later; then there's an entry for the arrival of the West Saxons in 514 and Cerdic is said to succeed to the kingdom of the West Saxons in 519. It is possible there is an alternative explanation: Cerdic arrives in 495 and occupies the land the West Saxons later inhabit. Nineteen years later the West Saxons Stuf and Whitgar do arrive, and six years after that Cerdic succeeds to their kingdom.

But nineteen years is the same as an Easter cycle, so could easily be misdated by medieval writers. In addition, according to genealogy at the start, and the later entries in the *Chronicle*, it does appear that the first date is a mistake and Cerdic is actually dated to 514. He then succeeds to the kingdom of the West Saxons in 519. This could be significant if the date for Badon is 516 as per the *Annales Cambriae*. Plus, the timespan for Cerdic and Cynric arriving in 495 and being succeeded in 560 by Ceawlin seems rather long.

Asser's ninth-century *Life of King Alfred* records a Creoda between Cerdic and Cynric which would make the time span more realistic, but it doesn't take away the apparent double entry. The reference to the taking of the Isle of Wight in 530 could be seen as a retreat from the mainland. It could be that further expansion inland was impossible, but that would be highly speculative. Yet we have this gap of a generation or two from the early 500s to further expansion of the West Saxons from the 550s onwards. This does seem to tie in with Gildas talking about a generation of peace.

I would use caution with the literary sources as there is a heavy influence from Gildas, who influenced Bede, who in turn influenced the *Anglo-Saxon Chronicles*. It's hard to speculate the extent of that influence, and what (and how valid) their other sources were. It may be important to note the differences: Gildas focuses on Saxons, while Bede is careful to name the Angles as those fighting at Badon.

There is another important point about the West Saxons which seems to contradict the narrative in the *Chronicles*. There is a suspicion that the whole line has been artificially extended, and a much more likely date would be 532[5] for Cerdic's arrival. In fact, Bede states that this area of South Hampshire and the Isle of Wight were Jutish until the West Saxon king Caedwalla conquered them in 686–8. Thus it would be impossible to place the origins in these Jutish territories.

The best claim for their origin is the upper Thames valley.[6] The first site of a West Saxon episcopal see was Dorchester, and the battles of 552, 556 and 571 seem to suggest a swathe of territory twenty miles north and south of the river Thames, culminating in the battle of Dyrham in the west in 577 where Bath, Gloucester and Cirencester were captured. It is also important to note that Bede stated the West Saxons were formally known as the 'Geuissae' or 'Gewisse'. They only started being called West Saxons after Caedwalla's time in the seventh century. Gewisse means 'certain' or 'sure' and may be a reference to their reliability.

Another group, the Hwicce, are occasionally conflated with them but they have separate entries in a later source, *The Tribal Hidage*, which we will examine later, plus there is no etymological link. They may well have bordered each other at some point, with the Hwicce running alongside the east of the river Severn. Geoffrey of Monmouth labels Vortigern as 'leader of the Gewissei. Additionally, in Nennius, after his confrontation with the boy Merlin, Emrys Ambrosius, Vortigern leaves the western part of Britain in his hands and goes to the northern part, to Caer Gwrtheyrn in the region called 'Gwynessi'. Caer Gwrtheyrn is identified as being an Iron Age hill fort in West Wales, which isn't north of any of the places in that part of the story. Vortigern takes Ambrosius from South Wales to sacrifice him before building a castle near mount

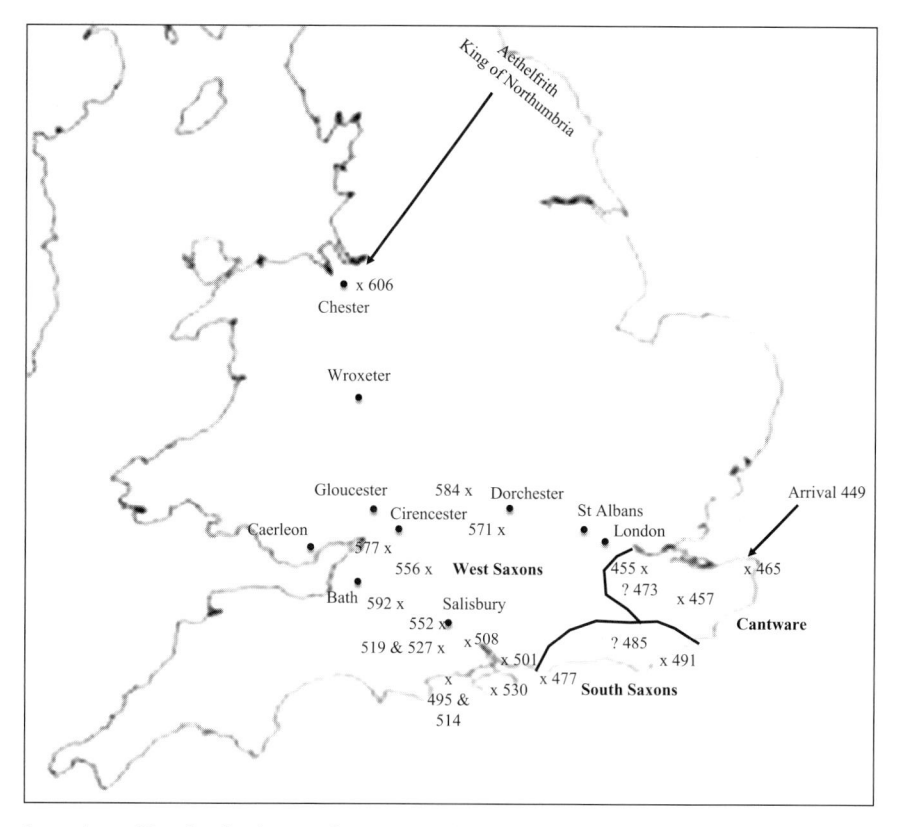

Location of battles in the *Anglo-Saxon Chronicles*.

Snowdon. There is no evidence for any speculation on this. The early entries in the *Chronicles* are highly suspect and we simply don't know enough about the origins of the West Saxons or Gewisse.

In summary, the *Anglo-Saxon Chronicles* broadly follow Bede and describe a narrative of an appeal, arrival and subsequent revolt. There then follows three distinct areas and periods of conflict. The first involves Hengist and Horsa in Kent, and intriguingly confirms the battle mentioned in the *Historia Brittonum*, where Horsa fell. The second involves Aelle in Sussex, Bede's first Bretwalda. The last involves the arrival of Cerdic and the West Saxons. There then follows an apparent break in victories until after 550, which on the face of it supports Gildas and a generation 'free from external wars'. Unfortunately, no entries before the middle of the sixth century can be confirmed. What is clear is Arthur does not appear in any way.

Chapter 9

Archaeology and Other Evidence

The origins of settlers can be identified through pottery, metalwork and burials. Angles from Schleswig-Holstein settled in mid-, eastern and northern England in the fifth century, along with some Saxons. Shortly after, towards the end of the fifth century, there was some movement from Norway into Norfolk and Humberside. Saxons left their home in North Germany and evidence is found along the Thames valley as well as Wessex and Sussex. Jutes from Jutland appear in east Kent and parts of the New Forest and the Isle of Wight,[1] and permanent settlements were established in the last quarter of the fifth century.[2]

This appears to corroborate Bede's description of three main tribes. Procopius, writing a century after, names the three races inhabiting Britain as the Angiloi, Frissones and Britons. Linguistic analysis has found Frisian as the most closely related language.[3] This Procopius passage is important as it also describes reverse migration of Angles and Frisians back to the Continent in the first half of the sixth century. Theuderich, king of the Franks, allowed Angles from Britain to settle after the Thuringian war in 531. This suggests there was pressure on Germanic peoples to move from Britain to the Continent from 500 onwards. Procopius states Theuderic's son, Theudebert (king of the Franks 534–48), boasted to Justinian that he had overlordship of part of Britain, presumably because of his support of Anglo immigrants into his kingdom. It may be important to note that archaeological links to Frankish Gaul are most prominent in Kent, and Christianity was reintroduced via a Frankish-Christian princess marrying a Saxon king of Kent, Aethelberht, in the last quarter of the sixth century.

Additionally, Bede's list of seven kings has Aelle of Sussex and Caewlin of Wessex separated by over fifty years between 500 and 560.[4] This further points to a lull in Anglo-Saxon advance and corroborates the idea of a British resurgence. However, the picture is not consistent across the whole country. There is a strong correlation between Anglian areas and

Archaeology and Other Evidence

cremation, and Saxon regions and burial.[5] So we have a South and Eastern divide. In addition there seems to be corroboration that the areas of Kent and Isle of Wight were Jutish. There is evidence that the New Forest area had once been Jutish land and Asser, King Alfred's biographer, records that Stuf and Wihtgar were Cerdic's nephews and of Jutish Origin.[6]

We can't conclude there is total support for the literary sources that suggest Germanic tribes arrived in Britain after the 450s. Aside from evidence of Germanic mercenaries during Roman Britain, the archaeological evidence is at odds with Gildas and Bede in that it

Fifth-century archaeological evidence.

King Arthur: Man or Myth?

suggests Saxon presence in 430s and perhaps even a generation earlier,[7] rather than after an appeal to Aetius before 449. Given the description of the southern coastal forts as the 'Saxon Shore' it really is impossible to say whether the forts were defended *against* Saxons or *by* Saxons, or whether the area was already settled by Saxons.

The evidence supports the idea of a Saxon presence before 450 and a later Angle presence after. This could explain both the *Gallic Chronicle* entry regarding Saxons in 440 and the later Gildas and Bede references concerning the arrival of mercenaries around 450. They could be mislabelling Angles and Jutes as Saxons. The evidence for cultural, linguistic and genetic change is for population movements from even before the Roman invasion.[8] The main evidence relates to eastern Britain from across the North Sea. Strabo, writing in the first century, contrasts Britons with Celts, and Tacitus describes Caledonians as having Germanic origin and the inhabitants of Britain 'nearest the Gauls' having similar language. The tribe nearest the Gauls were the Belgae and there is evidence from Caesar's *Gallic Wars* that the Belgae were a Germanic people. Gallo-Belgic coins were found in Britain across the same area affected by the alleged later Saxon invasion.[9] The Roman name for Winchester was 'Venta Belgarum', meaning the meeting place of the Belgae. There is also the interesting fact that after Roman Britain, inscribed stones were found everywhere except the southeast, suggesting further cultural difference. A similar difference occurs in the distribution of rune markings appearing in Angle and Jutish areas, but not supposed Saxon ones.[10]

As early as the late third century, Frankish and Saxon raiders began to attack the channel coasts.[11] However, the forts of the so called Saxon Shore seem to have been built in the wrong time and place for defence[12] and it is possible that Saxons were already present along the South Coast in the early fourth century. A Saxon site at Mucking in Essex shows late Roman bronzes in Saxon huts, and graves dated to 400. It is worth remembering Procopius writing in Byzantium in 550; he tells of a Frankish embassy accompanied by Angles, over whom the Franks claim to have dominion. The Angles tell of three populous nations: Britons, Angles and Friesians. They don't mention Saxons. This could be ignorance, but the Saxon homeland was adjacent to Angeln and it's unlikely Angles would have misidentified them. Far more likely this was a group who were linguistically and culturally different from both Angles and Saxons, or perhaps people who had settled many decades earlier and enough time lapsed for cultural and linguistic changes to take place.

There is genetic, linguistic, literary and archaeological evidence for Germanic presence in Britain before 400. The colonisation of later Anglian, Jutish and Saxon areas would have been inconsistent and irregular, with complex and different timescales,[13] which makes for a very mixed and confusing picture. There is, therefore, evidence of Saxon presence much earlier than we previously thought. Then there's evidence of further arrivals that could suggest Angles in the East, Jutes in Kent and Hampshire and more Saxons on the south coast. It is possible that it's these later arrivals which are referred to in the sources, but it's important to remember that they did not arrive into a political or cultural vacuum.

We do not know how they initially interacted with the indigenous population, the political administration and what the ethnic mix was at the time. Regarding provincial boundaries, there is some similarity with earlier Roman provinces and boundaries of later Anglo-Saxon and British kingdoms.[14] Germanic settlement appears to take place in areas of Romano-British economic and political activity,[15] which suggests some possible continuity. There's even evidence that villa and estate boundaries stayed constant into the Middle Ages. I wouldn't take that too far, but it does show that there was no 'wiping clean of the slate', so to speak. The Romano-British civitates and populations were not exterminated and replaced wholesale.

What there does seem to be is a return to tribalism[16] with a patchwork of different tribal affiliations, some in line with civitates' administrative boundaries, others overlapping. It would then be wrong to view the situation as one of simply Britons vs Saxons. There may well have been ethnic aspects at times, but at others a better analogy might be 'rats in a sack'. In fact, if we look at the period from 550 to 700, we see the West Saxons fighting against Sussex and Kent as well as the Britons, Penda of Mercia in alliance with Cadwallon of Gwynedd fighting Northumbria, and a patchwork of shifting alliances involving Picts and the Irish Scotti in Dalriada, south-west Scotland.

There may have been a degree of continuity with civitates, or territories being taken over by warrior bands as going concerns. On the other hand we have Anglo-Saxon society developing after the breakdown of Roman territorial structures. Both these extremes may have occurred in different places. Examples of areas retaining Roman, and even pre-Roman, boundaries include Kent and Lyndsey. The Western Province Britannia Prima retained its identity, if not its integrity, as it shrunk into modern Wales. The Pre-Roman tribal area of the Dumnonii became Devon and Cornwall. Within Flavia Caesariensis, Lindsey appears to have retained

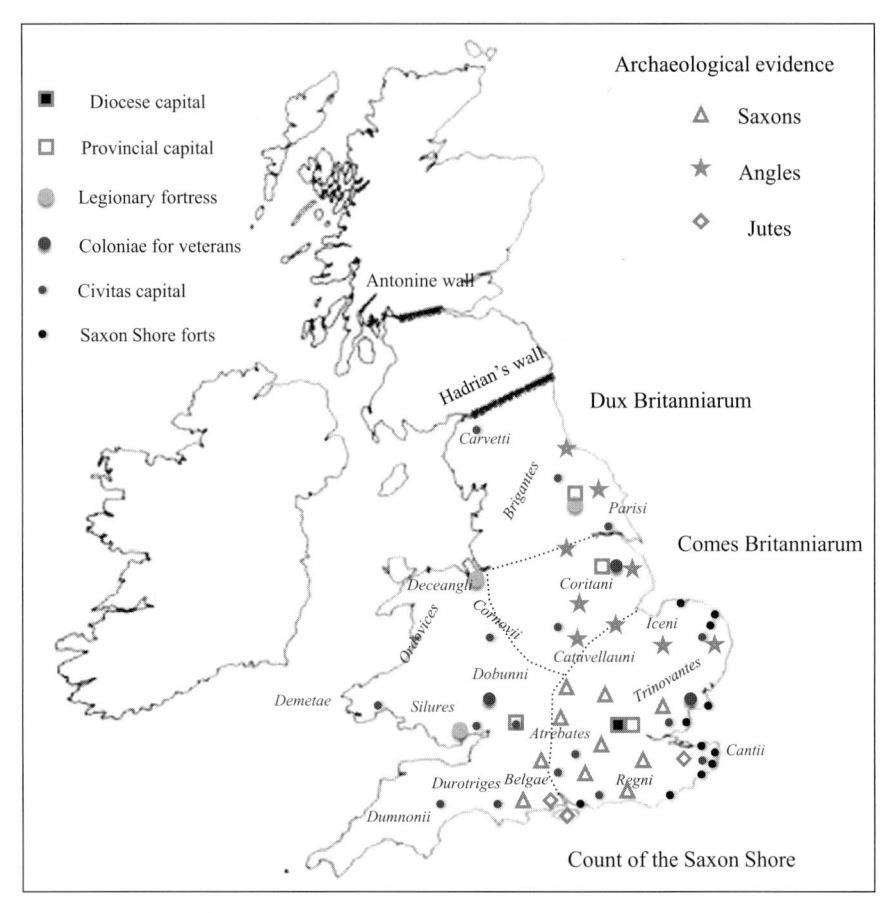

Post-Roman Britain.

some structure around Lincoln, while further west it later was home to the Mercians (literally boundary folk). In the southeast, Maxima Caesariensis retained at least one civitate, the Cantii, in modern Kent which may be connected with the legend of Hengist or Oisc founding or being given the county. In the northern province closely resembled the Northumbrian kingdom.

After the last legions left in the early fifth century, there was a steep decline in the Romano-British economy. The end of the coin supply and Roman governance after 400 destroyed the economic cycle, and parts of Roman life failed suddenly and irrevocably,[17] even if literary evidence suggests some aspects survived for several generations. However, the literary evidence implies a degree of governmental continuity rather than

Archaeology and Other Evidence

a rapid and wholesale collapse into petty kingships after 410, although it's likely that power was decentralised to the provinces and then civitates. There is a sharp contrast with what happened in Gaul, where incomers gradually adopted Gallo-Romano language, culture and religion. The evidence favours large scale continuity alongside significant migration although it must be noted the evidence for continental migration is actually higher in the Roman period than after.[18]

In terms of numbers, Britain was far more densely populated than was once thought with estimates ranging from 1 million to as high as 4 million.[19] There is evidence for climatic changes which, combined with increase in plague and famine, alongside military upheavals, put downward pressure on population in the fifth century.[20] A figure of 2 million is not unreasonable to compare with estimates of Germanic immigrants or invaders. The debate about the Anglo-Saxon invasions can be summarised as follows: on one hand, a large scale movement of people, possibly tens of thousands, took over significant areas by force. On the other hand, small warrior groups infiltrated specific civitates or areas over a prolonged period, possibly as low as a few thousand.

The view that there was a sudden or rapid mass migration or wholesale replacement of the Romano-British population by Germanic tribes is inconsistent with the evidence. Bede, writing 200 years later, may well have believed it based on Gildas. However, there is no physical evidence such as the burnt layer left in the archaeological record of Londinium by Boudica's destruction of the city. The change implied by the *Gallic Chronicles* or Gildas was political or military, rather than a mass migration. The archaeological evidence suggests cultural replacement rather than migration, there is simply no evidence for a military invasion.[21] That doesn't mean there weren't large scale invasions and warfare, just that there is no physical 'smoking gun' like widespread burnt remains at various urban sites. The literary evidence also does not state explicitly a one-off large invasion; rather it implies small, unrelated bands at various locations over a long period, each with a different context arriving in a usually small number of boats or Keels as they were known. These Saxon boats would have been around 23 metres long and carried approximately thirty men;[22] to transport 50,000 people would have required well over 1,500 such boats. That would equate to only thirty boats a week for a year, and we are talking about the last few decades of the fifth century and the whole eastern and southern coast. A boat a week over thirty years would have had the same effect in terms of moving a population. Therefore it is quite feasible for a large population of Germanic peoples to move into Britain, and there is evidence to suggest that did indeed happen. How much and in what circumstance is still open to question.

There is DNA evidence but it's a little mixed, although advances are being made all the time. It is difficult, if not impossible, to distinguish between Anglo-Saxon and later Viking influence. Welsh DNA is significantly different, however, as is Devon, Cornwall, Cumbria and Scotland.[23] There is a distinct difference in both maternal and paternal DNA between the East and the rest of the island, although overall the genetic structure across the British Isles is 'stubbornly Celtic'.[24] There has been some debate as to the interpretation of the evidence. One study found the most Continental influences amounting to 38 per cent in the expected areas of the North East, East Anglia and the Thames valley.[25] This could be due to large-scale replacement, but a warrior elite making up as little as 10 per cent could contribute as much as 50 per cent towards the gene pool within five generations due to reproductive advantages.[26] Thus the evidence does not favour dramatic population change; in fact, studies suggest principal traits within the British popularity were established 10,000 years ago after the last ice age.[27]

There is some DNA evidence to show a difference between what was to become the Anglo-Saxon kingdoms and the rest of the country, but there's also evidence to show continuity in all areas. It does suggest the indigenous population remained in large numbers in what became England. Nor were there large scale desertions of areas, as archaeology suggests considerable continuity of use across the British/Anglo-Saxon divide.[28] There is evidence of Romano-British presence from other sources too: The Law Code of King Ine of the West Saxons in 690 shows Britons were at a legal disadvantage similar to apartheid. The wergild ('man-value') of a British man was only half that of a Saxon. This would have encouraged some to adopt Saxon culture and language. The old English term for a Briton was Walh, which meant foreigner and came to mean 'un-free person' or slave. From this comes the modern 'Welsh', and can be seen in place names such as Walton or Wallasey. It is also worth noting there are British names in many of the Genealogies such as Cerdic, Cynic and later Caedwalla, all of whom were West Saxon kings.

Anglo-Saxon language appears to have been adopted by communities as part of a wider social and cultural change starting in the fifth century.[29]

Archaeology and Other Evidence

The English language adopted fewer than twenty words from British Latin of Brittonic before 600, and place-name studies suggest that few names from pre-Saxon times exist due to a near-complete replacement in England with English names. So language and place-name studies could support the idea of a mass migration, but might also show a subgroup taking on the language and culture of an elite.[30] This might be similar to how Norman French culture affected England after 1066.

The Tribal Hidage is thought to be compiled in the seventh century, although the earliest surviving copy is from the eleventh century. It contains a list of thirty-five tribes or territories and the number of hides assigned to each one. One hide is often equated with roughly thirty modern acres or 120,000 square meters. By contrast, modern Kent is over 31,000 hides compared to the 15,000 recorded in the *Hidage*. Alternatively, the measurement could refer to a unit for taxation purposes and thus not a geographical area. They are almost exclusively south of the Humber. The list is headed by Mercia, but Wessex is the largest at 100,000 hides. It includes all the major Anglo-Saxon kingdoms along with smaller tribal areas, some as little as 300 hides. Most historians agree it originated in Mercia. Although if it is a tribute list, the absence of Deira and Bernecia (or Northumbria) my indicate it originated there.

Table 16: The Tribal Hidage

Myrcna landes (Mercia) 30,000	North Gyrwa 600	Gifla 300	Hendrica 3,500	West Willa 600
Wocensaetna 7,000	East Wixna 300	Hicca 300	Unecungaga 1,200	**East Engle 30,000**
Westerna 7,000	West Wixna 600	Wihtgara 600	Arosaetna 600	**East Saxena 7,000**
Pecsaetna 1,200	Spalda 600	Noxgaga 5,000	Faerpinga 300	**Cantwarena 15,000**
Elmedsaetna 600	Wigesta 900	Ohtgaga 2,000	Bilmiga 600	**South Saxena 7,000**
Linesfarona 7,000	Herefinna 1,200	Hwinca 7,000	Widerigga 600	**West Saxena 100,000**
Suth Gyrwa 600	Sweordora 300	Cilternasaetna 4,000	East Willa 600	

King Arthur: Man or Myth?

Not all the tribes can be identified. However it is worth noting the relative size of Hwince, or the Hwicce, who were located south of the Severn. It shows that by the seventh century there was an extensive Anglo-Saxon presence which confirms much of the information in Bede and other sources. The Hwinca has the same number of hides as both the East and South Saxons. The Hwicce do appear to have been located south of the Severn, but there's no etymological link with Gewisse. Bede states the West Saxons were originally called the Gewisse but marks them distinct from the Hwicce, and as we can see they have the largest area of all at 100,000 hides.

One cemetery discovered in Wasperton in Warwickshire covers the period from the third to seventh centuries and apparently contains mostly

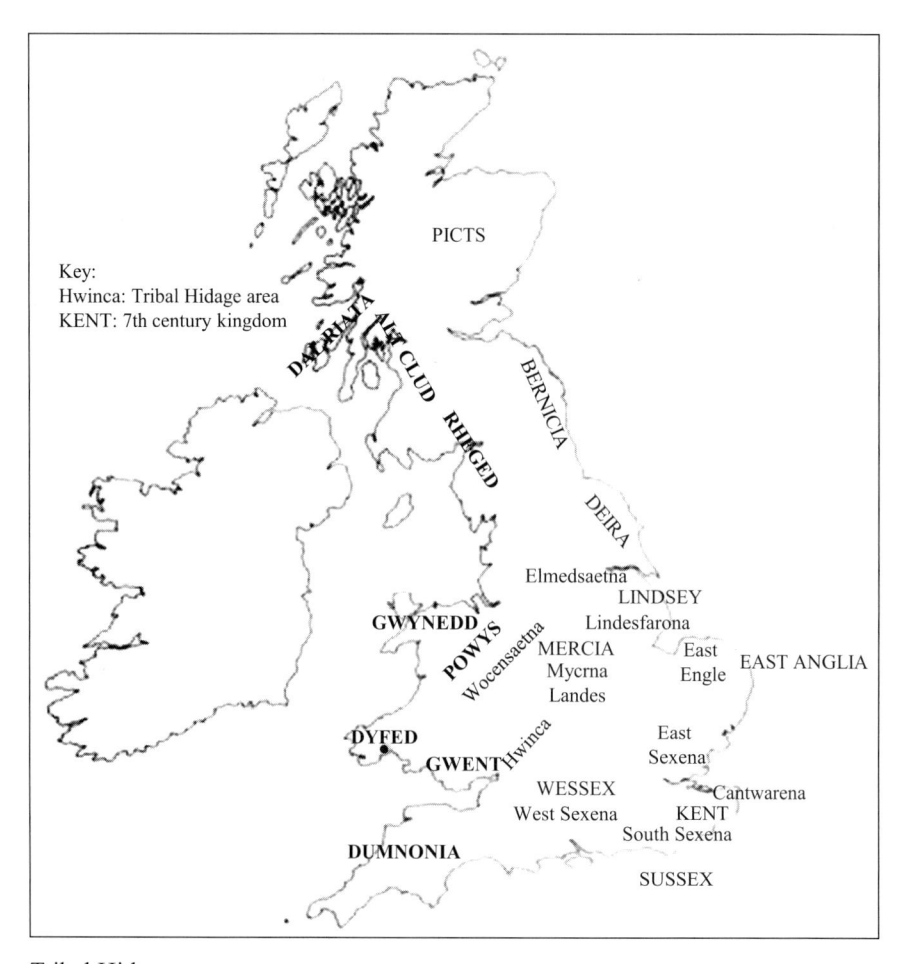

Tribal Hidage.

Archaeology and Other Evidence

local residents.[31] What it shows is a change from Roman to Anglo-Saxon burials alongside the adoption of other material possessions and culture. This village is north of the area supposedly conquered by the West Saxons in the late sixth century. It's precisely the area later covered by either Mercia or Hwince in the tribal hidage, but in the time of Ambrosius Aurelianus it is very likely to have been west of any 'partition of the island'. This does suggest something interesting, if only about this one small area. Here is a location with an apparently consistent population who slowly change and adopt cultural practices from Roman Britain, a post-Roman British controlled area to later Mercia. This doesn't mean other areas weren't conquered by the sword or that other populations weren't replaced. Towns and cities in general also show a marked change generally declining, yet some such as Canterbury, Wroxeter, St Albans and Carlisle show some perseverance.[32]

In summary, there has been much academic debate over whether there was a mass movement of tribes, small groups of warrior elites, or some combination of the two. The process may have been varied across time, geography and civitates, and involved many different Germanic groups coming at different times. Research generally has found both Bede and the *Anglo-Saxon Chronicles* inadequate as records of the arrival of the Saxons.[33] However, inadequate doesn't mean inaccurate or irrelevant. The spirit of what they are saying may be near the truth for a particular context in time or geography. There is still much debate about some of the figures referred to; stories about Vortigern and Hengist have had 'vigorous historical criticism which has exposed them as myth'.[34] However, while we cannot be sure of the process, we do know the outcome. The Anglo-Saxons slowly took control of Romano-British areas from east to west over a period of time, we can leave aside manner and exact circumstances. We have evidence of increased activity in Iron Age hill forts such as Cadbury, and refortification of sites like Viroconium near Wroxeter. What we don't know is by whom or for what reason. What we do know is that 200 years after the time of Arthur, Anglo-Saxon kingdoms are well entrenched in large parts of what later became England.

The question is, what was the situation at the time Arthur is supposed to have lived? This is pure speculation but we have some clues to go on. The *Anglo-Saxon Chronicle* records in 457 that the Britons fled to London, and there is archaeological evidence to suggest activity up to 450. Yet by 500 the archaeological record suggests London was deserted, not to be reoccupied until the time of Alfred the Great in the ninth century. At least, no evidence of any Anglo-Saxon presence has been found within the walls.[35] The decay was gradual rather than sudden. In fact, evidence to date appears to have disproved the theory of a surviving Romano-British enclave into the sixth century.[36] There is evidence, however, for some continuity outside London's walls from the fifth century and increased Anglo-Saxon presence around London from 450.[37] Instead, a new settlement, Lundenwic, grew up slightly to the west of the walled city around modern day Westminster. It wasn't until 886 that King Alfred established a settlement within the walls, a generation after Lundenwic had itself been abandoned due to Viking raids up the Thames.

Gildas, writing around 540, comments on the 'partition of the island' and being unable to access the shrines of the martyrs, including St Albans to the north east of London. The implication is that this had been the case since the time of Ambrosius Aurelianus. Taking the evidence from the *Gallic Chronicle*, Gildas and archaeology, this does seem to suggest that London and the southeast were already under Saxon control at the time Arthur is alleged to have lived. In 455, the Roman church changed the date of Easter, and evidence from later periods suggest the British church appeared to have adopted this change. Yet no later changes seem to have been made, suggesting that contact was lost sometime after this.[38]

If we trust the *Chronicle* and other literary sources, the south and east coast from the New Forest, round Kent and up to Hadrian's wall was affected by the presence, immigration, or invasion of Germanic warriors. The Gallic chronicler appears to believe, as early as 441, that Britain was lost. In around 540 Gildas claims he can no longer visit the shrines of the martyrs in St Albans and other places, but seems to imply this has been the case since the partition of the island which occurred in the time of Ambrosius Aurelianus. One can imagine a strip of land along the south and east coast that also, at one point, spread inland as far as St Albans. How deep this strip extended into the interior, or even how continuous around the coast it was, is unknown.

In the south the *Chronicle* records later expansion after 550 and in the north around the same time Ida becomes first king of Bernicia. Elmet, in the Leeds, area was not conquered until 616. This suggests that these areas were under British control in Arthur's time. Welsh sources also hint

Archaeology and Other Evidence

that eastern Powys, which spread deep into the midlands, was lost much later. We also have Urien of Rheged pushing the Bernicians almost into the sea in the last quarter of the sixth century. What this may indicate is that around 500, the British still controlled the bulk of what later became England. An arc from Dorset to Oxford, and perhaps even further to the Wash. Further north we can't say how much of Lincolnshire or Yorkshire was under Angle influence. But enough of the country was for Aelle to be described as Bretwalda by Bede.

Chapter 10

Timelines

In this chapter the conflicting timelines have been placed together. As we know, the dates and entries may not be accurate but we can compare them to the first column which we are from trusted sources. You will notice that the next three columns are somewhat similar. This is unsurprising as the *Chronicles* were influenced by Bede, who in turn was influenced by Gildas. The former two did use other sources. However Gildas's chronology depends on a number of assumptions:

- His reference to Agitius does mean Aetius.
- The 'thrice consul' comment referred to the time of the appeal and not added as a title.
- The passage about forty-four years does mean between Badon and the present, and not two other events.
- Maglocunnus is Maelgwn.
- The timeline for Gildas of circa 500 to 570 is correct.
- The reference to the descendants of Ambrosius does mean grandchildren and this suggests a fifty (or forty-four) year period (an elderly grandchild could be alive 100 years later).

If this is not the case then it brings into dispute the whole narrative and the subsequent narratives from Bede and the *Chronicles*. If, however, it is true then one is left to explain the *Gallic Chronicle* entry of 440/1: 'The Britons fell to the power of the Saxons.' The *Historia Brittonum* and *Annales Cambriae* leave us with even bigger problems, aside from the dubious mythology and magical wonders. On one hand it pulls the narrative earlier, starting in 425 with Vortigern's crowning, and dates the Saxon arrival a generation earlier in 428. This then pulls the whole story of the rebellion and Ambrosius into line with the *Gallic Chronicle*. Additionally it suggests St Germanus's second visit occurred before

440, otherwise he would have been expected to mention this momentous political or military upheaval. It also means all our assumptions about Gildas are wrong and Badon was a generation earlier.

However, later entries from the *Historia* and the *Annales Cambriae* leave the opposite problem. They have Arthur fighting Octha after Hengist dies, and then the Battle of Badon even later in 516. This increased timespan then creates an Ambrosius fighting at Wallop in 437 and at Badon in 493 or even 516. Some have tried to get round this by suggesting two Ambrosius Aurelianus, or even two Vortigerns. For the latter, as it's probably a title, this is possible. Also some texts refer to 'Vortigern the thin', suggesting a Vortigern the 'not so thin' elsewhere.

Whichever way one tries to adjust the timelines, one cannot get them to fit without ignoring whole parts, speculating on two characters with the same name or suggesting individuals were fighting battles fifty years or more apart. Then there is the archaeological evidence that suggests Saxons were already present during Roman times and there's no solid evidence for widespread Anglo-Saxon invasion causing the devastation Gildas describes. Given some of his historical errors such as Hadrian's wall and the purpose of his sermon, it's quite possible, his account of the Saxon revolt was grossly exaggerated and later mistakenly copied by Bede.

One could build a perfectly reasonable narrative to create a 'best fit' timeline to accommodate much of the source material. First, Vortigern ruling between 425 and the 450s is not unreasonable even if we ignore the possibility of two Vortigerns. Bede had other sources so it is likely his version is more reliable. However, the sources refer to reinforcements and further Saxon arrivals. One possibility is the earlier date in Nennius is correct and there was some political situation that caused the *Gallic Chronicle* in 440 to view Britain as being under Saxon control. This could be Vortigern marrying Hengist's daughter or handing control of Kent to them. Vortimer's battles could be a response to that and the appeal to Aetius refers to Saxons rather than Picts. There is then the reference in Nennius to Hengist returning and making peace with Vortigern and perhaps the 449 date in Bede and the *Chronicles* refers to that. The subsequent rebellion is recorded as Hengist's battles in the *Anglo-Saxon Chronicles* and this would put the rise of Ambrosius in the 460–70s. This may mean the victor at Wallop in 437 was his father or grandfather.

Table 17

Known sources	Gildas	Bede	Anglo-Saxon Chronicles	*Historia Brittonum* and *Annals Cambriae*
388 Maximus dies	Death of Maximus.	Death of Maximus Constantine dies		**425** Vortigern King
407 Constantine III				
411 Constantine dies	3 assaults by Picts and Scots. Seize north. Cities abandoned. Civil war, famine.	3 assaults from Picts and Scots.		**428** Hengist and Horsa arrive St Germanus. Saxons given Kent. Octa and Ebissa 40 ships to North.
423 Aetius Magister Militum				
429 St Germanus				
440/1 Gallic Chronicle				Vortimer drives Saxons back (Catigern and Horsa killed) Vortimer dies.
446 Aetius third Consul	Appeal to Agitus. Victory over Picts. Time of plenty. King anointed. Disease/plague Saxons invited.	**446** Appeal to Aetius Famine/plenty/plague. Vortigern/council. **449** Saxons arrive	**443** Appeal to Aetius **449** Saxons arrive	Hengist and Vortigern at peace. Night of long knives.
454 Aetius dies				
460s War in Gaul	Rebellion.	Rebellion.	**455-473** Hengist 4 battles (Horsa killed)	Vortigern dies. St Germanus returns to Gaul.
471 Riothamus				
476 Last Western Roman emperor	Ambrosius Aurelianus, war.	Ambrosius Aurelianus, war.	**477-491** Aelle's 3 battles (Sussex) **488** Hengist dies, Aesc succeeds	Hengist dies, Son Octha succeeds in Kent.
481 Clovis, King				
486 Last Roman enclave in Gaul destroyed				

507 Clovis made consul of Gaul	Battle of Badon.	493 Battle of Badon 44 years after arrisval of Saxons.	Arthurs 12 battles.
			516 Battle of Badon
531 Evidence of Saxon emigration		495-530 West Saxons arrival and battles	537 Battle of Camlann
			547 Maelgwn dies
550s Evidence of first Anglo-Saxon kingdoms	Gildas writes De Excidio.		
388 Death of Maximus	Death of Maximus.	552 Start of West Saxon expansion	570 Gildas dies
407 Constantine III			
411 Constantine dies	Constantine dies 411		425 Vortigern King
423 Aetius Magister Militum in Gaul	Two incursions by Picts and Scots followed by Roman intervention.	Death of Maximus	428 Hengist and Horsa with 3 ships St Germanus. Saxons – Kent Octa and Ebissa 40 ships to North. St Germanus confronts Vortigern (**437** Battle of Guoloppum: Ambrosius) Tale of Emrys Ambrosius.
	3 assaults from Picts and Scots. (follows Gildas's narrative)		
	Third incursion, Picts and Scots seize North. Britons abandon cities.		
440/1 Briton falls to power of Saxons (*Gallic Chronicle*)	Civil war. Famine.		Vortimer drives Saxons back.

(continued)

Table 17: (Continued)

446 Aetius third Consul	Appeal to Agitus. (Aetius 445-454?) Victory over Picts. Time of plenty. King anointed.	**446** Appeal to Aetius Famine/plenty/plague. Vortigern/council.	**443** Appeal to Aetius Saxons: more men Vortimer's 4 battles (Horsa and Catigern killed)
451 Hunnic war **454** Aetius dies **460s** Roman/Saxon/Breton/Visigoth war in Loire Valley	Disease/plague Saxons invited. Rebellion.	**449** Hengist and Horsa with 3 ships Rebellion.	**449** Hengist and Horsa with 3 ships **455-473** Hengist 4 battles (Horsa is killed), Kent. Hengist and Vortigern make peace. Night of long knives. Vortigern dies. St Germanus returns to Gaul.
471 Riothamus **476** Last Western Roman emperor	Ambrosius Aurelianus, war.	Ambrosius Aurelianus, war.	**488** Hengist dies, Aesc succeeds. Hengist dies, Son Octha succeeds in Kent. Then Arthur fought against them.
481 Clovis, King **488** Last Roman enclave in Gaul destroyed	Battle of Badon.	**493** Battle of Badon 44 years after arrisval of Saxons.	**477-491** Aelle's 3 battles (Sussex) **495** Cerdic and Cynric 5 ships **501** Port 2 ships **508** Cerdic battle of Netley Arthurs 12 battles.
507 Clovis made consul of Gaul	Gildas references 44 years (since Badon?)		

	514 Stuf and Whitgar 3 ships **519** Battle of Cerdic's Ford	**516** Battle of Badon
	527 Battle of Cerdic's Wood **530** Capture Isle of Wight	**537** Battle of Camlann **547** Maelgwn dies
531 Evidence of Saxon emigration	Ambrosius grandchildren alive at time of writing. King Maglocunnus in power at time of writing (Maelgwn of Gwynedd 534-547?)	
550s Evidence of first Anglo-Saxon kingdoms	**552** Start of West Saxon expansion	**570** Gildas dies

King Arthur: Man or Myth?

This would also make him a contemporary of Riothamus, if not the same person. Fighting in Kent, or even Gaul, in 460–70s would not necessarily negate the possibility of him fighting at Badon in 493. But that is not necessary because Nennius places Arthur fighting the Saxons after Hengist's death and after Ambrosius. It also has the happy coincidence of falling into line with the fall of the last Roman enclave in Western Europe, which may tie in with the narrative in Geoffrey of Monmouth, and Arthur's battles in Gaul and against the Romans. In this scenario one only has to correct the dates in *Annales Cambriae* by pushing the dates back a generation.

But there we run into the same problem others have before of over speculating: 'We only have to correct some dates'. Let me go through just some of the points there. We now have Hengist arriving fighting-fit in 428 and engaging in battle in 473, presumably in his seventies. Second, the appeal to Aetius (or Agitius) is most definitely concerning Picts and Scots and not the Saxons. The Saxons are invited because of that threat. Now it is true, it is just as likely this occurred in 420s as in the 440s. This would indeed satisfy the *Gallic Chronicle*. But it pushes back all the other dates and expands the timeframe to make individuals unrealistically old. It's not impossible that Ambrosius was in the 450s, Badon in the 470s, and Gildas wrote in 520. But then one has to explain all the other corrections necessary in the other sources.

Vortimer is associated with a battle in 455 when Horsa and Catigern die, not the 440s. If Arthur really is fighting battles in 516 and 537, why is Gildas not mentioning him? Why do the *Anglo-Saxon Chronicles* mention Vortigern but not Arthur? Why does Bede also not reference him? Why does the *Historia Brittonum* have most of the action occurring before St Germanus's final visit ended, suggesting 440s followed by Arthur's twelve battles? And yet the *Annales Cambriae* locate Arthur between approximately 500 and 537? I would invite the reader to attempt to adjust the different timelines to achieve a best fit.

There is a consensus from the experts that the narrative from Bede is roughly correct, or that Bede thought it was accurate and was attempting to be so. While there is archaeological evidence, however, it doesn't fully support this; one remembers the existence of Saxons in parts of the south much earlier. Additionally, the *Gallic Chronicle* is respected as a source and the 440 entry remains to be explained. There is no evidence whatsoever for an Arthur figure from any contemporary or later

Timelines

[Four maps of the British Isles showing:
- Top left: "Gallic Chronicle: Britain is lost to 'the power of the Saxons' c. 440"
- Top right: "c. 450 Mercenaries settled in 'east'"
- Bottom left: "Saxon revolt from Gildas and Historia c. 450-460" with labels Essex, Middlesex, Kent, Sussex
- Bottom right: "Partition of island since time of Ambrosius Aurelianus c. 474-491"]

Possible sequence of events.

respected source. The *Historia Brittonum* and *Annales Cambriae* do not have the same validity, but even if taken at face value they give widely contradictory statements and unlikely narratives. Additionally, the *Historia Brittonum* is the only reference to Arthur in the 300 years after he supposedly lived. Then over 100 years later we have two references in the Welsh Annals that may or may not have been added later to the text.

So to summarise, Arthur aside, we have sources that appear to contradict each other. For example the *Gallic Chronicle* against Bede. If you believe the material from the *Historia Brittonum* and *Annales Cambriae*, and that is the nub of the matter, this unfortunately still does not clarify any of the sources. Nevertheless, this is the first historical mention of Arthur. Also within these sources there is a rough consensus despite the contradictions. Something happened to cause an appeal, Germanic mercenaries arrived but later revolted. Ambrosius Aurelianus emerged to lead a fight-back culminating in the battle of Badon and a 'partition of the island' as Gildas puts it. Into this scenario, two late and disputed sources place our hero. How the legend changed and evolved over the centuries is impossible to know, but the next written sources to mention Arthur occur over 100 years after the *Annales Cambriae*.

Chapter 11

Saints' Lives

The saints' lives are semi-biographical accounts of various saints often written many hundreds of years later. They tend to contain miracles and wonders to demonstrate the saint's power. They are not regarded as being in any way historically accurate, but they contain historical elements in that they are intended to be believed. References to locations and characters may be included to demonstrate why the church has certain rights in an area. The earliest surviving texts concerning Arthur date from around 1100, before Geoffrey of Monmouth's work, although surviving copies are from later. Unless there have been major alterations, this suggests legends were common before he wrote. They are often designed to highlight the heroic nature of the saint involved and his victory and superiority over secular kings and lords such as Arthur.

For example, if I wished to prove a certain saint of this area was indeed powerful and holy, I might tell of how he defeated a dragon and link it to a king that I knew, or believed, to have lived at that time. Then if I wished to prove that I, or the church, had the right to this land or building, I might state in the story that the king then granted this land. If I wished to show the power of the church over secular power, I might write how the saint humbled that king in some way.

It is fair to ask whether it is relevant to include stories, centuries out of date, that include magic and monsters. Is there any historical value to this at all? They have value in the sense the writer wished the story to be believed. So the setting, location and characters would have to be believable, at least to the medieval mind. What they do suggest is that by the eleventh century Arthur was possibly seen as a real figure. On the other hand there's no proof as to what the writers believed. They may well have thought Arthur was as mythical as the dragon in the stories and knew the audience would understand the allusion. Also, their belief

500 years later is rather irrelevant as to the existence of Arthur. What we need for that is contemporary literary or archaeological evidence, but they are of interest and may provide clues although we must take this 'evidence' with a huge pinch of salt.

There are seven tales in all that reference Arthur, two of which are from Brittany. The first is possibly the most important if the date is correct. Although there is much debate about that.

In 1019, the Breton writer William, Chaplain of Bishop Eudo of Leon, wrote about St Goeznovius, a sixth/seventh-century saint from Cornwall who was a bishop in Brittany. There is some controversy around the date, but if true it predates Geoffrey of Monmouth's work by 100 years. William states that the information used in his preface came from *Ystoria Britanica*, unfortunately, a source now lost to us. It describes Vortigern inviting the Saxons and goes on to describe how 'presently their pride was checked by Arthur, king of the Britons'. Importantly, it could also be the first text to also describe his 'many victories which he won gloriously in Britain and in Gaul'.[1] It then describes a time of further incursions from Saxons and oppression of Britons and the church in particular. Many martyrs were made and some emigrated to Brittany.

What is meant by 'presently' is debatable, but it doesn't suggest a large time-span. Ambrosius Aurelianus isn't mentioned at all, but Vortigern is. It is also possibly the first time Arthur is referred to as a king. It demonstrates a Breton tradition which is also apparent after the Norman invasion and the increased interest from Norman and French writers after Geoffrey's work becomes popular. The book referenced, *Ystoria Britanica,* could be Nennius's *Historia Brittonum*, or one based on that. The inclusion of fighting in Gaul would suggest not, but that could have been from another, local source. The next saint is St Cadoc or Cadog.

St Cadoc was born around 497 and died in 580. He lived in South Wales and became abbott of Llancarfan. The life of St Cadoc, *Vita Cadoci,* was written around 1086 by Lifris of Llancarfan. In the prologue there is a tale of a King Gwynllyw, who abducts King Brychan's daughter, Gwladus. Brychan chases them to the border where he kills 200 of Gwynllyw's men. Two regions in South Wales are said to be named after these kings, Gwynlliog, and Brycheiniog. Arthur witnesses this with Kai and Bedwyr and at first has 'evil thoughts' about the girl. Cai and

Saints' Lives

Bedwyr encourage Arthur to act chivalrously and they chase Brychan's army away. Later the following tale is told:

> In that same time a certain very brave leader of the British [or Britons], called Ligessauc, the son of Eliman, also surnamed Llaw hir, that is, Long Hand, slew three soldiers of Arthur, most illustrious king of Britannia.

Arthur pursues him but St Cadoc gives him refuge for seven years in Gwynlliog. He is betrayed and Arthur comes with a 'very great force of soldiers' to the river Usk (South Wales). Cadoc intercedes and arranges for Arthur to receive three oxen for each man killed. Arthur reluctantly agrees but 'tauntingly' demands that the cows are half red and half white. The saint miraculously changes the cows as requested and drives them to the middle of the ford. When Cai and Bedwyr pull the cows to the other side the cows turn into bundles of fern. Arthur then asks and receives forgiveness for his behaviour before granting certain land rights. Arthur is referred to as king and this is again one of the earliest occasions he is given this title in Welsh sources.[2]

The next example is Gildas, whom we have already met. There are two versions of the *Life of St Gildas*. The first is by a monk of Rhuys and was likely written in the ninth century. He is said to be one of five sons of Caunus, King of Alt Clud (Strathclyde). He studied with St Iltud in Glamorgan together with St Samson and St Paul of Leon. He was later asked by the high king of Ireland to restore order to the church. Later he travelled to Brittany where he was asked to write the *De Excidio et Conquestu Britanniae*, discussed earlier. This version has him also travelling through Gaul during the time of Childeric (king of Franks, died 482) and meeting St Apollinaris (died 489), which would place Gildas much earlier than other traditions. To compound the confusion there is a miracle told within the text. A princess, the daughter of King Werocus and pregnant with child, is murdered by a Breton king, Conomerus (kings Waroch and Conomor both lived around 540). St Gildas brings her back to life (fixing her head back in place). The child born is also named Gildas, who the Bretons call Trechmorus so as not to confuse them. Arthur is not mentioned.

The second version is by Caradoc of Llancarfan dated to the twelfth century. In this, Gildas is the son of Nau, the King of Scotia and one of twenty-four brothers. At the time Arthur ruled in Britain and the brothers were always rising up against him. The eldest brother, Hueil, was eventually killed by Arthur. In the story Gildas forgives Arthur. Later, Melvas, king of the summer country, 'violated and carried off' Arthur's wife, Gwenhwyfar, to Glastonbury. Arthur searches for a year before besieging the town with an army from Cornwall and Devon. Gildas intercedes and brokers the return of Gwenhwyfar and peace. Both kings then grant extensive lands to the abbot of Glastonbury. The story places him in the time of King Trifinus in the district of Pepidiauc, which could refer to Triffyn of Dyfed in mid-fifth century.

So overall there is some confusion about whether Gildas was in the fifth or sixth centuries. Gerald of Wales, writing in 1190, explains how Gildas throws all the praise he had written on Arthur into the sea, the earliest attempt to explain Arthur's absence in *The Ruin of Britain*. The first 'life' has Gildas being buried in Brittany near Rhuys and the second has him buried at Glastonbury.

Saint Carannog or Saint Carantoc was a sixth-century abbot in Wales and the West Country. In the *Life of St Carannog*, written in the twelfth century, he is said to have visited Ireland and met St Patrick, placing him in the mid-fifth century. Later he returned to Ceredigion in West Wales and churches in both Cornwall and Brittany are said to be founded by him. The story goes as follows:

> And Christ gave him an honourable altar from heaven, the colour of which no one fathomed. And afterwards he came to the Severn river [i.e., the Severn sea], that he might sail across, and he cast the altar into the sea, which also preceded him whither God wished him to go.
>
> In those times Cadwy and Arthur were reigning in that country, dwelling in Dindraithov (Dunstan Castle, Exmoor). And Arthur came wandering about that he might find a most formidable serpent, huge and terrible, which had been ravaging twelve portions of the land of Carrum.

Carannog and Arthur meet, and Arthur agrees to tell the saint where the altar is if he catches the serpent. The saint prays, the serpent comes forward and is miraculously subdued and led 'like a lamb', raising neither 'wings or claws'. Arthur returns the altar after finding 'whatever was placed upon it was thrown to a distance'. He gives the saint land rights in the area of Carrum (Carhampton in Somerset) presumably as compensation. Cadwy appears in many of the legends as a king of Dumnonia and Arthur's half brother.

St Padarn founded St Padarn's church in Ceredigion, dying in 550. The *Life of St Padern* states he was originally from Brittany before travelling to Ireland then later to Britain. He defeats two of Maelgwn of Gwynedd's heralds and later cures him of his illness when he begs forgiveness. Later, Arthur, 'a certain tyrant', is filled with avarice for a tunic owned by Padarn. He flies into a rage and is determined to take the tunic. Padarn claims the earth will swallow him, which it does – up to his chin. Arthur begs forgiveness and is released. This may be linked to 'Padarn Redcoat' whose coat was one of the 'Thirteen Treasures of the Island of Britain' listed in fifteenth century texts.

The *Life of St Iltud* was probably written in Glamorgan in the twelfth century. There is just one reference that concerns us when the saint visits Arthur's court. St Iltud in the *Vita Sancti Sampsonis*, written in Dol, Brittany, about 600, is said to be a Disciple of St Germanus, which would place him in the mid-fifth century. A later, more untrustworthy, Norman tale has him as a Breton prince and cousin of King Arthur.

The *Life of St Efflam* is a Breton tale from possibly 1090, involving Arthur's attempt to slay a dragon, living in a cave, in Brittany. Arthur is exhausted after a long battle with the beast and weak with thirst. St Efflam draws water from a rock for Arthur and then uses prayer to defeat the monster who vanishes into the sea.

Table 18: Arthur in the Saints' lives

Saint	Written	Story
St Goeznovius ?–675	Possibly 1019, Brittany.	Preface refers to the great Arthur, king of the Britons, who subdues the Saxons and wins victories in Britain and Gaul.
St Cadoc 497–580	1086 Llancarfan, S. Wales.	1. Set in South Wales, aids one king against another.
		2. St Cadoc settles dispute between Arthur and another by the river Usk in South Wales and is granted land rights.

(continued)

Table 18: (Continued)

Saint	Written	Story
St Efflam 448–512	Possibly eleventh century, Brittany.	St Efflam assists Arthur in defeating a dragon.
St Gildas 500–570	Twelfth century, Llancarfan, S. Wales.	1. Arthur kills Hueil, brother of Gildas but is forgiven. 2. King Melvas abducts Arthur's wife. Arthur besieges Glastonbury but Gildas brokers peace. Abbot granted land rights.
St Carannog sixth century	Twelfth century, Pembrokeshire, S. Wales.	Set in Somerset. Carannog subdues serpent for Arthur in return for magical altar. Carannog granted land rights in Somerset.
St Padarn ?–550	Twelfth century, Pembrokeshire, S. Wales.	1. Defeats Maelgwn's henchmen. 2. Arthur attempts to steal Padarn's tunic and is swallowed by the earth up to his chin.
St Illtud (AKA Hildutus) fifth century	Twelfth century, Pembrokeshire, S. Wales.	St Illtud travels from Brittany to visit his cousin King Arthur before leaving for Poulentus, king of Glamorgan. Founded a religious school in Glamorgan that later taught St Gildas, St Samson and Samson of Dol.

It is interesting they are mostly fifth- and sixth-century figures and there are no references outside this time period but it has to be said they can't all be correct. The time span is too wide. At least one predates Geoffrey of Monmouth and so demonstrates a tradition that survived the centuries. Of course none of them are contemporary or valid in any way. It has already been stated that none of them are considered credible historical sources. Other saints' lives have also been connected with the Arthurian legend and we can see them below.

Table 19: Saints connected to aspects of legend

Saint	Written	Story
St Dubricius (St Dyfrig c. 465–550)	In the book of Landaff, twelfth century	Illegitimate son of daughter of King of Ergyng, south-east Wales. Friends with St Illtud and St Samson of Dol. Attended synod of Brefi in 545 to condemn Pelagism. Resigned see in favour of St David. Geoffrey of Monmouth claims he crowned Arthur.
St David c. 500–89	Eleventh century by Rhygyfarch	Son of St Non and grandson of Ceredig ap Cunedda. Became bishop of the region after the synod of Brefi around 550. Some legends name him as a cousin of Arthur.
St Samson of Dol c. 485–575	Vita Sancti Samsonis, Seventh–ninth century	Son of Anna of Gwent, daughter of Meurig ap Tewdrig. Pupil of St Illtud along with Gildas and Paul Aurelian. Staes Illtud was a disciple of Germanus of Auxerre (this may be far too early if Germanus died in 437). Ordained bishop by Dubricius in 521. Travelled to Guernsey (patron saint) and Brittany where he founded a monastery at Dol. Attended council in Paris between 556 and 573.
Paul Aurelian c. 500–75	884 by Wrmonoc of Landevennec Abbey, Brittany.	Son of a Welsh chieftain Perphirius ('clad in purple') from Penychen, Glamorgan. Studied with Gildas and Samson under St Illtud. In life of Cadoc, his father Gwynllyw has a brother called Pawl from Penychen. Some suggestion he is connected to Ambrosius Aurelianus.
St Germanus of Man c. 410–474	Baring-Gould	Baring-Gould argues that two Germanus's have been confused and that Illtud is a pupil of this St Germanus, or St Garmon.

(continued)

Table 19: (Continued)

Saint	Written	Story
St Teilo c. 500–60	In the book of Llandaff, twelfth century	Grandson of Ceredig ap Cunedda. Disciple of Dubricius. Friend of St David. Became Bishop of Llandaff.
St Kentigern aka Mungo early 500s–612	Jocelyn of Furness 1185	Born in what is now Lothian, son of Owain map Urien of Rheged and grandson of Lot, King of Lothian who in other sources is brother-in-law to Arthur. Stayed with St David. A later fifteenth-century source shows him in conflict with Lailoken, a mad prophet, linked to the battle of Arfdeydd in 573. Lailoken is seen as the same as the Myrddin Wylit of Welsh sources (and the basis of Geoffrey's Merlin).

In general they are eleventh- or twelfth-century compositions written to magnify the saint's name. There is often a local element which is used to justify or explain certain land rights or privileges for particular monasteries or churches. These are ecclesiastical 'hero tales' to demonstrate the power of the church over the secular power represented by kings and lords. Arthur is often shown in stark contrast to other Welsh legends and poems as being avaricious and arrogant before being humbled and begging for forgiveness. They also show Arthur as being one of a number of different kings. However, on present evidence, no region can claim Arthur for its own and it is possible his title of king was a literary invention to add status to the saint's story.[3]

Many of these dates are suspect, Paul Aurelian, for example, is recorded as being 140 when he died. St David's birth is recorded as 462 in the *Annales Cambriae* and his death in other sources in 589. St Samson's Father, Meurig, elsewhere is recorded as being born 100 years after him. There are a number of contradictions and impossible lifespans. Despite the contradictions and inconsistencies it is possible to build a coherent timeline.

Putting them in chronological order, first we have St Illtud and St Dubricius, both born around 470. Illtud is said to be Arthur's cousin.

Saints' Lives

An Arthur born around 480 would be fighting-fit at 500 and at any possible battle of Badon. He would also be the next generation on from Ambrosius who, according to Bede, was militarily active in the time of Zeno, 474–91. The next generation of saints are all recorded as being born around 500. Gildas, Samson and Paul are all disciples of Illtud. St David is said to be succeed Dubricius and is the nephew of Arthur, which fits perfectly with being a generation after. The Lives of Cadoc, Carannog and Padarn are all contemporary with this same generation in the early sixth century. They are all active in the same region of Wales and many of the tales place Arthur in this specific area in south-east Wales and around the river Severn. Yet these saints, alongside St David, are likely to have been born around 500 and been 'professionally' active from 520 onwards. For a historical Arthur to have interacted with them he would have had to have been in position in the 520s–530s. We will see from the genealogical evidence later that many of these figures are reported to be the great grandsons of Cunedda and thus allegedly of the same generation of Arthur and Maelgwn. Inconsistencies aside, an Arthur being born in the 480s and dying in 530s wouldn't be incompatible with the majority of these sources, while remembering that as evidence they are severely lacking in validity.

St Illtud and St Dubricious have been connected with St Germanus of Auxerre. This has caused some to claim that all the dates should be moved back a generation or more, and others to dismiss the stories as mere fables. An interesting theory[4] posits that this Germanus has been confused with St Garmon, who is known to have been in Wales in the 460s and died on the Isle of Man in 474. The only reason to reject St Illtud being taught by St Germanus of Auxerre and replacing him with this St Garmon is purely to explain away the obvious inconsistencies. The latest that St Germanus of Auxerre could have interacted with Illtud was the 440s, which pulls all the other saints' lives, and of course Arthur, back two generations. Yet in the *Life of St Germanus*, Constantius mentions none of the story in the *Historia*, so it is possible the latter refers to a completely different person.

In summary we have sources full of contradictory dates, dragons, serpents, magic altars and cloaks. On the point of timelines we could build a very tenuous link for St Germanus (or Garmon) to St Dubricious and St Illtud. There then follows a second generation born around the time of the battle of Badon. The *Annales Cambriae* suggests Arthur perished at Camlann twenty-one years later, so Cadoc, Padarn and Carannog would have been less than 21 when interacting with him if

Badon was before 500. But a Badon fought in 516 and a Camlan in 537, as stated in the *Annals Cambriae*, would be compatible. The problem is these saints' lives, genealogies and later legends were all written long after the *Annales Cambriae* and *Historia*. They may well have simply fitted their stories around what was believed at the time.

Even if we ignore all the inconsistencies, contradictions and absurdities, we still have a body of work written 600 years after his time. A body of work written today about Henry VIII is not at all relevant unless it includes evidence from contemporary sources. Evidence that has to be validated. Even a contemporary source can be false and has to be supported by other evidence. What we have here is little better than someone in 500 years using half-forgotten stories of superheroes to prove Spiderman was real. Nevertheless, it's odd that all these saints are clustered around the end of the fifth and beginning of the sixth century, and mostly located in South Wales. One could well argue that hagiographers would only attach their favoured saints to a figure connected with a specific time. The fact that Arthur was connected with this period in the mind of a medieval writer 600 years later doesn't prove he was real. However, at the very least it shows medieval writers placing the figure of Arthur, historical or mythical, a generation or more either side of AD 500. It also demonstrates some links with South Wales and the West Country.

Chapter 12

The History of the Kings of Britain by Geoffrey of Monmouth

The next source is perhaps the greatest source for the legend. *The History of the Kings of Britain* was written by Geoffrey of Monmouth in 1136. The purpose of the book was to trace the history of Britain through 1,900 years. The inspiration was a patriotic one aimed at the Welsh and Bretons. We know Geoffrey had some connection with Monmouth and frequently mentions Caerleon-on-Usk in South Wales. He is named in a number of charters and there is evidence he lived in Oxford and London for a time. However, he appears to be from Welsh or Breton stock. The book is dedicated to Robert, Earl of Gloucester, the son of Henry I and Waleron, Count of Mellent, son of Robert de Beaumont. Three times in the book he mentions Walter, Archdeacon of Oxford, who he claims provided him with a, now lost, ancient book in Welsh.

It is important to be aware of the historical and political situation. Just seventy years earlier, William the Conqueror had taken the throne of England from the Saxon King Harold at the battle of Hastings. For 500 years prior to that the Saxon kingdoms, and later England, had expanded at the expense of the Romano-British. The Welsh, Cornish and Strathclyde were the descendants of these, as were the Bretons in modern Brittany. Saxons were their common enemy. One third of William's army at Hastings were Bretons and many Breton lords were given land throughout England after the conquest.

We can't say what these Bretons thought about Britain or the Saxons, but it is not a coincidence the interest in Arthur occurred after the Norman conquest. The Breton link is, I think, important. The Arthur of local legends and magical animals was the dominant one until the twelfth century.[1] It was Geoffrey of Monmouth who propelled Arthur into literary fame. The French romance novels further developed the stories to the legend we know today. Indeed, many of the concepts were added at this point: the Round Table, Excalibur, the sword in the stone, even Merlin. The original story is as Nennius describes in the *Historia Brittonum* around 829: Arthur is a soldier, a leader of battle, leading the kings of Britain against the Saxons in twelve battles culminating in Baden. The Welsh legends and poems weren't written down until after Geoffrey and may have been influenced by him. The same may be said of the saints' lives, and both sets of 'evidence' are viewed as ahistorical.

Geoffrey makes Arthur a king and one that conquers a vast empire including Norway, Iceland and Gaul. He then engages in a battle against Rome on the Continent. So in Geoffrey's work, Arthur's Continental adventures are a major part. The most significant character added to the story is arguably Merlin, but this appears to be manufactured from the Ambrosius of the *Historia Brittonum* (itself possibly derived form the Ambrosius Aurelianus of Gildas) and the Myrddin Wylit of the *Annales Cambriae*.

Similar to other medieval historians in Europe, he believed the country was founded by a Trojan prince after the fall of Troy. So Brutus is the first of three main characters in the book, Arthur being the third. Brutus comes to Britain and, after defeating various giants, gives the island its name. A long list of kings and adventures follows, including King Lear of Shakespeare fame. We then have the story of Belinus and Brennius, two brothers who conquer Gaul and Rome.

Brennus was a chieftain of the Senones, a Gaulish tribe, that did indeed sack Rome in 387 BC which demonstrates, as with other characters, that Geoffrey was not averse to being economical with the truth or giving his characters storylines lifted from other figures. There's no evidence for many of his kings, although as he moves through history he does include more established figures such as Julius Caesar and Claudius. We then go through further kings, who apparently ruled alongside the Romans, until we get to Magnus Maximus, or Maximianus as Geoffrey calls him.

We will take it from there and follow the story up to just before Arthur so we can compare it with Nennius, Gildas and Bede. Geoffrey leaves Maximus having appointed Gracianus in charge, who immediately has to ward off invasions by the Picts and Huns led by Wanius and Malgo. Needless to say, evidence for the veracity of this is absent. There then follows what seems to be a repeat of Gildas with a legion returning, building the wall and a repeating of the Rescript of Honorius. Enemies

The History of the Kings of Britain by Geoffrey of Monmouth

return, this time Norwegians and Danes, and seize territory up to the wall. So a garbled version of Gildas and Bede with Huns, Danes and Norwegians thrown in for a twelfth-century audience.

We then have the appeal to Agicius, which may well mean Aetius, in 445–54, but Geoffrey seems to be placing this around 410. It doesn't help that he gives no dates. Around this time he names the Archbishop of London as Guithelinus, a name that may have relevance in the genealogy of Vortigern. He travels to Armorica, modern Brittany, to ask for help from King Aldoneus. The king's brother, Constantine, comes to Britain with an army and accepts the crown.

Immediately one is confronted with contradictory dates. Is this Constantine the same Constantine III who declares himself emperor from Britain and invades Gaul? On one hand, aside from the appeal of Aetius, the chronology would suggest yes. On the other, Geoffrey gives his children different names and has him ruling for ten years. Constantine III had Constans and Julianus and ruled for four years before being killed in Gaul. Geoffrey's Constantine also has a son named Constans, but he adds Ambrosius Aurelianus and Uther Pendragon. This will lead to problems later because an Arthur born to Uther in the early or mid-fifth century is unlikely to be fighting at Badon in 516, let alone Camlann in 542, the latter being the only date Geoffrey does give us.

So his chronology is a little muddled to say the least. After Constantine's death, his son Constans is given the throne but Vortigern, his advisor, conspires to have him killed and takes the throne. We then have the arrival of Hengist and Horsa, but this time settling in Lindsey around Lincoln. Reinforcements arrive and Hengist builds a fortress. Unlike Nennius, however, Geoffrey names the daughter that Vortigern falls for as Renwein. They marry and Hengist is given Kent, removing the British earl, Gorangonus. We then meet St Germanus who, as we know, in reality visited in 429. Octa and Ebissa arrive with 300 more ships and are allowed to settle in Northumberland. Vortigern is deposed and his son Vortimer made king, fighting four battles and forcing the Saxons to leave.

Geoffrey is roughly following Nennius rather than Bede, but with added information. Renwein poisons Vortimer allowing Vortigern to take back the crown and Hengist to return with 300,000 men. The British princes plot to rebel so Hengist arranges for a peace conference. This becomes known as 'The Night of the Long Knives' because, on a prearranged signal, Vortigern is captured and 300 British nobles murdered with only one escaping. The Saxons take London, York, Winchester and Lincoln. The timeline is closer to Nennius and any of the events above, such as Vortigern's marriage, the gifting of Kent, slaughter of the British nobles or the fall of the cities mentioned, could be linked to the entry for 440 in the *Gallic Chronicle*. However, it makes far more sense with regard to the other sources for these events to be after 450. Whether we take this as a separate event to the *Gallic Chronicle* or not, there is something worth noting. Despite the discrepancies there are some similarities between Gildas and Bede on one hand, and Geoffrey and Nennius on the other.

We have to remember that there's no evidence for any of this. It could be Geoffrey that possessed a now lost manuscript, but it's equally possible he made the whole thing up. To continue, Vortigern then flees to Wales and attempts to build a fortress. We then have the introduction of Merlin into the story. Geoffrey combines two characters here. The first is the Myrddin

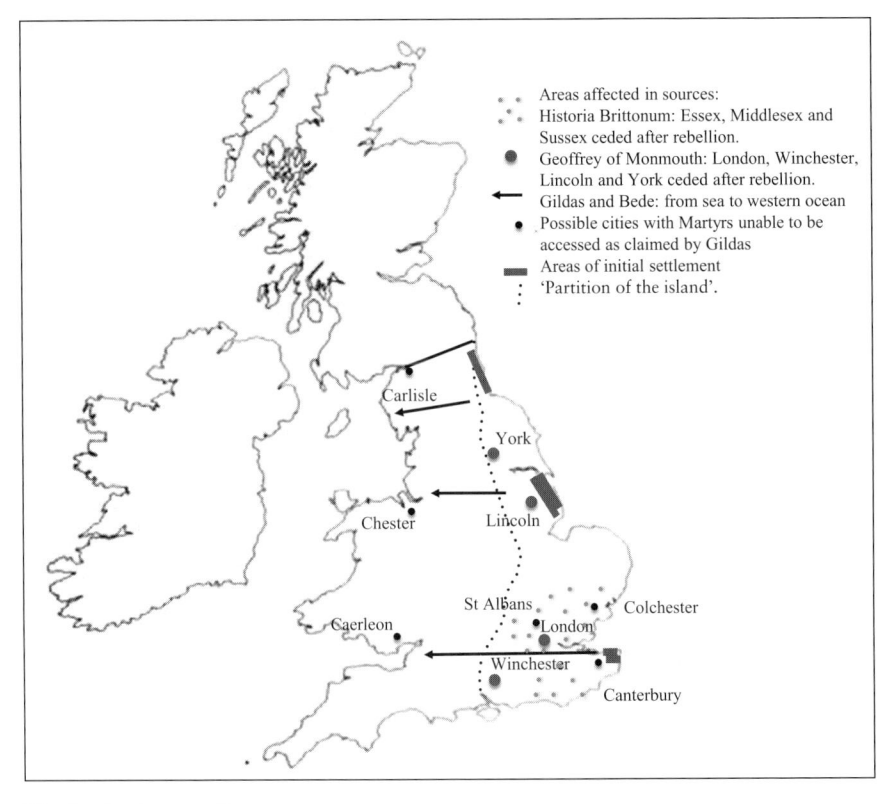

The barbarian revolt.

Wyllt (Mryddin the wild), mentioned in the *Annales Cambriae* and other Welsh legends as being at the Battle of Arfderydd in 573. The second is Emrys Ambrosius mentioned by Nennius and associated with Vortigern. So he has combined two figures, one from a generation before Arthur and the other from two generations after. Then he's changed the name to Merlin. Norman French 'Mryddin' is a little too close in sound to 'Merde', which has a rather impolite meaning. He then devotes much time describing a series of prophecies by Merlin, most notably the story of the red and white dragons with the red one eventually winning over the Saxon white dragon.

It is significant that Geoffrey, a Welshman or Breton, is writing for a Norman Lord – both would see Saxons as a common enemy. The portrayal of the Saxons as poisoners and betrayers is in line with this. Ambrosius and Uther then land and catch Vortigern in the castle of Genoreu in South Wales, where the castle and it's occupants are burned to the ground. Ambrosius is crowned king and defeats the Saxons in two battles, Maisbeli and Kaerconan, before executing Hengist. Octa and Eossa surrender and are given Bernicia in Northumberland, while Ambrosius rules from York. We then have an aside where Merlin is called from the land of Geweissi to magically transport the giants ring from Ireland to build Stonehenge as a suitable burial place for the 300 nobles slaughtered by the Saxons. Uther leads an army to Ireland to achieve this. On Uther's return Vortigern's son and the Irish king invade. While Uther is defeating them, Ambrosius is poisoned by the Saxons. Still we have no dates.

There is a mention of Uther's battle where he sees a two-headed dragon in the sky with a fiery tail. Geoffrey uses this to explain Uther's title of 'Pendragon'. Some have equated this with Haley's Comet which would have been around 451. But the mention of St Samson (circa 485–565) being given the Bishopric of York and St Dubricius (465–555) the City of the Legions doesn't tie in with this. Nor does an Arthur being born soon after, and fighting a battle in 542. There are two records of comets in the fifth century; the first recorded for 497 in a fourteenth-century text, *Flores Historiarum*. The second is seen from Brittany in 457 and is recorded by a Conrad Wolffart in the sixteenth century. They both have a similar description and may well be influenced by Geoffrey. If not though we once again have more than one possible date, which makes a timeline difficult.

Uther, now king, has to contend with Octa and Eossa who rebel, are defeated and taken prisoner. We then get the famous story of Merlin

King Arthur: Man or Myth?

helping Uther magically change his appearance to seduce Ygraine at Tintagel, and it is this union that produces Arthur. Uther is able to marry Ygraine after her husband dies in battle. Arthur has a sister, Anna, who is married to King Loth of Lothian who assists Uther in fighting the Saxons, Octa having escaped. Uther defeats them before being poisoned at St Albans. We now come to Arthur who occupies a good third of the book. Arthur is crowned by St Dubricius at the age of 15, the same age, incidentally, that Clovis I of the Franks was crowned. The author is more than willing to borrow from other people's history and make things up, and this could be another example. Arthur defeats the Saxons, now led by Colgrin and Baldulf, at a battle at the river Douglas before besieging York, which is possibly a reference to the City of the Legions in Nennius. He's forced to retreat to Lincoln before requesting assistance from Hoel of Brittany, son of Arthur's sister and King Budicius.

Geoffrey doesn't make clear whether this is a second marriage or a second sister. He does state that Loth and Anna have two sons, Mordred and Gawain. Arthur then gains two victories at Kaerluideoit, Lincoln, and at Caledon Wood, both possible nods to Nennius's battle list. The Saxons then promise to leave, but break this immediately by sailing round to Devon. Arthur defeats them at the Battle of Badon near Bath. His cousin, Cador, Duke of Cornwall pursues the Saxons to Thanet, reminiscent of Vortimer's four battles. Arthur then fights three battles against the Picts, another at Loch Lomond and one against a King Gilmarius of Ireland. He marries Guinevere before invading Ireland and receiving the surrender of the Orkneys and Gotland.

Twelve years go by, meaning Arthur is now 27 in the story, and he invades Norway and Denmark before marching on Paris, defeating a Frollo in single combat, and subduing Gaul. It goes without saying there is no evidence for any of this. We know there were Britons fighting in the Loire valley in the 460s and of course Riothomus in 471, but whether these are from Britain or Brittany is impossible to say. Otherwise we have Frankish expansion into Brittany that might be the basis for a British leader fighting in France either side of 500. But there was certainly no conquest of Norway or Ireland at this time. It may well be that he has stolen the story of Maximus, or one of the other Roman leaders declared emperor from Britain who then invaded Gaul.

Nine years go by, making Arthur 36, and we then come to the main part of the narrative. One that is often forgotten in subsequent stories.

While in court in Caerleon-on-Usk, messengers from the Roman Procurator, Lucius Hiberius arrive, demanding tribute and submission. This is said to be in the time of the Roman emperor Leo. In fact the eastern emperor, Leo I, reigned from 457–74 and Leo II in 474. There was a Pope Leo in 440–61, but that seems too early. There is no record of a Lucius Hiberius, although a western emperor Glycerus (473–4) was sometimes misspelled as Lucerius. If true, this would place Arthur's birth around 438, which would not tie in with any of the other implied dates, or indeed fighting at Camlan aged 96. Arthur refuses on the basis that Brennius and Constantine the Great had defeated Rome and so Rome owed allegiance to Britain. This is quite important; Geoffrey is telling his audience that Britain has a glorious past that gives it authority over other nations. To push the point further he has Arthur take an army to Gaul to fight the Romans, leaving his nephew Mordred in charge of Britain. There is a short story of Arthur defeating a giant at Mont St Michel in which he remembers another giant-killing act. He describes in great detail a huge battle in the Saussy region between Langres and Autun, near Dijon in Eastern France. Needless to say, there is no such record of British or even Roman military activity in this area at this time. Arthur is, of course victorious, and prepares to invade Italy and take Rome.

At this point he learns that Mordred and Guinivere have betrayed him and have allied with Saxons led by Chelric. Arthur returns to Britain and defeats Mordred at the battles of Richborough and Winchester, possibly referring to Fort Guinnion. Mordred is finally killed at the battle of Camlann in Cornwall. Arthur is fatally wounded and taken to the Isle of Avalon so that 'his wounds might be attended to'. Arthur orders that his cousin Constantine takes the crown. Nothing more is said and his death is not confirmed beyond the fatal wounding comment. So we see the legend we know today start taking shape. But you may notice the absence of Excalibur, the Round Table, Lancelot and the Grail. Geoffrey actually names the sword 'Caliburn', but these later concepts were added by other authors inspired by Geoffrey's work.

Geoffrey states the battle of Camlann was in 542 and assuming this was a year after his Roman war, he died aged about 37. So, working backwards, we have a birth date around 505 and a battle of Badon after his crowning at 15, placing it after 520. Uther reigns at least fifteen years, suggesting the comet in 497 is the more likely one to be connected. This does put Ambrosius reigning in the 490s slightly at odds with Bede's statement that it was in the time of Zeno, 474–91. It also pulls Vortigern right up towards the later part of the fifth century. While we can't trust any of the narrative or dates, there is one glaring problem with the text. There simply was no British army victoriously rampaging across Roman Gaul in either the fifth or sixth centuries. We know there was a Romano-Saxon war in the 460s and the Romans later requested help from a British king, Riothamus. But his battle was against the Goths and he lost, never to be heard of again. The history of sixth-century Gaul is fairly well known and neither British or Roman armies featured. We will discuss the relationship between Bretons and Franks later, but we can be fairly certain this part is inaccurate.

After Camlann, Geoffrey then proceeds to list four of the five kings denounced by Gildas: Constantine is the first, followed by Aurelius Conanus, Vortiporus, and Malgo (Maelgwn). He misses out Cuneglasse. This is the king Gildas accuses of rejecting his wife and taking her sister from 'holy orders'. He goes on to call him: 'Bear; Driver of the chariot of the bear's stronghold; Red butcher; and with arms special to yourself.' Could it be because Geoffrey has already mentioned him? The Bear, 'arth-' in Welsh, being possibly an epitaph for Arthur? That, I'm afraid, is hugely speculative. Many have tried to suggest it, and he is one of the candidates that people have put forward, but he's one among many. I would add also that Gildas appears to be delivering his sermon as all five kings are ruling. Geoffrey has them coming sequentially.

It is accepted that he had access to Gildas, Nennius, *Annales Cambriae*, *Harleian Genealogies* and a number of Welsh legends and poems. His account does not stop there though. He then describes a King Keredic and the invasion by Gormund, king of the Africans, with an army of 160,000 aided by Isembard nephew of Louis, king of the Franks. This does seem complete fabrication. He ends in 689 with the death of Cadwallader, the seventh-century King of Gwynedd and the last Welsh king to claim lordship over Britain. He finishes by berating the Welsh for their tendency to civil war and claiming the Saxons behaved more wisely and kept the peace among themselves.

The book as a whole does have a particular message: it is the first attempt at a full historical narrative for Britain. It shows a great and glorious past descended from the kings of Troy and equal to the Romans. Arthur is simply one of three main characters, Brutus, Brennius and

The History of the Kings of Britain by Geoffrey of Monmouth

Arthur. It shows that the Welsh and Bretons have a proud history and the prophecies are there to demonstrate they will rise again if they avoid the civil wars and discord. To help this narrative Geoffrey is quite happy to include fictitious characters and events alongside giants and magic. It also also provides a link between Britain, Brittany and France, at the same time demonstrating the dangers of discord and civil wars. The Saxons and the Romans provide a common enemy for the Welsh and the whole narrative would not offend his Norman sponsors. In fact, Arthur emerged as a popular character only after the Norman conquest.[2] Prior to that Arthur is the more mystical and magical character of Welsh poems and legends that weren't written down until much later.

It is quite possible that Geoffrey made the whole thing up. But it's also possible he took that one reference in Nennius and added an elaborate tale using bits of other historical characters, myths and legends. The author of the translation I have been using does state 'most of the material in the History is fictional and someone did invent it,' yet 'history keeps peeping through the fiction'.[3] For example, Geoffrey describes the Venedoti decapitating a whole Roman legion in London and then throwing their heads into a stream called Nantgallum, or Galobroc in Saxon. In 1860 a large number of skulls were indeed found in the bed of the Walbrook in London.

Contemporary writers had something to say about Geoffrey. William of Newburgh writing around 1198 in *History of English Affairs*:

> For the purpose of washing out those stains from the character of the Britons, a writer in our times has started up and invented the most ridiculous fictions concerning them, and with unblushing effrontery, extols them far above the Macedonians and Romans. He is called Geoffrey, surnamed Arthur, from having given, in a Latin version, the fabulous exploits of Arthur, drawn from the traditional fictions of the Britons, with additions of his own, and endeavored to dignify them with the name of authentic history.

Ranulf Higden of Chester writing in 1352:

> Many men wonder about this Arthur, whom Geoffrey extols so much singly, how the things that are said of him could be

true, for, as Geoffrey repeats, he conquered thirty realms. If he subdued the king of France to him, and did slay Lucius the Procurator of Rome, Italy, then it is astonishing that the chronicles of Rome, of France, and of the Saxons should not have spoken of so noble a prince in their stories, which mentioned little things about men of low degree. Geoffrey says that Arthur overcame Frollo, King of France, but there is no record of such a name among men of France. Also, he says that Arthur slew Lucius Hiberius, Procurator of the city of Rome in the time of Leo the Emperor, yet according to all the stories of the Romans Lucius did not govern, in that time nor was Arthur born, nor did he live then, but in the time of Justinian, who was the fifth emperor after Leo. Geoffrey says that he has marveled that Gildas and Bede make no mention of Arthur in their writings; however, I suppose it is rather to be marvelled why Geoffrey praises him so much, whom old authors, true and famous writers of stories, leave untouched. But perhaps it is the custom of every nation to extol some of their blood-relations excessively, as the Greeks great Alexander, the Romans Octavian, Englishmen King Richard, Frenchmen Charles; and so the Britons extolled Arthur. Which thing happens, as Josephus says, either for fairness of the story, or for the delectation of the readers, or for exaltation of their own blood.

We also have writers with the opposite view. William of Malmesbury in *The Deeds of the kings of England* (*De Gestis Regum Anglorum*) c.1125:

> ...the strength of the Britons diminished and all hope left them. They would soon have been altogether destroyed if Ambrosius, the sole survivor of the Romans who became king after Vortigern, had not defeated the presumptuous barbarians with the powerful aid of the warlike Arthur. This is that Arthur of whom the trifling of the Britons talks such nonsense even today; a man clearly worthy not to be dreamed of in fallacious fables, but to be proclaimed in veracious histories, as one who long sustained his tottering country, and gave the shattered minds of his fellow citizens an edge for war.

The History of the Kings of Britain by Geoffrey of Monmouth

Then Henry of Huntingdon, *History of the English* (*Historia Anglorum*) c.1130:

> The valiant Arthur, who was at that time the commander of the soldiers and kings of Britain, fought against the invaders invincibly. Twelve times he led in battle. Twelve times was he victorious in battle. The twelfth and hardest battle that Arthur fought against the Saxons was on Mount Badon, where 440 of his men died in the attack that day, and no Briton stayed to support him, the Lord alone strengthening him.

Both these examples pre-date Geoffrey's work but are clearly derived from Nennius. But concerning Geoffrey's work: what value can there be in a book, written 600 years after the event, that contains so much false history not to mention giants and magic? Yet he also names lots of historical figures too. There have been some modern historians who have agreed.

Leslie Alcock, *Arthur's Britain* (1971):

> There is acceptable historical evidence that Arthur was a genuine historical figure, not a mere figment of myth or romance.

John Morris, *The Age of Arthur* (1973):

> …he was as real as Alfred the Great or William the Conqueror.

Others take a different view.

Michael Wood, *In Search of the Dark Ages* (1987):

> Yet, reluctantly we must conclude that there is no definite evidence that Arthur ever existed.

David Dumville, *Histories and Pseudo-histories* (1990):

> The fact is that there is no historical evidence about Arthur; we must reject him from our histories and, above all, from the titles of our books.

King Arthur: Man or Myth?

After the *History of the Kings of Britain* was written in 1136 there was a rapid increase in interest and subsequent works. Fifty years later the monks of Glastonbury claimed to have made a remarkable discovery. In 1184 a great fire destroyed many buildings at Glastonbury Abbey. A chronicler at the abbey of Margam records that a monk had begged to be buried at a certain spot. When he died in 1191 the monks duly obeyed his request. Digging down they came across three coffins. The first contained the bones of a woman claimed to be Guinevere. The second, a man supposedly Mordred, 'his nephew'. The last, with a leaden cross fixed, were the bones of a large man. The inscription stated:

> Here lies the famous King Arthur buried in the Isle of Avalon.

He goes on to explain that the place was once surrounded by marshes, and is called the Isle of Avalon, that is 'the isle of apples'. Explaining that 'aval' means, in British, an apple.

Gerald of Wales, writing shortly after, also recorded what happened. It is slightly different but he at least visited the site and handled the cross. Acting supposedly on the word of Henry II before he died in 1189, two years later they discovered, 16 ft below the ground, a hollowed oak tree that contained two skeletons. Under the covering stone was a lead cross bearing the following inscription.

> Here lies buried the famous *Arthurus* with *Wenneveria* his second wife in the isle of Avalon.

Ralph of Coggeshall, writing in 1193, also mentioned it and supports the Margram version:

> Here lies the famous King Arturius, buried in the Isle of Avalon.

Historical records differ on the number of tombs, skeletal remains and exact inscription. The majority appear to suggest two bodies and the reference to Arthurius and Isle of Avalon. The bones were transferred to a marble tomb in the Lady Chapel. A hundred years later during a visit by Edward I, there was a ceremony to move the bones again, this time to a black marble tomb in front of the altar of the larger church. The bones disappeared during the dissolution of the monasteries under Henry VIII. The leaden cross apparently survived.

Excavations in the 1960s suggest that there was a grave in that spot. We also know the cross was real. Leland described it in 1534 and William Camden sketched one side in 1607, it's inscription supporting that of the *Margam Chronicle* and thus bringing into doubt Gerald of Wales (although leaving open to question what was on the other side). He admits he sketched it from the original copy and some of his copies differ in the shape of the letters. Sadly the cross went missing in the eighteenth century. Modern academics dismiss the find as a hoax for a number of reasons. First, following the devastating fire and the death of their greatest benefactor, the king, pilgrims and money had dried up. The scale of false religious artefacts and forgeries by the church in the Middle Ages should give pause for thought. Second, the letterforms are not consistent with the fifth century, but appear to be tenth century, as does the shape of the cross. The monks also had a history of similar claims. William of Malmesbury, writing shortly before Geoffrey, claimed that St Patrick was buried there in 472, dying aged 111. Like Geoffrey, he makes no link between Glastonbury and Arthur's grave, claiming Arthur's resting place is 'nowhere to be seen'. William also claims the name Glastonbury comes from the founder, Glasteing. Indeed, the earliest record is *Glestingaburg* in the seventh century. There is no mention of islands or apples. Another legend also has it that Joseph of Arithamea founded the abbey in the first century and this is linked to Robert de Boron's twelfth-century poems: *The Holy Grail, Joseph of d'Arimathe* and *Merlin*, all of which post-date Geoffrey of Monmouth.

The abbey itself was not built until the seventh century and was extended in the tenth. There is no evidence for any of these legends and no archaeological evidence for earlier activity on this site. Geoffrey of Monmouth did not connect Avalon with the site. In his *Life of Merlin*, he does call Avalon *Insula Pumorum,* or Isle of Apples; in his *History* it is Insula Avallonis. He does not associate this with Glastonbury. In the *Life of St Gildas* written by Caradoc of Llancarfan in 1130–50, he tells the story of Melwas capturing Guinevere, and Arthur coming to Glastonbury to release her. Gildas intervenes and is later buried in the floor of St Mary's church, despite all the other legends and evidence which place his resting place at Rhuys in Brittany. The same author also includes Arthur in the *Life of St Cadoc*. There is no mention of Avalon or any association with Glastonbury.

In the *Brut y Brenhinedd*, a mid-thirteenth century copy of Geoffrey's work, this becomes Ynys Afallach. This suggests an island belonging to someone called Afallach, an attested Welsh name. This is similar to a King Avallo mentioned by Geoffrey. However, there are also similarities to other Welsh legends. In the *Preiddeu Annwn*, a cauldron, sought by Arthur, is guarded by nine maidens and it is a place where neither age or injury can hurt. In another Welsh myth, Afallach is the King of Annwn and father to the goddess Modron. Gerald of Wales also relates how Margan, a goddess of Annwfyn, hid Arthur in Ynys Afallach. In fact as early as the first century, a Roman geographer, Pomponius Mela, described an island, Sena, off the coast of Brittany. There, nine virgin priestesses cared for the oracle of a Gaulish god.

What all this demonstrates is that the association of Glastonbury with Avalon came after Geoffrey of Monmouth. Prior to this, Arthur's resting place is seen as distinctly mythical and in part of the legend he wasn't dead at all but would return in time of need. It also shows that separate to Arthur there were tales of islands, nine virgin priestesses and cauldrons. We also have a historical account of a first-century island off Brittany. It may also show the willingness of medieval writers to blend stories and legends and be willing to create myths and foundation stories to boost claims and revenue. This is something to bear in mind when reading the saints' lives. Importantly it also demonstrates there was no particular consensus in the Middle Ages about Arthur's resting place or even historicity. Tales and stories emerging 600 years after Arthur's alleged time can hardly be held up as evidence.

In 1981 someone claimed the cross had been found in a lake in Enfield. The man took it to the British Museum and an employee who saw the cross described it as just over 6 in high, not the 1 ft Leland described in 1532. The finder, however, refused to hand the cross over and his description of the cross included the same wording and size as the William Camden sketch. Despite the council's attempts, the cross was never recovered. The gentleman in question was apparently a lead-pattern worker for a local toy maker and was involved in the manufacture of lead models of cars. He was also a member of the Enfield Archaeological Society.

One possibility is that this was a hoax concerning an earlier hoax and highlights the need to treat any evidence with a healthy scepticism. There

The History of the Kings of Britain by Geoffrey of Monmouth

is a tendency to view evidence from the twelfth century, for example, with greater weight than it deserves; certainly more than a story written in modern times. While a modern story may have no historical value, we forget many of these tales were written 700 years or more after Arthur is supposed to have lived. In a similar vein, many modern theorists selectively pick out certain aspects of Geoffrey and other stories and mix them together in an attempt to build a coherent theory, neglecting to lay out the 90 per cent that has been cast aside. Later we will cover the genealogies that were also written many hundreds of years later. Theorists have used these and many of the names in Geoffrey's work to build up a family tree. It is vital the reader looks to the original sources and not take the evidence at face value. There are a number of authors who have misrepresented and misspelt names to fit in with their theory. The reader will discover that many an 'Arthur' is not an Arthur at all, but Anthun, Atroys or Arthwys. There are as many people today willing to manipulate the evidence, or even lie for whatever purpose, as there were at any time since the fifth century.

In summary, we have a twelfth-century text, written 600 years after the events. It is contradictory and full of suspect material. Yet history does indeed 'peep through the cracks'. On one hand the author is wholly unreliable, but on the other it shows a persistence of the legend and a receptive audience in the twelfth century. Additionally, as we shall see later, there is a way of interpreting the narrative that does not contradict other sources at all. This interpretation shouldn't, of course, be mistaken for proof.

Chapter 13

The French Romances and Welsh Legends

We will now cover the other sources for the legend. They can be split into two parts. The first are the French romances, all of which post-date Geoffrey of Monmouth. They were inspired by his work and we can see how the story evolved to include many of the elements we now consider part of the Arthurian tale. It does suggest there was a tradition in Normandy and France that was receptive to this. There may well have been a Breton influence. The second are the Welsh legends. Some of these are thought to pre-date Geoffrey's work and thus are an invaluable source of clues as to what the legend may have appeared like to audiences pre-tenth century. Unfortunately, the only surviving copies are much later and so it is difficult to ascertain how much they have been corrupted. It is worth noting when specific concepts were introduced, such as the Round Table or sword in the stone.

It is a fruitless task to look at these stories in any great depth or detail as they are corrupted and contradictory. Theories built on such 'evidence' start by building on sand and relying on tenuous links and tautology. Written down over 500 years and as much as 1,000 years after the events, they can tell us little about how the stories developed prior to that. We will therefore only briefly list the most famous texts. On their own they prove very little, if anything, but as a body they do demonstrate a 'market' for Arthurian stories in the Middle Ages. So we have a list of works in the first table below, written mostly 600 years after Arthur is supposed to have lived and derived or influenced almost entirely by Geoffrey of Monmouth's work.

The French Romances and Welsh Legends

Table 20: The French romances

Literary source	Comments
Roman de Brut by Wace 1155 Norman French poem.	Literary history of Britain based on Geoffrey of Monmouth's work. First introduction of the Round Table.

Tristan and Iseult
Twelfth century various:
  Thomas of Britain 1170s
  Beroul 1170s
  Folie Tristan d'Oxford 1175–1200
  Prose Tristan 1230–40
  Sir Tristram 1300 (first English version)
	Love affair between a Cornish knight and an Irish princess, fiancée of King Mark of Cornwall.
	Linked to Arthur for the first time in 1230s and through the later Welsh legends.

Joseph of Arimathea and **Merlin** Robert de Boron Late twelfth-century French poem	Joseph of Arimathea brings the Grail to Britain to the valley of Avaron, later translated to Avalon and identified with Glastonbury. Traditional tale of Merlin in connection with Arthur. Introduces sword in an anvil placed on a stone. First to connect the Grail with Jesus. Introduces 'Rich Fisher' version of the later Fisher King.
romance poems Chretien de Troyes 1170–90 French	Includes Arthur's court and the knights of the Round Table. Eric and Enide 1170 Cliges 1176 Yvain, the Knight of the Lion 1180 Lancelot, the knight of the Cart 1180 Percival, le conte du Graal 1190 The first to feature Lancelot as a main character and the affair between him and Guinevere. Introduces the quest for the Holy Grail and The Fisher King.

(continued)

Table 20: (Continued)

Literary source	Comments
Vulgate Cylcle or Prose Lancelot Unknown 1210–30 French	Five prose volumes introducing more Christian themes. Estoire del Saint Grail Estoire de Merlin Lancelot Propre Quest del Saint Graal Mort Artu Galahad's quest for the Grail.
Post Vulgate Cycle Unknown 1230–40 French	Similar to Vulgate Cycle and one of the biggest influences of Mallory's later work. Estoire del Saint Grail Estoire de Merlin Quest del Saint Graal Mort Artu Introduces Arthur's incestuous affair which produces Mordred. Introduces the receiving of Excalibur from the Lady in the Lake. Links Tristan to the Grail quest.
Le Morte d'Arthur Thomas Mallory 1485 Middle English	Combines many of the themes from Geoffrey together with all the romance poems and stories. One of the best known works of Arthurian literature and the basis of many later and modern adaptations.

The Welsh legends almost certainly pre-date both the French romances and Geoffrey of Monmouth's book. However, they weren't actually written down until much later and can be seen in the following manuscripts:

1. White Book of Rhydderch, c.1350 (*Llyfr Gwyn Rhydderch*, National Library of Wales, Peniarth MS 4-5).
2. *Black Book of Carmarthen*, c. 1350 (*Llyfr Du Caerfyrddin* National Library of Wales, Peniarth MS 1).

The French Romances and Welsh Legends

3. *Red Book of Hergest*, after 1382 (*Llyfr Coch Hergest*, Jesus College Oxford MS 111).
4. *The Book of Taliesin*, dated to first half of fourteenth century but may include material from the tenth century, although not as far back as a sixth-century poet called Taliesin (*Llyfr Du Caerfyrddin* National Library of Wales, Peniarth MS 2).
5. *Book of Aneirin*, dated to around 1265 but thought to be a copy of a ninth-century original. It contains the poem, *Y Gododdin* concerning a battle in 600, and the sixth-century poet Aneirin that may be contemporary.
6. *Triads of Britain*, dated to thirteenth century, containing both mythic and historical figures and events (*Trioedd Ynys Prydein*, National Library of Wales, Peniarth MS 16).
7. *Mabinogion* is a collection of many of the works already mentioned, brought together in an eighteenth-century compilation. The stories contained are believed to have originated in the twelfth century and may have pre-dated Geoffrey of Monmouth.

Below is a brief outline of the relevant stories:

Table 21: Welsh legends

Literary source	Comments
Preiddeu Annfwn 'The spoils of Annwfn' Preserved in the *Book of Taliesin* dated to the early fourteenth century. Possibly originated tenth century. Estimates range for original version from 600 to 900.	Arthur undertakes a dangerous journey to Annfwn, Welsh name for the Celtic Otherworld (realm of deities or the dead). Out of three boatloads of warriors only seven return. Arthur's ship is named Prydwen. The poem is not clear but a cauldron of the Chief of Annwn guarded by nine maidens appears to be one of the spoils taken. Similar to the Cauldron of Diwrnach which Arthur takes from Ireland in Culhwch and Olwen. Also similar to story of Bran and Branwen in the *Mabinogion*. Possibly the basis of the Grail legends.

(continued)

Table 21: (Continued)

Literary source	Comments
Pa Gur 'who is the gatekeeper' Possibly originated tenth century. From the Black Book of Carmarthen in mid-thirteenth century.	Dialogue between Arthur and a gatekeeper in which Arthur boasts of his prowess and that of his companions including Cat the Fair. Mentions son of Uthr Pendragon's servant. Another fought at the Battle of Tryfrwyd, along with Bedwyr and Arthur, one the twelve battles in *Historia Brittonum*. Mentions Arthur fighting first a witch and then mythical 'dog-heads' at Edinburgh. Cai fights nine witches at the peak of Ystafngwn and a terrible cat of Palug. The former may be a reference to the nine maidens in 'The Spoils of Annwfn', the nine witches of Gloucester in Peredur or in the *Life of St Samson*.
Stanzas of the Graves Ninth- or tenth-century origin. Preserved in the *Black Book of Carmarthen* mid-thirteenth century.	A number of short verses of renowned persons. One verse ends with: 'The grave of Arthur is a mystery'.
Elegy of Geraint son of Erbin Ninth- or tenth-century origin. Preserved in the *Black Book of Carmarthen* mid-thirteenth century.	Poem celebrating Geraint and his deeds at the Battle of Llongborth. 'In Llongborth I saw Arthur, And brave men who hewed down with steel, emperor and conductor of the toil.' Llongborth may be identified with Langport in Somerset or Portsmouth in Hampshire. Geraint may also be referred to in the early poem *Y Gododdin* as 'Geraint of the South'. A later Welsh poem, *Geraint and Enid*, is linked to Erec and Enide by Chretien de Troyes.
Triads of Britain Eleventh to fourteenth century Found in: Peniarth 16 manuscript, thirteenth century.	A rhetorical poem that groups things into threes. Multiple mentions of Arthur and related themes. For example: Three unfortunate counsels of the Island of Britain: To give place for their horses' fore-feet ... to Julius Carsar; to allow Horsa and Hengist and Rhonwen into this island; the three fold dividing by Arthur of his men with Medrawd at Camlan.

The French Romances and Welsh Legends

Red book of Hergest 1400 Fragment in *White Book of Rhydderch* 1325.	Mentions various other characters: Urien, Uther, Owain, Gwenhwyfar, Medrawd, Emrys Weldig (Ambrosius), Gwrtheyrn the Thin (Vortigern), Gwerthefyr (Vortimer), Llachau son of Arthur, Cei, Geraint and Camlan.
Culhwch and Olwen anonymous Original possibly eleventh century. Found in: *Red book of Hergest* 1400 Fragment in *White Book of Rhydderch* 1325.	Culhwch wishes to marry Olwen, daughter of the giant Ysbadden. He travels to Arthur's court in Celliwig, Cornwall to get Arthur's help in a number of tasks the giant sets him. Only a small number are recorded including: The hunt for the boar Twrch Trwyth referenced in *Historia Brittonum*. The rescue of Mabon from a watery prison. The quest for the cauldron of Diwrnach in Ireland. Arthur kills The Black Witch. The tasks completed, the giant is killed and the lovers marry. Many of the tasks are similar to tales in other Irish legends.
Geraint and Enid Found in: *Red book of Hergest* 1400 Fragment in *White Book of Rhydderch* 1325.	Geraint, one of Arthur's knights and son of Erbin of Dumnonia, and his romance with Enid. Likely derived from Chretien de Troyes's *Erec and Enide*.
Owain or Lady of the Fountain Original possibly eleventh century. Found in: *Red book of Hergest* 1400 and *White Book of Rhydderch* 1325.	Owain, one of Arthur's knights, based on historical Owain son of Urien, in a romance with the Lady of the Fountain. Likely derived from Chretien de Troyes's *Yvain, the knight of the lion*. Similar also to tale in Life of St Mungo (aka St Kentigern) where the saint's father, Owain, tries to woo Lot of Lothian's daughter.
Peredur son of Efrawg Found in: *Red book of Hergest* 1400 and *White Book of Rhydderch* 1325.	Peredur travels to King Arthur's court and proceeds on a number of adventures including a similarity with the Fisher King, although the Grail is replaced by a severed head in this version. Likely derived from Chretien de Troyes's *Perceval, the Story of the Grail*.

(continued)

Table 21: (Continued)

Literary source	Comments
Brut by Layamon Late twelfth century	First English version of Geoffrey of Monmouth's *History of the Kings of Britain*
Brut y Brenhinedd Thirteenth century.	Middle Welsh version of Geoffrey of Monmouth's *History of the Kings of Britain*
Brut Tysilio Fifteenth century.	Initially attributed to the seventh-century Welsh saint, Tysilio. Scholars now believe it derives from Geoffrey of Monmouth.
Dream of Rhonabwy Written end of twelfth century, found in: *Red Book of Hergest* 1400.	Set in twelfth century. Rhonabwy falls asleep and dreams he is back in Arthur's time. He meets Iddawg, 'the Churn of Britain', called this because he caused the battle of Camlann by distorting messages between the king, or emperor as he is titled here, and his enemy Medrawd. He is led to Arthur's camp before the Battle of Badon. Arthur is playing gwyddbwyll, a chess-like game, with Owain, son of Urien. The same Urien who is mentioned in *Historia Brittonum* and other sources as King of Rheged (Cumbria/Southern Scotland area) in the late sixth century. The Saxons, led by Osla Gyllellfawr (Osla big knife), ask for and receive a truce. Arthur's army heads for Cornwall and Rhonabwy wakes up. Osla is recorded in Culhwch and Olwen as part of Arthur's retinue. Alternatively, it could refer to Octa, son or grandson of Hengist and King of Kent in the early sixth century.
Y Gododdin Book of Aneurin thirteenth century	Welsh poem about the men of the kingdom of Gododdin, around Din Eidyn (Edinburgh). 300 fought the Angles of Deira and Bernicia at Catraeth (possibly Catterick) around 600, and only one returned. Arthur is mentioned in passing in comparison to another warrior.

The French Romances and Welsh Legends

dated to seventh–eleventh century.	'He charged before three hundred of the finest, He cut down both centre and wing, He excelled in the forefront of the noblest host, He gave gifts of horses from the herd in winter. He fed black ravens on the rampart of a fortress **Though he was no Arthur** Among the powerful ones in battle, In the front rank, Gwawrddur was a palisade.'
The Chair of the Prince Preserved in the *Book of Taliesin* dated to the early fourteenth century. Possibly originated tenth century.	'Has he not brought from Annwn The horses of the pale burden bearer The princely old man, The third deeply wise one, Is the blessed Arthur. **Arthur the blessed**, Renowned in song, In the front of battle, He was full of activity.'
The Elegy of Uther Pendragon Preserved in the *Book of Taliesin* dated to the early fourteenth century. Possibly originated tenth century.	'Do I not share my protection **a ninth part to the battling Arthur**'
Journey to Deganwy Preserved in the *Book of Taliesin* dated to the early fourteenth century. Possibly originated tenth century.	'Silent as fools, as at the **battle of Badon** With **Arthur, chief giver of feasts**, with his tall blades red, from the battle which all men remember.'

You will notice that the Welsh stories are more mythical in nature and don't contain many of the themes of the French stories. Below I have shown when some of these themes were added to the story. You will note that many of those we associate with Arthur are actually very late additions to the legend.

King Arthur: Man or Myth?

Table 22: Arthurian themes

Concept and date	Comments
Round table 1155	First introduced by Wace's *Roman de Brut* in 1155. Created to prevent quarrels among his barons. *Brut by Layamon* added that it was made by a Cornish carpenter after violence at a Christmas feast.
	There are no references in the Welsh sources.
	Charlemagne (742–814) is said to have possessed a round table decorated with a map of Rome.
	Celtic custom of warriors sitting in a circle round the king or lead warrior was often depicted in legends.
Merlin Tenth century	First reference is in the tenth century *Annales Cambriae* for 573 and the battle of Arfderydd after which 'Myrddin went mad' (which places him thirty-six years after Arthur's death at Camlan according to same source).
	Legend of Myrddin Wylit (the Wild) is similar to Lailoken, who features in a twelfth-century *Life of St Kentigern* (or Mungo, who lived in the Strathclyde area circa 600).
	The *Book of Taliesin* also contains an early reference in the 'Great Prophesy of Britain', although it may be a different person, Merdin son of Madog. Another Taliesin poem appears to suggest the author is known as Taliesin and Merddin.
	The *Black Book of Carmarthen* contain a 'dialogue between Myrddin and Taliesin' and three other poems. The *Red Book of Hengist* contains 'the conversation between Myrddin and his sister Gwenddydd' and two other poems.
	Geoffrey of Monmouth combines Myrddin Wylit and Emrys Ambrosius from Nennius to create Merlin and place him before and during Arthur's reign.
	Later French romances and Welsh literary sources come after this.
Uther Pendragon or Uthyr Bendragon. 1136 by Geoffrey of Monmouth.	Geoffrey of Monmouth records first detailed biography in 1136.
	He is also mentioned in various Welsh poems and Triads some of which name him as Arthur's father.
	In Robert de Boron's (twelfth-century) *Merlin*, Uther kills Hengist and Merlin creates the Round Table for him.

The French Romances and Welsh Legends

Could be an epithet: 'head dragon/chief leader'.	In *Prose Lancelot* (thirteenth century), Uther takes an army to Brittany to fight near his home town of Bourges, similar to the historical character Riothamus in 471.
Igraine or Eigyr 1136 by Geoffrey of Monmouth	Welsh sources and genealogies name her as daughter of Amlawdd Wledig. Her sister Gwyar is the mother of Gwalchmai (Gawain). Geoffrey states she is the wife of Gorlois, Duke of Cornwall. Later romances derive from Geoffrey and also place her at Tintagel.
Guinevere or Gwenhwyfar 1136	The earliest mention is in *Culhwch and Olwen*, eleventh century. Geoffrey of Monmouth 1136 named her as Guanhumara. Welsh sources name her Gwenhwyfar (*Culhwch and Olwen*; *Life of St Gildas*). Abducted by Melwas (*Life of St Gildas*) or Meleagant (Chretien de Troyes). Affair with Mordred (Geoffrey) or Lancelot (Chretien de Troyes). Welsh Triads name three Gwenhwyfars as wives of Arthur. A sister, Gwenhwyfach, is mentioned in *Culhwch and Olwen*. Additionally in two Triads a feud between the sisters is said to have caused the Battle of Camlan.
Kingship	The first description is 'dux bellorum', or leader of battles in the ninth-century *Historia Brittonum*. This doesn't preclude a royal status, but is probably a biblical analogy as it is similar to the description of Joshua. The suggestion it is a late reflection of a Roman military title has also been made. The earliest Welsh sources that describe him as a king come in the eleventh century. One early poem, *Geraint son of Erbin*, possibly refers to him as *ameraudur*, which could be translated as emperor or general/commander. Geoffrey of Monmouth describes a vast Empire from Norway to the Alps.

(continued)

137

Table 22: (Continued)

Concept and date	Comments
Sword in the stone Twelfth century	First described by Robert de Boron in the poem *Merlin*. The sword was in an anvil on a stone in a churchyard in London. Later renditions changed it to in the stone itself. A number of suggestions have been put forward: A medieval sword of Saint Galgano (1148–81) is embedded in rock in the Abbey of San Galgano in Italy and may have influenced Robert who was writing soon after. The 'London Stone' is a block of limestone that was once a medieval landmark. Striking a stone with a sword was a popular medieval concept to signal authority. In John Cade's rebellion in 1450 he is said to have struck the stone with his sword and declared himself Lord Mayor. The use of a stone mould to cast metal would result in the sword being drawn from the stone once cooled. Possible confusion between Latin word for stone, saxum similar to Saxonum for Saxon.
Excalibur Twelfth century	Derives from the Welsh Caledfwlch (e.g *Culhwch and Olwen*) meaning hard cleft, possibly borrowed from Irish mythology and the sword Caladblog. Geoffrey of Monmouth Latinised the name to Caliburnus. In French sources this became Caliburc, Escaliborc, Escalibor, Excalibor and finally Excalibur. Early legends have the sword being drawn from an anvil on a stone, then a stone itself. Later the Post Vulgate Cycle, 1230–40, has Arthur receive Excalibur from the Lady in the Lake.
Other weapons Twelfth century	In the Welsh Triads: Rhongomiant his spear, Carnwennan his dagger and Caledfwich his sword. *Culhwch and Olwen* refers to 'Carnwennan' (white hilt). Geoffrey of Monmouth refers to his lance *Ron*. In fifteenth-century *Thirteen Treasures of the Island of Britain* there is another 'White-Hilt', Drynwyn, belonging to Rhydderch Hael (580–614). It can only be drawn by a worthy man and the blade blazes with fire. Irish mythology also has a 'sword of light' ('Claiomh Solais').

The French Romances and Welsh Legends

Lady in the lake Twelfth century	Chretien de Troyes first mentions Lancelot's upbringing by a fairy in a lake. Called Nimue or Vivienne in later romances. In some stories she captures Merlin in a tree or beneath a stone. Morgan is also later said to be either a sister or the Lady herself. Descriptions of her as a fairy queen are also similar to Geoffrey's depiction of Morgan on the Isle of Avalon to whom Arthur is taken to be healed after Camlan.
Lancelot Twelfth century	Lancelot du Lac (of the lake) or Launcelot. First appeared in Chretien de Troyes in the twelfth century, the first to feature the love affair with Guinevere. Later works introduce his relationship with the Lady in the Lake and also the Grail quest.
Morgan le Fay 1136	First mentioned by Geoffrey of Monmouth but has no relation to Arthur. In his later *Vitae Merlini* she is the leader of nine magical sisters of Avalon or The Fortunate Isle. This is similar to many other legends and myths in Britain, Ireland and Gaul, hence Le Fay or Faerie. Chretien de Troyes is the first to name her as a half-sister to Arthur and also names her as a healer. In later stories she developed into a sorceress or witchlike character and even a seducer of Arthur and mother to Mordred (early tales name her sister Morgause in this role).
Modred Medrawt Medraut Tenth century	First mentioned in *Annales Cambriae* written in the tenth century. The entry for 537 refers to 'The strife of Camlann, in which Arthur and Medrawt fell.' There is no mention of them being enemies. In fact some Welsh texts describe him in positive terms. His notorious reputation begins with Geoffrey of Monmouth. Early Welsh texts record him as nephew of Arthur and son of either Morgause or Arthur's sister Anna, married to King Lot of Lothian. The references to him being Arthur's son from an incestuous liaison came much later.
Arthur's sons from 830	**Amr** in *Historia Brittonum* c.830 (Amhar in *Geraint and Enid*). **Llacheu** is named in the Triads and Pa Gur. **Loholt** mentioned in the French romance *Perlesvaus* and Vulgate Cycle thirteenth century.

(continued)

Table 22: (Continued)

Concept and date	Comments
	Duran said to have died at Camlan in a fifteenth-century Welsh text.
	Cydfan
	Gwydre
	Modred is first described as a nephew but later texts change the relationship.
Camelot Twelfth century	The earliest written source, *Culhwch and Olwen* from the eleventh century places Arthur's court at Celliwig (forest grove) in Cornwall.
	In the Welsh Triads (Peniarth MS 54, fifteenth century) Arthur's courts are at Pen Rhionydd in the north, Celliwig in Cornwall and Mynyw in Wales (St David's). The first two are unidentified although the former is likely to be within the later kingdom of Rheged.
	Geoffrey of Monmouth bases Arthur at Caerleon in South Wales.
	Camelot is mentioned for the first time, in passing, by Chretien de Troyes and he distinguishes it from Arthur's chief court at Caerleon.
	In thirteenth-century Lancelot-Grail and Post-Vulgate Cycle, Camelot begins to supersede Caerleon but it is not until Malory in the fifteenth century that the Camelot of modern times emerges.
	Other sites are also mentioned as courts of Arthur:
	Quimper in Brittany in Lancelot romance.
	Carduel, Wales in Chretien's *The Knight and the Lion* (unidentified).
	Cardigan in Chretien's *Eric and Enide*.
	Stirling in Beroul's twelfth-century *Tristan*.
Avalon 1136	First mentioned by Geoffrey of Monmouth as the place where Arthur is taken after Camlan to be healed by Morgan Le Fay. Insula Avallonis means Isle of fruit (or apple) trees. In later Welsh texts it is Ynys Afallon or Afallach. May be linked to Irish legends concerning Emain Abhlach, a mythical island paradise also identified with Isle of Man or Arran. Geoffrey's *Vita Merlini* indicates a sea voyage is necessary to get there and it is named the Isle of Apples.

The French Romances and Welsh Legends

Later French romances identified it with Glastonbury. This was aided in 1190 by the 'discovery' of a burial on the site of the abbey with a cross inscribed with a reference to Arthur and Avalon. This discovery is believed to be a fake by the monks.

There is an Avallon in Burgundy close to where Riothamus campaigned. Other suggested possible cities include Aballava or Avallana, a Roman fort at the western end of Hadrian's Wall and Ile d'Aval of the coast of Brittany.

As early as AD 45 Mela gives account of an island off Brittany, home to nine holy priestesses. Similar to nine maidens in 'The spoils of Annwfn' and later stories connected to Morgan Le Fay.

The Grail

1190

First appears in Chretien's 1190 *Perceval*.

The German poet Wolfram von Eschenbach, based his work on Chretien, but perceived the Grail as a stone later linked to The Philosopher's Stone.

Around 1200, Robert de Boron linked the Grail to the last supper and the collection of Christ's blood on the cross. Joseph of Arimathea then transports the Grail to England and founds a dynasty of Grail keepers.

The Vulgate Cycle expands on this and includes other characters such as Lancelot and Galahad.

The Grail has also been linked to earlier Welsh and Irish folk tales concerning cauldrons and vessels similar to Arthur and the cauldron in Spoils of Annwfn.

The Fisher King

1190

First introduced by Chretien de Troyes. The Fisher King is the last of a long line of Grail Keepers, usually wounded in the groin or leg. All he is able to do is fish from a small boat near his castle in later legends called Corbenic (blessed horn/body).

Initially linked to Percival later stories include Galahad and Bors.

Could be derived from the Welsh legend 'Bran the Blessed' in the *Mabinogion* which is independent of Arthurian and Grail literature.

(continued)

Table 22: (Continued)

Concept and date	Comments
Bedivere	Bedwyr first mentioned in tenth century *Pa Gur*. Also in *Culhwch and Olwen*, *Stanzas of the Graves*, Welsh Triads and *Life of St Cadoc*. Becomes Bedivere after Geoffrey of Monmouth.
Gawain	First appears in *Culhwch and Olwen* eleventh century. Then in French romances from Chretien onwards.
Kay or Cai	First mentioned in tenth-century *Pa Gur*. Also in *Life of St Cadoc*, *Culhwch and Olwen* and later French sources. Maybe derivative of Latin Caius.
Owain or Ywain	Possibly based on Owain, son of Urien, King of Rheged at the end of the sixth century. Both Owain and Urien have multiple references in Welsh sources. Appears in Geoffrey of Monmouth and later romances as one of Arthur's knights.
Percival or Peredur	Introduced by Chretien de Troyes.
Lot, Loth or Leudonus	Introduced by Geoffrey as Arthur's brother-in-law and King of Lothian. Married to either Anna or Morgause depending on later legends. In the Life of St Kentigern (Mungo) written in 1185, he is said to be the saint's grandfather after Teneu is raped by Owain mab Urien making him a contemporary of Urien of Rheged. Welsh sources make him king of the Gododdin.

Thus many of our current concepts were not present in the early myths and stories. Merlin, the sword in the stone, the Round Table, Excalibur, the Grail, Camelot, and Avalon were all added in the twelfth century and we can see how the trend developed. Merlin, for example, is not mentioned by Nennius. In the *Historia Brittonum* the story of the two dragons attributed by Geoffrey to Merlin is actually given to Emrys Ambrosius, who is quite clearly the Ambrosius Aurelianus of Gildas. This is then a 'Merlin' a generation before any Arthur. However, the attached *Annales Cambriae* references a 'Myrddin the wild' in 573 which would be a generation or more after any Arthur. Geoffrey combines both characters many hundreds of years later and Latinises the name to Merlinus to avoid French or Latin speakers' blushes from associating the word Myrddin with 'merde' or 'merda', despite the fact that in speech a Welsh -dd sounds like -th.

The French Romances and Welsh Legends

An early fourteenth-century tale, *Sir Perceval of Galles,* is another example of an entirely different story compared to Chretien de Troyes over a hundred years before. There is no Grail or Fisher King. Instead there is a magic ring. It is written in a style of parody and was used later by Geoffrey Chaucer. What this shows is how quickly stories develop and change. So when looking at Chretien's stories in the twelfth century or the earliest Welsh legends, it is worth remembering the hundreds of years between the late fifth or early sixth century when these stories are supposedly set, and the earliest sources that have survived to the present.

Essentially, the Welsh tales leave us with an Arthur devoid of the trappings or stories we associate him with. In fact he's a more mythical and magical figure fighting giants and giant boars. Yet the stories did appear. One wonders where the French writers got their inspiration if not from the stories of the day. And even if these are found to be false, we are still left with an Arthur figure and references to at least some of the characters connected to him, such as Uther and Guinevere. If one looks at the consistency in Arthur's father and mother across all the different traditions:

Table 23: Arthur's family

Source	Father	Mother	Sisters	Wife	Sons
Welsh sources	Uthr Bendragon	Eigyr	Gwyar	Gwenhwyfar or Gwenhwyvar	Llacheu, Gwydre, Amhar
Geoffrey of Monmouth	Uther	Ygerne	Anna	Guinevere	
Chretien de Troyes	Uther Pendragon	Igerne	Morgan le Fay	Guinevere	
Vulgate cycle	Uther	Ygraine or Igerne	Morgawse, Blasine, Brimesent, unnamed, Morgan le Fay	Guenevere	Loholt
Thomas Malory	Uther	Igraine	Morgause, Elaine, Morgan le Fay	Guenevere	Borre

King Arthur: Man or Myth?

There is certainly some consistency regarding his parents. However, the proposed family trees differ significantly across the sources. In the traditional Welsh legends Igraine's father is Amlawdd Wledig who marries a daughter of Cunedda. This places Arthur three generations after Cunedda and the same generation as Maelgwn and this contemporary with the five kings of Gildas. In Geoffrey of Monmouth's version he is the grandson of Constantine, and Ambrosius is his uncle. The later romance versions build on this with various sisters and cousins. We have little information on Amlawdd Wledig, there's more than one genealogy and none that are contemporary or credible historical sources. In short, we have a jumble of contradictory sources that lack any validity regarding a family tree. If we were to attempt a genealogy from the earliest sources it would look slightly different to Geoffrey of Monmouth and later French romances.

It is possible to see where some of the other concepts come from. The sword in the stone does have its equivalence in the medieval story of Saint Galgano (1148–81) where a sword is embedded in rock in the Abbey of San Galgano in Italy, and may have influenced Robert de Boron who was writing soon after.

In the Welsh Triads 'Pen Rhionydd' is listed as one of Arthur's northern courts. It has been suggested this is Penrith in Cumbria and it may be worth noting a Neolithic stone ring called King Arthur's Round Table is nearby. There are many such sites all over Britain: twenty-two Arthur's stones, thirty Arthur's Quoits (discus shaped stone); five tables and three round tables; eight seats; six Halls, camps or other types of residence; five graves and fifteen other sites referring to Arthur.[1] They can't all be connected to Arthur, and beyond local myth and legend there is absolutely no evidence linking any of them.

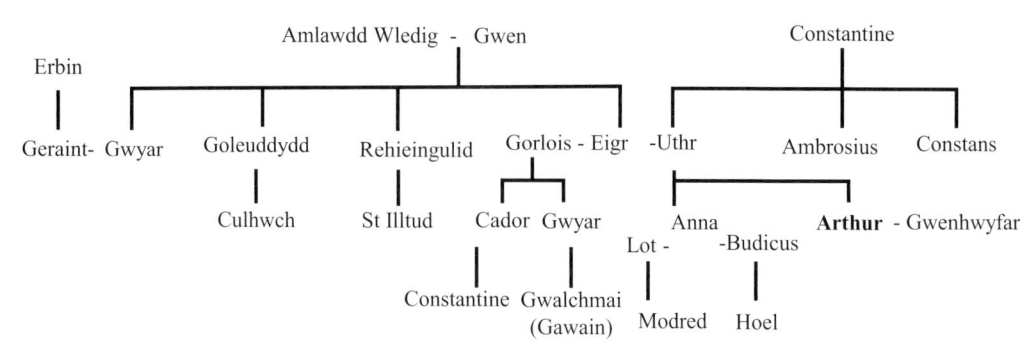

Genealogy of Arthur.

The French Romances and Welsh Legends

However, it is worth noting the absence of such sites in the south east. They are heavily concentrated around the Welsh coastline, with a smaller number in Cornwall, Somerset and the north. Similarly, the stories in the saints' lives are mostly located in South Wales with the West Country also featuring alongside two references to Armorica. Additionally, while the alleged twelve battles can't be located with any confidence, it is interesting that most of the credible theories do not involve the south east.

In summary, what we have is a single reference to Arthur in 830 by Nennius, 300 hundred years after he was supposed to have lived. There is one passing reference in the *Y Gododdin* which may originate between the seventh and eleventh centuries but wasn't written down until the thirteenth. We have two lines referring to Badon and Camlann

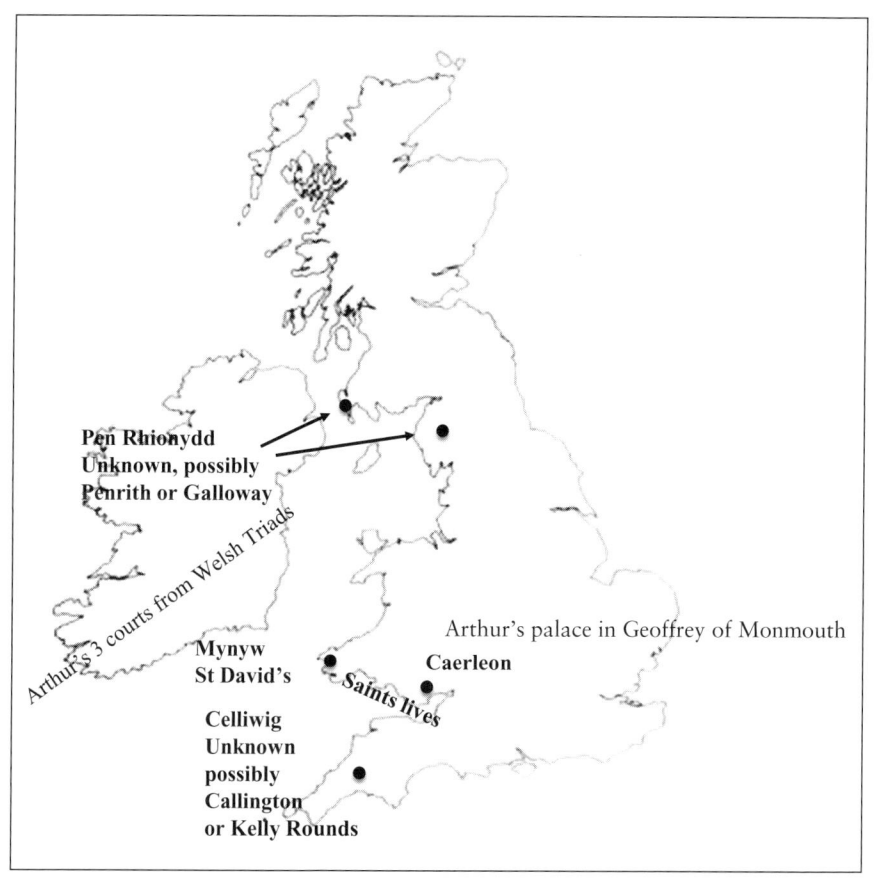

Arthurian locations in Welsh legends.

King Arthur: Man or Myth?

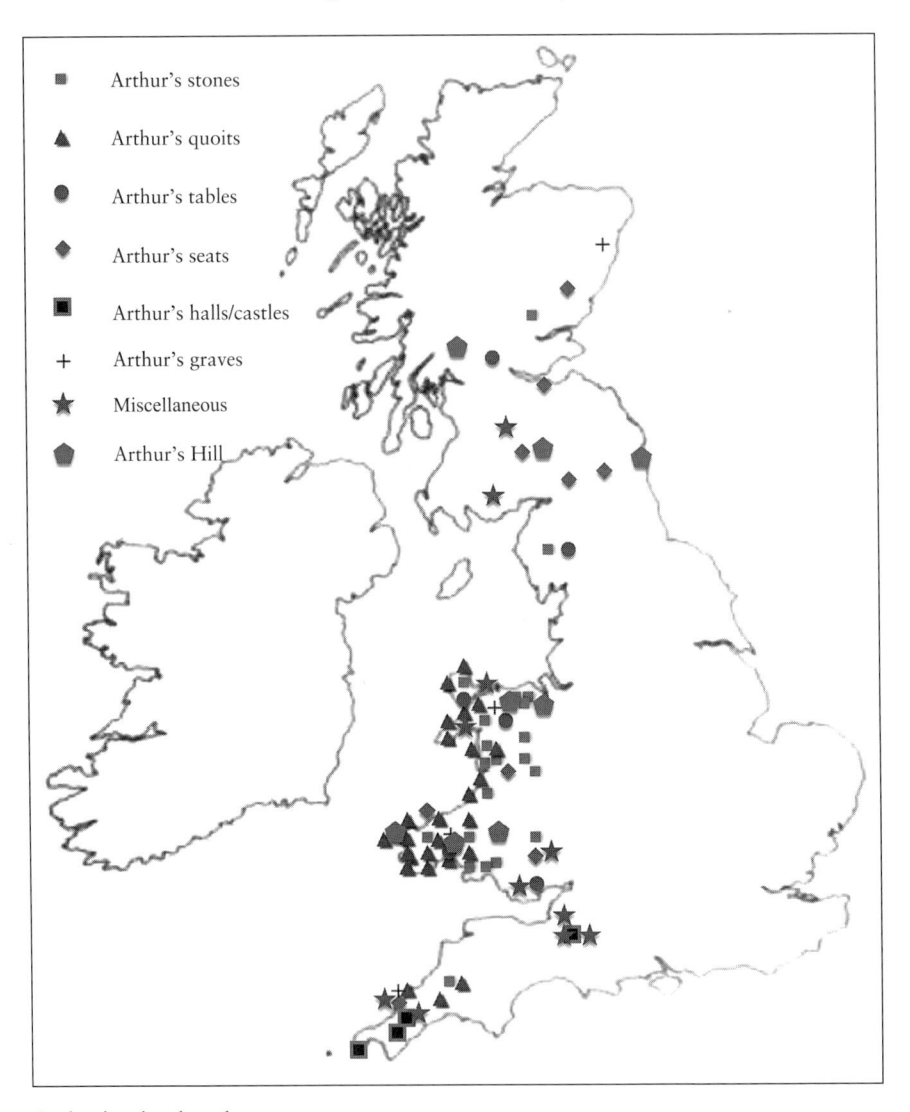

- ■ Arthur's stones
- ▲ Arthur's quoits
- ● Arthur's tables
- ◆ Arthur's seats
- ◼ Arthur's halls/castles
- + Arthur's graves
- ★ Miscellaneous
- ⬠ Arthur's Hill

Arthurian landmarks.

in the *Annales Cambriae* written in the tenth century, which, though it may reflect earlier composition, the lines themselves may have been added much later.

Then we have Geoffrey of Monmouth's work in the twelfth century which is highly suspect and in turn inspires an explosion of Arthurian stories. Many of the concepts we now associate with Arthur are added to the story then. Much later, Welsh stories and legends are written down

The French Romances and Welsh Legends

and these reflect a more mythical and magical Arthur. It is debatable if they reflect an earlier tradition of stories, or if Geoffrey based some of his story on them. On that basis some might say the only evidence we have is the reference by Nennius in 830 and subsequent lines in the *Annals Cambriae*. All the other works are 500 years or more after any historical figure and could easily be based on a completely mythical character. Or indeed all based on the reference in Nennius, which itself is highly suspect and lacks credibility.

Let us look at the line in *Y Gododdin*:

> In one sense rather weak evidence, however there is a consensus that this poem is contemporary and thus was written around 600. So we possibly have an authentic voice from the end of the sixth century mentioning Arthur in passing. In some ways this very casual reference does show that the author and his readers would recognise and accept the comparison with this famous person. However, first I would argue that one could equally say today: 'though he was no superman or Hercules'. That would not prove the existence of either. Second, we know from the historical record that there were indeed persons called Arthur towards the end of the sixth century. This appearance and sudden popularity of the name has often been used as an argument that they were named after some famous warrior. We shall come across this later. While many have been put forward as *the* Arthur, I would say they can't possibly *all* be Arthur.

For example, we have a prince of Dal Riata in the Strathclyde area. Arthur mac Aeden was the son of Aeden mac Gabrain, king of the Dal Riata. He lived and fought towards the end of the sixth century in precisely the area near the area of the Gododdin. At that time Dal Riata, Rheged, the Picts, Bernicia and Deira, Elmet and the Gododdin around Edinburgh were all vying for control. This reference in *Y Gododdin* could just as easily be about this Arthur rather than the Arthur referenced in Nennius. Equally, it could just as easily be proof that Arthur was a mythical figure with no basis in reality to whom warriors were routinely compared. People get very excited about this one line but there is only circumstantial evidence that it is contemporary and none that it is a reference to a historical figure, let alone the Arthur of legend.

Yet we have a body of myths and legends that did develop to produce a variety of stories in Welsh legend, which inspired the later French and Norman stories. These didn't appear out of thin air. In any event we still have the reference in Nennius and entries in the *Annales Cambriae*, even if we were to do away with all the later stories. Unfortunately we simply don't know the origins of the many stories or how they developed over time. The Welsh legends paint a very different picture from Geoffrey or the French romance stories. I've provided the table below to illustrate the many of the lesser known concepts form Welsh legend.[2]

Table 24: Welsh legends

Father: Uthr Bendragon	**Mother:** Eigr	**Daughter:** Archfedd	**Sons:** Amhar, Gwydre, Llacheu, Cydfan, Smerbe.
Half-brothers: Madog ab Other, Cadwr ap Gwrlais, Gormany ap Rhica.	**Sisters:** Anna, Elen, Gwyar, Morgen.	**Nephews:** Gwalchmai, Gwalhafed, Medrod,	**Wife:** Gwenhwyfar (thtree times in some sources).
Ships: Prydwen, Gwennan.	**Hall:** Ehangwen.	**Courts:** Caerllion ar Wysg, Celliwig, Penrhyn Rhionydd.	**Porter:** Glewlwyd Gafaelfawr.
Assistant porters: Huandaw, Gogigwr, Llaesgymyn, Penpingion.	**First fighter:** Gwenwynwyn ap Naf.	**Mantle (cloak):** Gwen.	**Mistresses:** Indeg, Garden, Gwyl.
Sword: Caledfwlch.	**Servants:** Cacamwri, Hygwydd, Hir Eiddyl, Hir Amren.		

The French Romances and Welsh Legends

So how would we describe an Arthur devoid of all these transparent additions? We would be left with a battle leader, perhaps a king, but not necessarily. If a king, he might be a ruler of a tribal area, civitas or even one of the old Roman provinces. Perhaps the holder of some leftover Roman administrative or military authority. There would be no Excalibur, no sword in the stone, no Merlin, Round Table, knights, Camelot, Avalon and no Holy Grail. The earlier Welsh traditions do mention Guinevere, Uther, Igraine and Cai, Bedivere and Gawain, but the Welsh versions of these names would be unrecognisable to most and there would be no Lancelot or Percival. He would be far more localised and involved in civil strife. There would be no Arthurian empire or conquests on the Continent.

We have a large body of legends, myths and stories written 600 to 800 years after any supposed historical figure. These stories can be split into two broad groups. The first tend to be of French, Norman or Breton origin. They were inspired by Geoffrey of Monmouth's work in the twelfth century and possibly by other myths circulating at the time; they were written down from the twelfth century. Many of the concepts we associate with Arthur appear to have been added to the story at that point. The second group are of Welsh origin and though written down after the French romances, may have originated much earlier. This second group present a more mythic and magical figure. They also portray a far darker and morally ambiguous figure. He is simply one of many warriors or kings who is often in conflict with his peers or the church.

Both these traditions would have interacted and helped evolve and change the story through the centuries. The nearest contemporary references are sparse and include the *Historia Brittonum* in 830, the *Annales Cambriae* compiled around 954 and the single reference in *Y Gododdin* which, though written down in the thirteenth century, may have been contemporary with the sixth. The reader will have to decide what weight he or she give to all the legends, stories, romances, saints' lives written many hundreds of years later. Whether we can dismiss them all as unreliable and too late, or whether we can believe they may reflect a surviving element of fact. The reader will also have to decide the weight to give to the three earlier sources just mentioned.

Chapter 14

The Brittany Connection

We have seen how important this region is to the development of the story. Not forgetting of course that a large part of Geoffrey of Monmouth's story concerned Arthur's battles on the Continent. We do of course have a reasonably detailed historical record concerning the decades before and after the Continental Western Empire and we can be quite sure there was no Arthur or British army rampaging across Gaul. But there maybe other less dramatic explanations for Geoffrey's embellishments and exaggerations. We have some evidence of British presence in the middle of the fifth century, although that doesn't mean there was not earlier movement. Certainly Emperor Maximus moved through Brittany to secure Gaul in 388, as did Constantine III twenty years later. Western Brittany saw a mass movement in the fifth century.

There are two main points that come out of Geoffrey's narrative concerning Gaul. The first is simply that Arthur fought there; we will leave aside which part of modern France, or against whom for a moment. The second point, often overlooked even more than the Gaulish connection itself, is the arrival of the Roman messengers that start this war. Linked to that, this is placed at the end of his reign. He is forced to return from these wars to fight at Camlann. It would be useful to pinpoint not just periods of possible warfare, but incidents that might have precipitated a delegation from the Continent.

The first strong evidence for British presence is the Council of Tours in 461 and the presence of Bishop Mansuetus of the Britons. The next indication of strong British influence was the invitation of British army led by King Riothamus. This was part of Emperor Anthemius's (467–72) coalition against the Visigoths. In 469 there is a letter by Sidonius Apollinaris on behalf of Prefect Arvandus from Lyon to Euric, king of the Goths urging him to reject alliance with Anthemius and attack the Britons situated 'on the far side of the Loire', which appears to mean Armorica. Gregory of Tours does not name Riothamus but talks of the Britons being defeated at Bourg de Deols in 469. Jordane's History of the Goths names Riothamus as being defeated after coming 'by way of the sea'. Whether this means via the Channel from Britain, the Loire, or east coast from Brittany has been questioned. A further letter from Sidonius to Riothamus appears to suggest he has some judicial power and thus is based in the area. This suggests it's probable that Riothamus was based north of the Loire rather than Britain.[1] By this time there must have been substantial Saxon settlement in the Loire Valley, as Gregory of Tours also reports around this time a great war between Romans and Saxons.

This resulted in the Saxons being defeated and the Franks subsequently capturing their islands and many being killed. It doesn't state where the Saxons fled to. Aegidius had been the magister militum of Gaul serving under Aetius. He rebelled against General Ricimer when the Emperor Majorian was deposed in 461. Initially on good terms with Childeric, king of the Franks, he formed the kingdom of Soissons in northern France. His son Syagrius succeeded him in 465. Clovis succeeded his father as king of the Salian Franks in 481 and proceeded to dominate the other Frankish tribes before defeating the last Roman state in northern Gaul in 486. The Bretons bordered the west of Soissons and now the border became a Frankish-Breton one.

This Frankish expansion and disintegration of Roman Gaul in the second-half of the fifth century ties in with the information in Bede and the *Anglo-Saxon Chronicles* concerning the arrival of Hengist, Aelle and later, Cerdic. There's no hard evidence there's any connection, or that these people even existed, but it doesn't contradict the known record. The narratives are not incompatible; we can put it no stronger than that. So, we have Britons or Bretons involved in wars in the Loire region in the 460s; we then have the last Roman kingdom at war with the Franks in the 480s. Either of these could have caused requests for help or involvement from Britain. Though speculative, this could explain Geoffrey of Monmouth's inclusion of Roman emissaries attending Arthur's court and demanding tribute. Another curious incident occurred during the siege of Rome in 538. The Ostrogothic army led by Vitiges was besieging an Eastern Empire force led by Balisarius. During negotiations the Goths were made the following offer recorded by Procopius:

> And we on our side permit the Goths to have the whole of Britain, which is much larger than Sicily and was subject to the Romans in early times.

This didn't materialise, but one wonders how the Romans could have offered a province that had been lost to them for over 100 years. The suspicion is that it was simply a ruse. However, it is interesting to speculate what response a visiting Byzantine ambassador might have got from a British ruler if he turned up suggesting the Romans were now taking back control and had promised 150,000 Goths they could pitch up in Britain. So we have a number of events that could have caused an embassy to arrive either from Rome, Constantinople or the Franks. Starting with the request to Riothamus around 470, if he was based in Britain. Then we have the war between Clovis and Syagrius in 487, and the suspected treaty between Franks and Bretons in 497. Then in 508 the eastern emperor offered Clovis the consulship, which may have prompted some sort of overture to the British. Then we have the Goths being offered Britain in 538 and finally, a war between the Breton king, Conomor, and the Franks around 560.

There's no evidence for any friction or any other relationship involving Britain or Brittany. The relationship in the sixth century between Britons and Franks was one of peace and there are clues that there was even a treaty around 497.[2] Procopius describes the Armoricans fighting off the Franks so that they were forced to make them 'their companions and relations by marriage'.[3] Clovis expanded his dominion not over the Bretons, but the Burgundians and Visigoths defeating the latter at the Battle of Vouille in 507. It was after this battle he was granted Consul by the eastern emperor Anastasius and he died in 511. Gregory of Tours states that from the time of Clovis the Breton rulers ceased to be called kings, but were merely counts and subjects of the Franks. If this is true it would call into question any Arthurian connection in the sixth century. Two bits of evidence suggest Frankish influence even spread across the Channel. First, one part of the Frankish law code referred to retrieving slaves from across the sea. Second, Procopius states a Frankish emissary visiting the Eastern Empire in 553 were accompanied by Angles.

History of the Wars 8.20.6-10:

> Three very populous nations inhabit the Island of Brittia, and one king is set over each of them. And the names of these nations are Angles, Frisians, and Britons who have the same name as the island. So great apparently is the multitude of these peoples that every year in large groups they migrate from there with their women and children and go to the

Franks. And they [the Franks] are settling them in what seems to be the more desolate part of their land, and as a result of this they say they are gaining possession of the island. So that not long ago the king of the Franks actually sent some of his friends to the Emperor Justinian in Byzantium, and despatched with them the men of the Angles, claiming that this island [Britain], too, is ruled by him. Such then are the matters concerning the island called Brittia.

Certainly by the end of the sixth century it is a Frankish Christian Princess that marries Aethelbert, King of Kent, who eventually welcomes St Augustine from Pope Gregory in AD 597. However, Gregory of Tours later relates the Frankish-Breton war against Waroch in 578 and he quotes Regalis, the Bishop of Vannes, near the border, as saying, 'we have to do as the Bretons tell us'. Both these points seem to contradict his earlier statement or suggest there was a resurgence of Breton independence after Clovis.

Clovis certainly expanded the Frankish kingdom considerably. He defeated the Thuringians in 491, the Goths in 507 and Alemanni in 508. After his death in 511 the kingdom was split into four smaller kingdoms, each ruled by one of his four sons. There then followed further expansion against the Thuringians in 531, Burgundians in 534, Provence region in 537, the Visigoths in northern Spain in 542 and a Saxon war in 555–6. There was also a fair amount of internal rivalry, civil wars and assassinations. The kingdom was finally unified once more under Clothar in 558. On his death in 561, four of his sons inherited the four separate kingdoms again. Just before he died, one of his rebellious sons, Charm, joined forces with Conomer a leader of the Bretons. A subsequent war ended in the death of both Conomer and Charm around 561. Further wars erupted involving Waroch II and the Frankish kings Chilperic in 578, and Guntram in 589.

So we have a record of Breton military activity from 460–470s. Then there is an expansion of Frankish power, first by Clovis then Clothar. The next mention of military action involving Bretons is 560. When considering at what point could a British Arthur have been fighting in Gaul, there is no clue from the sources. We can certainly dismiss Geoffrey's tale of Arthur fighting the Romans and penetrating as far as Burgundian territory. This is simply fantasy. But an Arthur fighting border wars in the fifth or sixth century is possible. Geoffrey's tale of a Roman embassy demanding tribute could equally be made up. But the war between Clovis and Syagrius might have resulted in a request for help from either side. Likewise, Clovis receiving the consulship from the eastern emperor in 508 and the later allegations of Frankish overlordship of the Angles may have created a political backdrop to some sort of demand of rulers in Britain.

Brittany was maybe the main, if not only, route by which the legend entered the Continent.[4] The *Historia Brittonum*, Geoffrey's *History* and *The Dream of Mascen Wledig*, based on Magnus Maximus in the *Mabinogion*, all describe a foundation story for Brittany. Despite these legends there is little evidence to precisely date the British migrations. What we do know is a substantial part of William the Conqueror's army in 1066 was Breton. Up to that point all the earlier Welsh legends, even if they can be dated to the eleventh century or earlier, portray a mythical and magical Arthur. He is often a petty king or tyrant. Geoffrey of Monmouth wrote *History of the Kings of Britain* in 1136 and all the French romances from Wace and Chretien de Troyes came after.

So we can see two Arthurs. An original war leader with mythical and magical aspects of Welsh legend, followed by the chivalric knight of Norman and French romance we now know. Arthur is only an occasional figure in literary sources between 850 and 1000 and is omitted from the bulk of the saga poetry that survives. The only figure we come across in that early period belongs in the world of myth and magic.[5] The question remains: in what way did Breton traditions influence the legend? There was certainly a common belief in Brittany, Cornwall and Wales for Arthur's existence.[6]

In his commentary on Geoffrey of Monmouth's *Prophecies of Merlin*, Alain de Lille (1128–1202) states:

> What place is there within the bounds of the empire of Christendom to which the winged praise of Arthur the Briton has not extended? Who is there, I ask, who does not speak of Arthur the Briton, since he is but little less known to the peoples of Asia than to the Bretons as we are informed by our palmers who return from the countries to the East?

The Brittany Connection

In 1139 Henry of Huntingdon in a letter states that Arthur:

> received so many wounds that he fell; although his kinsmen the Britons deny he was mortally wounded and seriously expect he will come again.

Adam of Tewksbury writing in 1170 states:

> His departure will be obscured by doubt, which is indeed true, for there are today varying opinions as to his life and death. If you do not believe me, go to the Kingdom of Armorica, that is, lesser Britain, and preach in the villages and market-places that Arthur the Briton died as other men die; and then if you escape unharmed, for you will either be cursed or stoned by your hearers, you will indeed discover that Merlin the prophet spoke truly when he said that Arthur's departure would be obscured by doubt.

Below is a timeline of events for Britain and Gaul that may indicate when an embassy and subsequent conflict could have occurred:

Table 25: Britain and Gaul

Britain	Gaul
429 first visit of St Germanus.	
440 'Britain falls to power of Saxons' (*Gallic Chronicles*).	
446–456 Appeal to Aetius (Gildas/Bede)	
449 Saxons invited (Bede).	
450s Saxon rebellion (Bede, *Anglo-Saxon Chronicles*).	460s Romano–Saxon war. Britons in Loire fighting Goths (Gregory of Tours).
	470 Riothamus leading 12,000 men (Jordannes).
470s Ambrosius Aurelianus emerges as British leader.	476 Last western Roman emperor deposed.
	481 Clovis I crowned.
	486 Clovis defeats Syagrius last king of the Romans and captures Soissons.

(continued)

Table 25: (Continued)

Britain	Gaul
493 Battle of Badon (Bede's forty-four years after arrival).	497 Possible treaty between Franks and Bretons. 507–8 Clovis defeats Goths and Alemanni. Receives consulship. Baptised. 511 Clovis dies, 'Breton rulers ceased to be called kings but were merely counts and subjects of the Franks' (Gregory of Tours). Four sons expand Frankish territory against surrounding kingdoms, Brittany not mentioned.
516 Battle of Badon (*Annales Cambriae*).	
	531 Thuringian war, Saxon immigrants from Britain assist Franks
	538 Siege of Rome. Balisarius offers Goths Britain.
537 Battle of Camlann (*Annales Cambriae*).	
540 Britain is now partitioned and has numerous kings.	
	553 Procopius.
542 Battle of Camlann (Geoffrey of Monmouth).	555–6 Frankish–Saxon war. 558 Clothar unifies Frankish kingdom. 560 War against Breton ruler Conomer.
	578 and 589 War against Breton ruler Waroch II.

Thus a belief in Arthur's continued life was sufficiently powerful in 1113 to almost cause a riot in Cornwall when it was contradicted by sceptical French canons: 'many men rushed into the church with arms', and if local passions had not been calmed, 'it would certainly have come to the spilling of blood'.

On the other hand, outside Geoffrey of Monmouth and the disputed life of St Goeznovius, there is no reference anywhere in any of the legends of Arthur fighting in Gaul, Brittany or anywhere outside of Britain. Given Geoffrey's flight's of fancy, known embellishments and downright lies concerning the characters in the same book, it's about

The Brittany Connection

time we put this to rest. But we have a body of literature and a belief in the Middle Ages that this is historical. Not to mention the explosion of interest after the Norman conquest.

In summary, we have very scant evidence concerning Brittany in the fifth and sixth centuries and none concerning any Arthur figure. However, several hundred years later there was a belief and body of legends that existed and influenced the evolution of the legend after the Norman conquest in 1066. It would be possible to dismiss the whole Brittany and Gaul connection as fantasy. It would certainly make things simpler and it may be the most likely explanation. If it is to be considered, however, it is interesting that the most likely period for military activity by a British leader is exactly in the same period we focus on for an Arthur in Britain. The possible timeframes for an embassy from the Continent and subsequent warfare are as follows:

1. 460–70 Romano-Saxon war and appeal to Riothamus for help.
2. 480s Frankish–Roman war results in defeat of last Roman enclave.
3. 497 Treaty between Franks and Bretons.
4. 508 Clovis offered consulship by eastern emperor.
5. 538 Romans offer Britain to the Goths.

The war involving Conomor and the Franks around 560 seems too late. Aside from the dubious account in the *Life of St Gildas*, he has been linked to the *Tristan and Iseult* story. Yet his identification as *Marcus Quonomorius,* or King Mark, in the ninth century *Life of St Paul Aurelian* is dubious. Likewise, a sixth-century inscribed stone in Cornwall is often translated as 'Drustanus hic jacit cunomori filius' (here lies Tristan, son of Conomor). In fact the earliest transcriptions translate as dedicated to Clusius. A life of another sixth-century saint, Tudwal, describes Conomor as a 'prefect' of the king of the Franks. Thus suggesting political and military dominance of the Franks by the mid-sixth century.

Chapter 15

Genealogies and Kings

There are a number of sources for the available genealogies. None are contemporary and none can be completely trusted with reference to their earlier entries. They were compiled much later, often for dynastic reasons. I will cover the Welsh tables first, for which there are three main sources; first, however, it might be useful to show the material we do have for Arthur's family tree. According to Geoffrey of Monmouth in *History of the Kings of Britain*, we have a Conanus Meriodocus placed as ruler of Armorica by Magnus Maximus before 388. This could make him a contemporary of the Cunedda mentioned in the *Historia Brittonum*, if the reference of 146 years before Maelgwn of Gwynedd is taken at face value. Aldroneus is the fourth King of Armorica after Conanus. His brother, Constantius, is invited to Britain by Guithelinus, Archbishop of London. This is interesting as the name Guithelinus is similar and could be a derivative of Vortigern. This Constantius may be synonymous with Constantine III, a British western emperor until 411. However, neither the manner of his death nor the names of his three sons match with this figure. The ten-year rule of Constantius and short reign of his eldest son, Constans, do tie in with the narrative in the *Historia Brittonum*, which suggests Vortigern takes the throne in 425. There is another historical figure, Flavius Constantius, who was consul and then emperor in 421, but again there is no record of any connection with Britain or Arthurian characters. In the story, the two younger sons of Constantius, Ambrosius and Uther, were still young children and had to escape across the channel, fostered by King Budicus of Armorica. They return when adults, so presumably in the 440s (following this timeline), defeat Vortigern and Ambrosius rules for four years. Uther marries Igerna and they have two children, Arthur and Anna. Anna marries Loth of Lodonesia, or Lothian, and they have two children, Gualguainus and Modred.

Genealogies and Kings

The *Bonedd Y Saint* or *Descent of the Saints* are a thirteenth- to eighteenth-century compilation of saint and royal genealogies. They do mention Arthur, Uther and Igraine. There are also several claiming descent from Cunedda, Malewyn of Gwynedd and Vortigern. One example shows a granddaughter of Cunedda, Eigr, marrying Uthyr Bendragon. However, these are all highly suspect and not trusted by historians as credible. There are three other sources that have more weight.

1. Harleian genealogies, British library MS 3859. These contain the *Annales Cambriae* and *Historia Brittonum* dated to 1100. It shows the paternal and maternal genealogy of Owain Hywel Dda who died in 988, so they were probably compiled before that date. The tables detail the lineage of the kings of a number of Welsh kingdoms including Dyfed, Gwynedd and Powys.

2. *Bonedd Gwyr y Gogledd* (*Descent of the Men of the North*) shows supposed sixth-century kings of Hen Ogledd (the Old North). The earliest manuscript is Peniarth MS 45, dated to late thirteenth century. This contains two main sections. The first is the descendants of Coel Hen. These include Urien of Rheged, who we know was a historical late sixth-century figure and is here a great-great-great-grandson, placing Coel presumably at the start of the fifth century when the Romans left. Another great-grandson, Arthwys, is elsewhere identified as a king in the Pennine area in the late fifth century. The second branch involves Dyfnwal Hen, a supposed grandson of Magnus Maximus. He is listed as a great grandfather of Rhydderch Hael of Alt Clut. Rhydderch and figures from the Coel branch, Gwendoleu, Peredur and Gwrgi are elsewhere said to have been at the Battle of Arfderydd, mentioned in the *Annales Cambriae*, when Myrddin went mad.

3. Genealogies from Jesus College (MS 20) compiled in late fourteenth century and includes number of Welsh lineages especially those of South Wales

Again, it's important to remember there are no contemporary records for the fifth and sixth centuries. The texts that do exist can be seen as late dynastic propaganda.[1] Concerning the genealogical evidence for

Gildas's five kings and using the Harleian manuscripts, it is possible to identify Guortepir for Vortipor in Dyfed and Malicun for Maglocunnus in Gwynedd.[2] However, this is not certain and there is no reliable or sufficient early genealogy evidence to be confident in identifying anyone. There is an Arthur in these pedigrees but he is Arthur, son of Pedr, who himself is a grandson of Gildas's Vortipor. There is no other information and he appears to be too late for any historical Arthur.

The Harleian MS 3859 highlights the status of one particular king, Owain ap Hywel of Dyfed, it gives a broad survey of the royalty of the Britons and it concludes with the migration of Cunedda as a possible foundation myth for many Welsh dynasties.[3] Cunedda is also mentioned in the *Historia Brittonum*. It states that 146 years before the reign of Maelgwn of Gwynedd, his ancestor Cunedda came from the land of Manaw Gododdin, modern Lothian in Scotland, with eight sons. They expelled the Irish with 'immense slaughter'. It is precisely these sons that are the founding kings of the various Welsh kingdoms in the Harleian genealogies. The latter sources make Maelgwn a great-grandson and thus it is debatable if 146 years is a likely timeframe. There is a complete absence of Arthur from any of the early Welsh genealogies.[4]

However, we do have this mass of later evidence. Although contradictory and corrupted, still it persists. One would have to explain what was the motivation for people hundreds of years later to compile such lists? Additionally, for all their errors and corruptions, some tantalising clues poke through. A tradition persisted that led to people believing figures such as Cunedda and Vortigern were historical, and the genealogies do support this. Unfortunately there is no corresponding evidence of Arthur. This lack of evidence might suggest he was from a dynasty that was overwhelmed at an early stage by Anglo-Saxon domination.[5] The kingdom of Elmet in Yorkshire or Lindsey around the Lincoln area would be examples. As we know, four of the twelve battles in Nennius were in the 'Linnuis', which is likely to be Lincoln. Kent itself is another possibility, although the Anglo-Saxon takeover appears to have occurred much earlier. The *Historia Brittonum* states Hengist's son, Octha, succeeded him to the kingdom of Kent and *then* Arthur fought against them, which suggests Arthur came after the takeover of Kent. Alternatively, it could be that he was seen at an early stage as a mythical figure who was only later became seen as historical.

Genealogies and Kings

But this is all just speculation. The genealogical evidence we do have is sparse, late, suspect and makes no mention of any Arthur. One may legitimately ask how can we possibly comment on evidence we don't have? It's worth remembering the original reference in the *Historia Brittonum* does not label him as a king at all but a 'Dux Bellorum', leader of battles fighting *with* the kings of Britain. So there's no reason why he could not have held some administrative or military command that survived from the old Roman structure. The *Notitia Dignitatum*, which has been dated to around 425, does indeed show the military and civilian structure in Gaul and Britain surviving past 409. Then, in the *Life of Saint Germanus* in around 429, we have a bishop with former military experience, taking charge of a British army against Picts and Saxons. Lastly, we have the account of Gildas and Bede who tell of Ambrosius Aurelianus, whose parents 'wore the purple', taking command and leading the resistance which culminated with the Battle of Badon. Additionally, we have the rise of petty kings and kingdoms that we do have evidence for from the fifth century onwards. Some of these kingdoms, such as Kent, have exactly the same boundaries as former civitates and tribal areas and persist as counties even to this day. Clearly there were structures and positions of power.

Contrary to this is, first: the dating of the *Notitia* is not certain and it's contents impossible to verify. One man leading a force, whether it be Germanus or Ambrosius, does not prove the case for any political or military structure. Second: with no evidence, the existence of other petty kings does not prove the existence of one particular king. It could be that he was seen at an early stage as a mythical figure who was only later became seen as historical. There is no reference to Ambrosius in the genealogies and yet it is accepted he was a historical figure referenced by both Gildas and Bede. So absence from the genealogies does not prove anything either. It is the absence of any evidence from any credible source that is troubling.

Perhaps there are references to some of the other characters associated with Arthur? We do have two engraved stones dated from that time that are considered relevant. The first is a fifth- or sixth-century stone in south-west Wales which bears a Latin inscription alongside Irish Ogham text. Found in Castell Dwyran, Carmarthenshire, it is now in Carmarthen museum. The Latin inscription says: 'Memoria Voteporigis Protictoris', meaning 'Monument of Voteproix Protector'. The Irish text simply gives the Irish form of his name, Votecorigas. It has been suggested this stone refers to Vortiporus of Dyfed, one of Gildas's five kings and the only one identified with some confidence. He is also listed in the Harleian genealogies under Dyfed:

> ...Arthur map Petr map Cincar map Guortepir map Aircol map Triphun (map) Clotri map Gloitguin map Nimet map Dimet map Maxim gulecic (map)...

Guortepir is regarded as synonymous with Vortiporus in Gildas and he is seen as being seven generations after Maxim Gulecic, who is often regarded as Magnus Maximus who declared himself emperor from Britain and took control of the Western Empire before being killed in 388. An average of twenty years for each reign would place Guortepir on the throne of Dyfed from 528 onwards making him a contemporary of, if not the same as, Vortiporus. The same mathematical logic would place this Arthur, son of Petr, on the throne of Dyfed around 588 which seems far too late aside from the lack of any other evidence.

Even if true, it just verifies the identity of one of Gildas's five kings and has no bearing on the matter at hand. In fact, if we are to merely support the narrative provided by Gildas or Bede, then we have no need for any Arthur at all, although their narrative does not necessarily exclude him. The second engraved stone is the Pillar of Eliseg in Denbighshire, North Wales, which was erected by Cyngen ap Cadell, King of Powys, who died in 855. It was to honour his great grandfather Elisedd ap Gwylog and an accepted translation of the inscription reads as follows:

> Concenn son of Cattell, Cattell son of Brochmail, Brochmail son of Eliseg, Eliseg son of Guoillauc.
>
> And that Concenn, great-grandson of Eliseg, erected this stone for his great-grandfather Eliseg.
>
> The same Eliseg, who joined together the inheritance of Powys ... throughout nine [years?] out of the power of the Angles with his sword and with fire.
>
> Whosoever shall read this hand-inscribed stone, let him give a blessing on the soul of Eliseg.

Genealogies and Kings

> This is that Concenn who captured with his hand eleven hundred acres which used to belong to his kingdom of Powys ... and which ... the mountain
>
> [the column is then broken with a line or two lost]
>
> ... the monarchy ... *Maximus* ... of Britain ... Concenn, Pascent, Maun, Annan.
>
> Britu son of *Vortigern*, whom Germanus blessed, and whom *Sevira* bore to him, daughter of Maximus the king, who killed the king of the Romans.
>
> Conmarch painted this writing at the request of king Concenn.
>
> The blessing of the Lord be upon Concenn and upon his entire household, and upon the entire region of Powys until the Day of Judgement.

So we have independent evidence for Vortigern, albeit late. In the *Historia* Vortigern is said to have had three sons: Vortimer, Cateryn and Pascent. Confusingly it goes on to mention a fourth son, Faustus, the result of incest with his daughter. This son is then blessed by St Germanus and adopted. He later founded a monastery at Riez, and indeed there was a Bishop Faustus of Riez thought to have lived between 410–90. This particular Faustus was British and was in correspondence with Sidonius Apollinaris. The actual Faustus of Riez became abbott of his monastery in 433 and bishop in 460. So it is unlikely he was a small boy at the time of St Germanus's first visit in 429. If anything, the inclusion of Faustus demonstrates Nennius cannot be trusted as a source. Concerning Brittu, this could be a fifth son, or maybe it's another name for one of the sons mentioned by Nennius.

This pillar was raised in 855 and the *Historia Brittonum* written around 830, so very close in time. Yet the pillar gives a different narrative completely. Aside from being connected to the kingdom of Powys, Vortigern seems to be regarded positively and worthy of praise. This is very different from Nennius who relates the story of the tyrant Benlii who was burned in his fortress during the visit of St Germanus, who then installs Cadell who was 'made a king from a servant, and all his sons were kings, and from their seed the whole country of Powys is ruled, even to this day.' Vortigern, on the other hand, is given a poor reputation.

King Arthur: Man or Myth?

He is first recorded as attempting to build a fortress near Snowdon, but eventually gives the boy Emrys Ambrosius this fortress, together with 'all the kingdoms of the western part of Britain'. Vortigern then travels to the 'northern part' called Gwynessi and builds a city, Caer Gwrtheyrn. This is slightly odd as Caer Gwrtheyrn is in south-west Wales and the Gwynessi have been linked to the Gewisse, an Anglo-Saxon people in the upper Thames near Dorchester. The genealogy of Vortigern in Nennius also links him to the Gloucester area through his great-grandfather Gloiu. It has to be said the suggestion that this Gloiu founded Gloucester has no merit at all.

So there are competing traditions being written down in the ninth century. They can't both be true. This seems to suggest we simply cannot trust this evidence, hundreds of years out of date, whether it be written in stone or parchment. It may show political rivalries. The Harleian manuscripts give various versions for Powys. There is indeed a Brittu, but he is shown as the son of Cattegirn. If we take twenty years per generation then we find this Cattegirn to be 400 years before Cincen, who is identified with Concern, who erected the stone around 850. So this would place him around 450, which ties in with the timeline in Nennius and the *Anglo-Saxon Chronicles*.

However, Catel Dunlurc has often been associated with the Cadell in Nennius, to whom St Germanus grants the kingdom of Powys. He is a mere thirteen generations back and while Cattegirn and Pascent both follow him in line, we then have to assume an average of thirty-five years per generation to place him back to the visit of St Germanus.

Dumville[6] suggests possible genealogies from Harleian 3859 with possible candidates for some of Gildas's five kings. The pillar of Elliseg, MS3859 and Nennius all have alternative pedigrees. I've supplied a table that demonstrates the contradictory lineages. Of these only Guortepir is identified with any confidence. There is no reliable pedigree for Dumnonia so the fifth king, Constantine, cannot be identified. If it refers to the Devon area rather than the Damnonia in the Strathclyde region, then much later regnal lists place a Custennin ap Cado, later Saint Constanine, around 530–60. However, none of these sources have any validity and are mostly derived from Geoffrey of Monmouth. The earliest figures are at the top of the table.

Genealogies and Kings

Table 26: Genealogies of Welsh kingdoms

DYFED Harleian 3859	GWYNEDD Harleian 3859	RHOS Harleian 3859	POWYS Dumville (1988: 59)	POWYS Harleian 3859	POWYS Pillar of Elliseg	Nennius Vortigern's Genealogy
			Guorthigirn (Vortigern)	Catell	Vortigern	Vortigern the thin
			Cattegirn	Cattegirn	Brittu	Pascent
Triphun	Cunedda	Cunedda	Brittu	Pascent		Briacat
Aircol	Enniaun	Enniaun	Camuir	Maucann		Idnerth
Guortepir *Vortipore: tyrant of the Demetians*	Catguolaun d.534 or Cadwallon Lawhir	Eugein Dantguin aka Owain 'whitetooth'	Millo	Cincen		Meuric
Cincar	**Mailcun c. 534-547 aka Maelgwn** *Maglocune: Dragon of the island*	**Cinglas** *Cuneglasse: Bear*	**Cinnin** *Aurelius Conanus: Lions whelp. Possible grandchild of Ambrosius Aurelianus*	Brochfael		Paul
Pedr	Run	Meic		**Cynan** *Aurelius Conanus: Lions whelp. Possible grandchild of Ambrosius Aurelianus*		
Arthur	Beli	Cangan				
Nougouy	Iacob d.613	Catgual				

This does seem to suggest that we have a confusing and contradictory mess. As has been mentioned before in these lists, Cunedda is listed as being a great-grandfather of Mailcun yet in the *Historia Brittonum* he

165

King Arthur: Man or Myth?

is said to have founded several dynasties 146 years before Maelgwn reigned, which places him in 388. This requires a fifty-year average for each reign which would be unusually long. A more reasonable 20–25 year average would place Cunedda around 460–80, which would place him after even Vortigern if he ruled in 425. So the genealogies do not seem to be consistent with Nennius.

In fact if you look at Dyfed there is an alternative Irish version. An Irish text, *The expulsion of the Deisi,* lays out the genealogy of the Deisi from Ireland who settled in Dyfed. It mirrors the Harleian version from Triphun to the eighth century. Prior to Triphun though it has a completely Irish content. It suggests the Harleian version was doctored to give a non-Irish and more acceptable Roman pedigree going back through Magnus Maximus to Constantine I; this is backed up by archaeological evidence for Irish settlement. It is worth noting that all the Arthurs who appear in the late sixth century in royal genealogies have Irish connections similar to Dyfed.

Rather than waste time trying to unpick a pile of contradictory and highly debatable material, we could accept the consensus among historians that there is nothing to be gained from these genealogies; we should accept they have no credibility and move on. This may be a little harsh in the sense that they do exist. Someone wrote them with the intent, or even expectation, that they would be believed. Whether people believe a story told about something 500 years after it happened is neither here nor there.

Thus the genealogies and annals do not give us reliable data.[7] The furthest the evidence takes us is the mid-sixth century. We certainly can't go before that point with any confidence. In fact without corroboration they can't be used as evidence before the tenth century.[8] Regarding the saints' lives there is even less support.[9] No copies of Welsh saints' lives survive before the eleventh century, nor do they provide any factual record of sixth- and seventh-century events. The chronological and logical inconsistencies are too great.

The Harleian genealogies were specifically for holding the status of one tenth-century king, Owain ap Hywel, to promote the royalty of the Britons and trace the lineage back to Cunedda.[10] They are not 'capable of sustaining historicity as far back as the sixth century', and the *Annales* are 'valueless' in constructing a historical Arthur.[11] Yet for some figures there is support.

Genealogies and Kings

There is no reasonable doubt, for example, that Vortigern is historical.[12] So there's a consensus that Ambrosius Aurelianus and Vortigern were historical figures. There's no evidence for Vortimer, and he may well be construct of Nennius. Bede qualifies his description of the Adventus Saxonum by saying their first leaders 'are said to be Hengist and Horsa'. He goes on to describe Horsa falling in battle and there being a monument in the eastern part of Kent. The lineage is then traced back to Woden.

This is a good point to draw the line under the Welsh evidence and move on to the Anglo-Saxon genealogies, but just to summarise, for the Welsh sources there are no contemporary records for this period. There are later royal genealogies and saints' lives written several hundred years after the supposed events. Many of these are, at best, highly suspect and not to be trusted for anything prior to the sixth century, and at worst, inventions for political or religious purposes at the time they were written. But nevertheless, there is a wide body of late evidence, albeit often contradictory, that would suggest a willing and receptive audience for the narrative.

Turning to the Anglo-Saxon sources. Nennius gives a number of genealogies for the following Anglo-Saxon kingdoms: Bernecia, Deira, Mercia, Kent. The *Anglo-Saxon Chronicles* also detail those of the West Saxons and Kent. Many of these trace their ancestry back to Woden and are also extremely suspect until around the middle of the sixth century. They are not contemporary, having also been written hundreds of years later. In other words, none of them can be trusted for the period in which we are interested.

Nennius records the following directly after his passage on Arthur:

> when they were defeated in all their campaigns, the English sought help from Germany and continually and considerably brought over their kings from Germany to rule over them in Britain, until the time Ida reigned, who was the son of Eobba. He was the first king in Bernicia, that is Berneich.

Bede records that Oessa was the first of the dynasty to arrive in Bernicia, but his grandson Ida was the first to rule 547–59.[13] The *Historia Brittonum* goes on to list the royal houses for Bernecia and Deira, later combined as Northumbria, alongside Mercia and East Anglia. It is noteworthy that they all cite Woden as a founding ancestor. However, these lists do not become credible before the middle of the sixth century. None of them appear to have any link to the Arthur legend. Nennius, however, does describe four British kings combining to push the English back to the island of Lindisfarne. This is placed in the reign of Theodric son of Ida, approximately 571–78. This would indicate the English in the north had not gained dominance until the very end of the sixth century. Detailed Bernicia history begins with Aethelfrith 592–616, grandson of Ida, while the first Deiran king that can be securely dated is Aelle who died in 616.[14] Bede describes Aethelfrith as 'a very brave king and most eager for glory ... he ravaged the Britons more extensively than any other English ruler.'

The *Anglo-Saxon Chronicles* also cite Woden as a founder of the West Saxons and list the descendants down to Cerdic and Cynric who supposedly landed in 495 with five ships. The *Chronicle* states in the introduction that after six years they conquered the West Saxon kingdom, implying they fought together in various battles. It also gives later dates of 514 and 519 for similar events. Cerdic then ruled for sixteen years, followed by Cynric for twenty-six years. Yet in the body of the *Chronicle*, Cerdic is said to pass away in 534, suggesting the earlier dates are a mistake. Cynric then continues fighting in 552 and 556, dying in 560. Aside from the mathematical contradiction and implausibility, there is no contemporary evidence for any of the kings mentioned until much later.

The Anglian Collection is a collection of eighth-century manuscripts that also list various genealogies of Anglo-Saxon kingdoms. What may be relevant are the references to Kent. Kent has the most detailed of the surviving legends although prior to the second-half of the sixth century are largely mythic.[15] Bede cites Oeric, whose second name was Oisc, as the founder of the dynasty known as the Oiscingas. The genealogy of Aethelbert II in the Anglian collection has Octa as Hengist's son and Oisc as the grandson. This confusion between the sources is compounded by a complete lack of evidence prior to Aethelbert.

Archeology supports Bede's assertion that Kent was Jutish in origin and the material culture of the area was predominantly Germanic by the sixth century. Kent is unique in having two bishoprics at Canterbury and Rochester, and indeed early records suggest two distinct petty kingdoms, east and west. The combination of the evidence suggests the early Kentish kingdom comprised only east Kent and may have grown out of the Romano-British province.[16] It is clear from Bede and charter evidence that it was normal for two kings to rule together with one being more dominant.[17]

Genealogies and Kings

Table 27: Genealogy of the kings of Kent

Nennius c. 830	***Anglo-Saxon chronicles* c. 900**	**Bede 730**	**Anglian collection Eighth century**
Woden	Woden	Woden	Woden
Wechta	Wechta	Wechta	Waegdaeg
Witta	Witta	Witta	Wihtgisl
Wichtgils	Wichtgils	Wichtgils	Witta
Hengist and Horsa	Hengist and Horsa 455 Hengist and Aesc succeed to kingdom	Hengist and Horsa 449	Hengist
Octha	Aesc 488 succeeds to kingdom of kent and rules 24 years	Oeric Oisc	Ocga
Ossa	512?	Octa	Oese
Eormenric		Eormenric	Eormenric
Aethelbert	Aethelberht 465 rules for 53 years	Aethelbert 596 Pope Gregory sends St Augustine	Aethelberht

Hengist's first kingdom may have been just the east of Kent. The verifiable historical horizon begins with Eormenric and the Frankish connection confirmed through archaeology and the marriage of Bertha, a Frankish Christian princess, to Aethelbert around 580. The reference in the ASC to Aethelberht reigning for fifty-three years may be a mistaken entry for his birth. It may be that all these genealogies derive from a common source or influenced each other. What is clear is that few of the names can be verified before the second-half of the sixth century.

The most we can say is that here we have a series of chronicles that appear to roughly agree. Or at the very least they were written with the expectations that they would be believed. So there had to be belief or tradition present in parts of eighth-century Britain concerning the origins of the kingdoms. The thing to remember is these genealogies were written hundreds of years later and would have had a political purpose as much as anything. Nevertheless, they place Octa either after Hengist or one generation later. This is vitally important if the *Historia* can be trusted, because it is quite clear when it places Arthur. After Hengist's death Octha came to Kent and then, 'Arthur fought against them'. If one works back we could speculate on the following likely floruits. Hengist arrives of fighting age around 450 and dies in 488 aged about 60. Octha (or Aesc) reigns from 488 to 512, followed by Ossa, Oese or another Octa. None of this is incompatible for Eormenric in the mid-sixth century and Aethelbert, whom we know reigned in the latter quarter. What this means is that Nennius is quite clear when he believes Arthur fought: either in the 490s or the 510s. He may well be wrong, as so many of his facts and dates are. He could be exaggerating or lying. But that is what he is implying. All the later saints' lives and genealogies, flawed as they are, do seem to roughly agree with a floruit sometime between 490–540.

Many of the lists begin with Woden which many have assumed to be a reference to the Saxon god. However, they also refer to Uoden Frealafing, which can be translated as 'Woden son of Frealaf'. It's often assumed they are simply associating their line with the Saxon god Woden, but it's at least possible some powerful Chieftain claimed divinity in the same way some Roman emperors were deified. One genealogy, Lindis or Lincoln, continues four further generations past Woden. Is it possible this demonstrates the Lincoln area was one of the first centres of Angle settlement? It's just impossible to know as there simply isn't any evidence to support the earlier entries to the regnal lists and none at all to date them. In practical terms, four generations between Woden and Hengist puts Woden in the late fourth century, and another four generations in the example of the Lindsey area puts us at the start of the fourth century. Nennius also records Hengist's genealogy stretching back five generations past Woden, with one name added to the Anglian list. But the suggestion that there were Anglo-Saxon kings in Lincoln stretching back to the Roman period has no evidence. Yet the archaeological evidence does show much earlier Germanic influence than was previously thought and it may be worth noting four of Arthur's twelve battles were in the region of the Linnuis and a fifth, on the river Glein, has also been associated with the area.

Genealogies and Kings

The origins of these genealogies are in the late eighth century,[18] but there is little to no evidence that surviving stories retained any consistency.[19] I've provided a table for the early genealogies. We must remember that there are other lists that contradict, differ in name and chronology or have additions. The first six kingdoms come from the Anglian collection.[20] The Wessex line comes from the *Anglo-Saxon Chronicles*, although later collections also provided a lineage back to Woden. The only mention of the South Saxons after Aelle comes in the seventh century, after which it is conquered by the expanding Wessex kingdom. The names at the top in bold are those for whom we have reliable evidence and are dateable.[21] I have aligned them all with Woden or Uoden to give some idea of alleged contemporary generations.

Bede lists seven 'Bretwaldas', roughly meaning 'Britain ruler'. The first four appear in the table; it is worth noting the long gap between Aelle of Sussex and Ceawlin of Wessex. What we see is a large number of dynasties starting around the end of the fifth century, followed by a period of little expansion, which fits in with the narrative of Gildas regarding forty-four years of relative peace since the battle of Badon. It also fits in with Frankish expansion in Gaul in the second-half of the fifth century, pushing Saxons out of the Loire valley and dissuading raids on northern Gaul.

From the start of the sixth century things appear to have changed. The battles involving the West Saxons are not all listed as victories and start to appear defensive: Cerdic's shore; Cerdic's Wood, Cerdic's Ford, before turning towards Isle of Wight in 530. Just after this time, Gregory of Tours is relating how Saxons are emigrating from Britain and being settled by the Franks in return for military help.

Concerning the West-Saxon line, it has been suggested that the 495 and 514 dates are duplicates. Also that the life span for Cynric seems unusually long. There is an alternative genealogy in the *Life of King Alfred* written by Asser in the ninth century, which lists a Creoda between Cerdic and Cynric. That would indeed make more sense chronologically speaking, but we don't know how valid any of this is before the latter part of the sixth century. However, we do seem to have an expansion by the West Saxons after 550. and then in Northumbria maybe a generation later.

Table 28: Early Anglo-Saxon genealogies

Kent AC	Bernicia AC	Deira AC	East Anglia AC	Mercia AC	Lindsey AC	Wessex ASC	South saxons ASC
Edilberht c.589–616 Bretwalda	Aethelfrith 592–616	Aelle c.590–600	Raedwald c.599–624 Bretwalda	Penda c.626–655		Cuthwine	No further info until 675
	Ecgfrid Osuio Edilfrid Edilric (Nennius differs here and includes Theodoric c.571–578)	Yffi	Alduulf Edilric Eni Wuffa c.578 Wehha 571	Pypba		Ceawlin c.560–92 Bretwalda	
Iumenric	Ida 547–559 Eoppa	Uuscfrea Uilgils		Crioda Cynewald	Aldfrid Eatta		
Oese	Oesa (first to come to Britain—Bede)	Uestor-ualcna		Cnebba	Eanferd	Cynric 534–60	
	Edilberht Angen-geot	Soemel Saefugul	Wilhelm	Icil c.520? Eamer	Biscop Beda		
Ocga c.488–512	Alusa	Saebald	Hryp	Angen-geot	Bubba	Cerdic 495–534	Aelle 477–491+
Hengest d.488	Ingibrand	Siggeot	Hrodmund	Offa	Caedbaed	Elesa	
Uitta	Wegbrand	Suebdaeg	Trygil	Uermund	Cueldgils	Esla	

Uihtgils	Beornric	Siggar	Tyttman	Uihtlaeg	Cretta	Gewis
Uegdaeg	Beldaeg	Uegdaeg	Caser	Weoldul-geot	Uinta	Wig
Uoden	**Uoden**	**Uoden**	**Uoden**	**Woden**	**Uuden**	Freawine
					Frealaf	Frithugar
					Friodulf	Brand
					Finn	Baeldaeg
					Godulf son of Geot	**Woden**

King Arthur: Man or Myth?

The legends are also contradictory in naming Arthur's adversaries. Geoffrey of Monmouth, for example, names Colgrin, but there is no identifiable person of that name in the genealogies. In later Welsh legends, 'Osla Big-Knive' is listed as both one of Arthur's men in *Culhwch and Olwen* and his protagonist at Badon in the *Dream of Rhonabwy*. It seems obvious to translate Osla as Octha. Having said that, it's also possible there has been confusion with the eighth-century Mercian king, Offa Kyllellvawr urenhin Lloegr (Offa Great-Knife, King of England). You could look at the genealogy tables and estimate which kings may have been contemporary, but it would be pure speculation. Nennius seems quite certain that Arthur is fighting in the time of Octha of Kent and thus Cerdic and later Cynric of the West Saxons and Aelle or his sons of the South Saxons.

In the North the British are strong enough, according to Nennius, to besiege the Bernicians on the island of Lindisfarne as late as the 570s. It is not until the start of the seventh century that the kingdom of Elmet in the Yorkshire area is destroyed. The following table shows some of the Welsh kings recorded in the Harleian manuscripts and is purely for information purposes. The possible kings in Gildas and Cunedda from Nennius are highlighted; it is unlikely that Cunedda was 146 years before Maelgwn. The earliest kings are at the bottom and all are from Harleian MS 3859.

Table 29: Early Welsh genealogies

Gwynedd	Rhos	Dunoding	Meironydd	Ceredigion	Dyfed	Powys
Catman	Enniaun	Iouanaul	Sualda	Arhgen	Cloten	Brocmayl
Jacob	Ytigoy	Eicaun	Iudris	Seisil	Nougoy	Elitet
Beli	Catgual	Brochmail	Gueinoth	Artgloys	Arthur	Guilauc
Run	Cangan	Ebiau	Glitnoth	Artbodglo	Petr	Eli
Mailcun c.534–49 (Maelgwn)	Meic	Mouric	Guurgint	Bodgu	Cincar	Eliud
Catoglaun	**Cinglas**	Dinacat	Gatgulart	Seguil	**Guortiper (Vortipor)**	Cincen
Lauhir	Eugein Dantguin (Owain 'white-tooth')	Ebiaun	Meriaun	Iusay	Aircol	Brochmail

Genealogies and Kings

Eniaun	Enniaun Girt	Dunaut	Typiaun	Ceretic	Triphun	Cincan
Cunedda	**Cunedda**	**Cunedda**	**Cunedda**	**Cunedda**	Clotri	Maucant
Aetern					Gloitguin	Pascent
Patern Pesrut					Nimet	Cattegirn c.450
Tacit					Dimet	Catell
Genealogy goes back to Anna 'cousin to the Virgin Mary'.					**Maxim Gulecic (Magnus Maximus d.388)**	

Partial genealogies also survive but it's not always obvious where they apply.

Table 30: Northern British genealogies

York?	Pennine region	Pennine region	Lothian? Elmet?	Rheged	Dumbarton?	Ystrad Clud Strathclyde
Gurci		Morgant		Urbgen Urien late sixth century	Riderch Rhydderch late sixth century	Riderch
Peretur		Cincar	Guallauc	Cinmarc	Tutagual	Eugein
Eleuther	Dunaut	Bran	Laenauc	Merchianum	Clinoch	Dumnagual
Ietlum	Pappo	Dumngual	Masguic	Gurgust	Dumgual	Teudebur
Ceneu	Ceneu	Garbaniaun	Ceneu	Ceneu		Beli
Coyl Hen Early fifth century?	Coyl Hen	Coyl Hen	Coyl Hen	Coyl Hen		Elfin

Not only do we have highly suspect sources lacking credibility once again, we also have no Arthur. Even the areas that were taken over first have no Arthur as such, although there is an Athrwys mentioned in later genealogies for the York area. This may seem promising, but Athrwys isn't at all the same name as Arthur. There's nothing connecting him to the legend and we know nothing about him other than a link in a late genealogy.[22] Moving on to other regions: Ceretic is described as a king of Elmet by Bede and being overrun by Edwin of Northumbria around 616. From later genealogies, and the *Historia Brittonum*, his father Guallauc fought with Urien, Rhydderch and Morcant against the Angles at Lindisfarne, which would be around 571–78 by Nennius's unreliable calculations. In general, 'the sources are potentially unreliable as sources of direct historical testimony but may be useful to the historian about the period of composition.'[23] They may simply be origin legends used by writers at the time. Similarly, saints' lives composed for the contemporary interests of the ecclesiastical sites often associated with these origin legends.

Nevertheless, we can speculate once more which kings are in the period suggested by Nennius. If we take the generation of Maelgwn of Gwynedd 534–47 as succeeding Arthur, then the two before include Cinglas, Cincen and Vortipor, at least one name with which we are already familiar from Gildas.

Another source, the *Llandaff Charters*, were compiled to further the territorial and jurisdictional claims of the church of Llandaff in the twelfth century. Some historians, such as Wendy Davies, disagree and see them as deriving from an early source.[24] Others say it's impossible to identify reliable texts before 1050.[25] There are 149 charters, mainly concerning the south east of Wales, Gwent and Ergyng. Some claim to represent charters from as early as the late sixth century. It covers 500 years of the diocese's history and includes lives of three saints: Dubricius, Teilo and Oudoceus. None of these reference Arthur. It has been suggested that some of the charters do mention Athrwys ap Meurig and that this is the Arthur of legend.

There are a number of reasons why that may be unlikely. First, in most texts his name is spelt Atroys, Andrus or Antres. Second, the evidence places him in the seventh century with parents named Meurig and Onbrawst; there is no connection to any of the names in the legend. Third, there is no evidence connecting him to any of the battles or other aspects of the legend. There are possibly two people named Athrwys ap Meurig,[26] which may be due to confusion of dating or may refer to two separate people. The charters place one of these as a contemporary of disciples of Bishop Dubricius. This would place him in the mid-sixth century and makes him a King of Gwent: *Arthuis rex Guenti*.

Genealogies and Kings

The second Athrwys is son of Meurig ap Tewdrig and a contemporary of St Oudoceus, placing him in the early seventh century. He is not named as king but his father and son are kings of Gwent and Glywysing. Later theorists have put forward this figure but there's no evidence other than an 'Arth-' sounding name. At best the *Llandaff Charters* are dubious for the time we are interested in and have nothing to say about anyone called Arthur. Magnus Maximus similarly appears in the line for Dyfed and Alt Clud as an ancestor of Vortipor and Rhydderch respectively. Needless to say, no such record exists for any sons of Maximus.

The summary will have to be similar to previous ones. We have a tradition reflected in a body of evidence written hundreds of years after the events recorded. We have evidence to support the various genealogies going back to the beginning of the seventh century. Beyond that the evidence thins before disappearing completely by the middle of the sixth century. It is not uncommon for such regnal lists to be corrupted or simply made up. There are certainly no archaeological or other historical sources to support them. There are references in these lists, both Welsh and Anglo-Saxon, to various characters that have been connected to our investigation, such as Vortigern and Hengist. On one hand there is a complete lack of evidence, on the other is the existence and repetition of the tradition over 300 years before our first written record appears.

What is clear is Arthur does not appear in any of the original genealogies and the inclusion of Uthr marrying Eigr, daughter of Amlawdd Wledig and Gwen, a daughter of Cunedda, doesn't appear until the Middle Ages. This hasn't stopped numerous theorists trawling through this late material and attempting to manufacture a narrative.

Nevertheless, it is possible to construct a family tree from the various sources and legends. There is no consensus and many contradictions across the various texts. Again, none are contemporary, all of them being several hundred years after the alleged people concerned. To simplify matters we have two families, that of Cunedda and of Coel Hen, linked by marriage. Many of the saints we have discussed can be seen as great-grandsons of Cunedda. Later Armorican lines were also linked through marriage and one of these is Uthr. They should be taken with a large pinch of salt, but they do at least clarify to which generation particular figures supposedly belonged, and the relationship between characters.

We know some facts from later sources. As late as the 570s the northern British pushed the Angles back to the island of Lindisfarne.

ARTHUR AND WELSH KINGS AND SAINTS

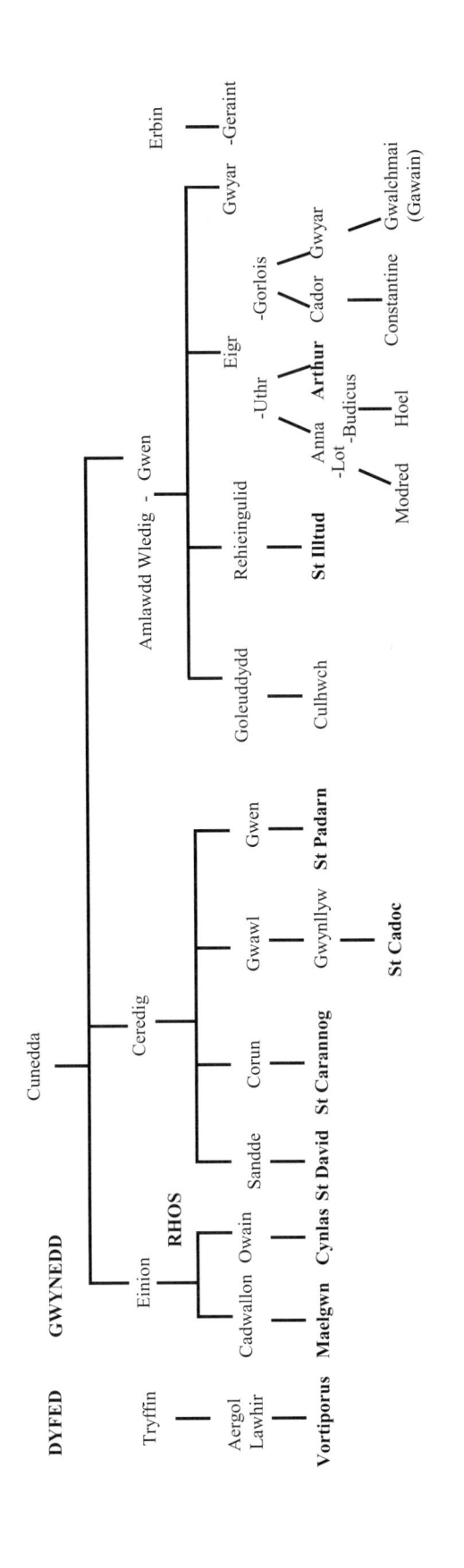

DYFED

Tryffin
— Aergol Lawhir
— **Vortiporus**

GWYNEDD

Cunedda
— Ceredig
— Einion

RHOS
- Cadwallon
- Owain
- **Maelgwn**
- **Cynlas**
- **St David**
- **St Carannog**

Ceredig's children: Sandde, Corun, Gwawl, Gwen
- Gwynllyw — **St Cadoc**
- **St Padarn**

Amlawdd Wledig — Gwen
- Goleuddydd — Culhwch
- Rehieingulid — **St Illtud**
- Eigr
  - —Uthr — Eigr — —Gorlois
    - Anna —Lot, **Arthur** —Budicus, Cador — Gwyar
      - Modred, Hoel, Constantine, Gwalchmai (Gawain)
- Gwyar — Erbin — Geraint

GENEALOGY OF THE 'OLD NORTH'

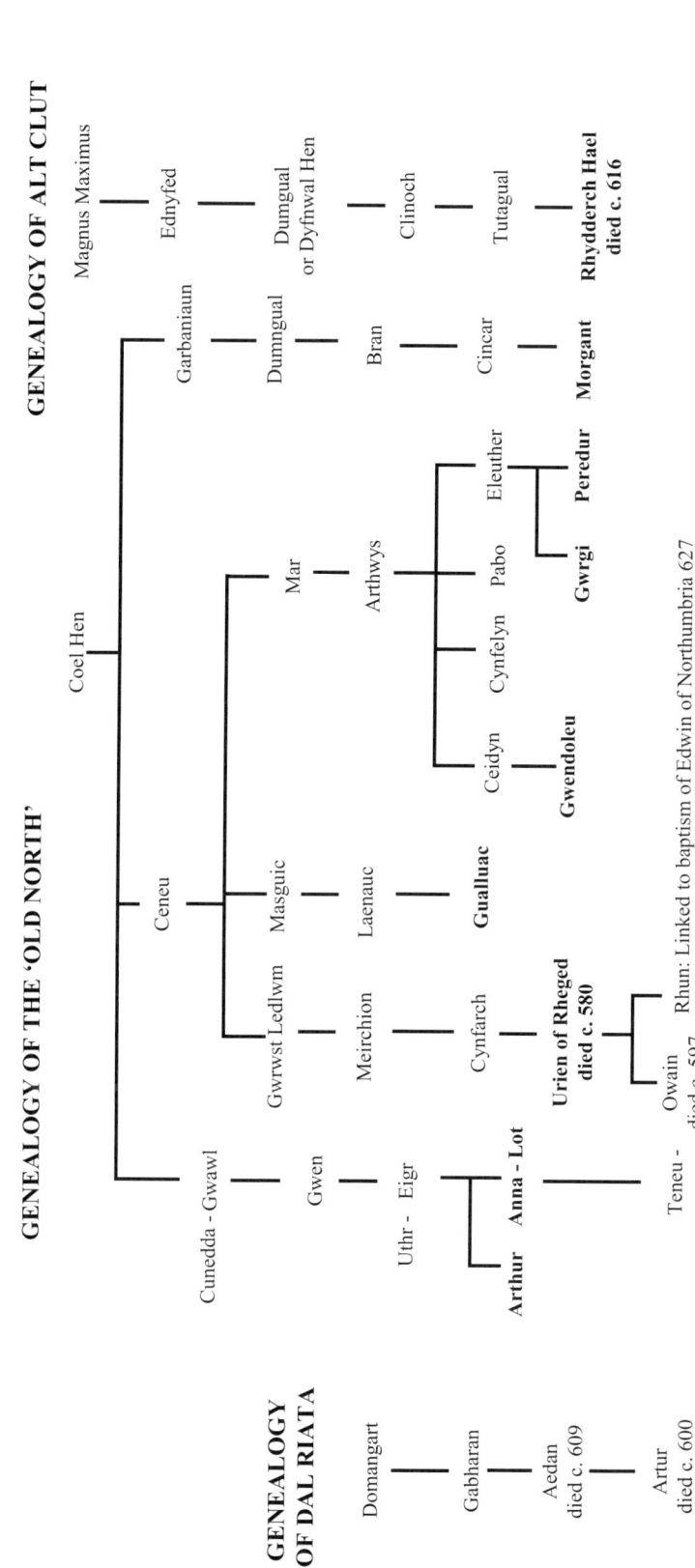

GENEALOGY OF ALT CLUT

Magnus Maximus
— Ednyfed
— Dumgual or Dyfnwal Hen
— Clinoch
— Tutagual
— **Rhydderch Hael died c. 616**

Coel Hen
├── Garbaniaun — Dummgual — Bran — Cincar — **Morgant**
└── Ceneu
    ├── Gwrwst Ledlwm — Meirchion — Cynfarch
    │   ├── **Urien of Rheged died c. 580**
    │   │   └── Owain died c. 597
    │   └── Teneu
    │   └── St Kentigern (St Mungo) died 614
    ├── Masguic — Laenauc — **Gualluac**
    └── Mar — Arthwys
        ├── Ceidyn — **Gwendoleu**
        ├── Cynfelyn
        ├── Pabo — **Gwrgi**
        └── Eleuther — **Peredur**

Cunedda - Gwawl
└── Gwen
    └── Uthr - Eigr
        └── **Arthur** — **Anna - Lot**

GENEALOGY OF DAL RIATA

Domangart — Gabharan — Aedan died c. 609 — Artur died c. 600

Rhun: Linked to baptism of Edwin of Northumbria 627
Linked to authorship of Chatres fragment of Historia Brittonum.

References and connected figures (in bold)
Annales Cambriae: Battle of Arfderydd c. 573: Rhydderch Hael, Gwrgi, Perdur vs Gwendoleu and possibly Aedan Mac Gabharan
Historia Brittonum: c. 570s: War against Bernicians: Urien, Gwallawg, Rhydderch Hen and Morcant

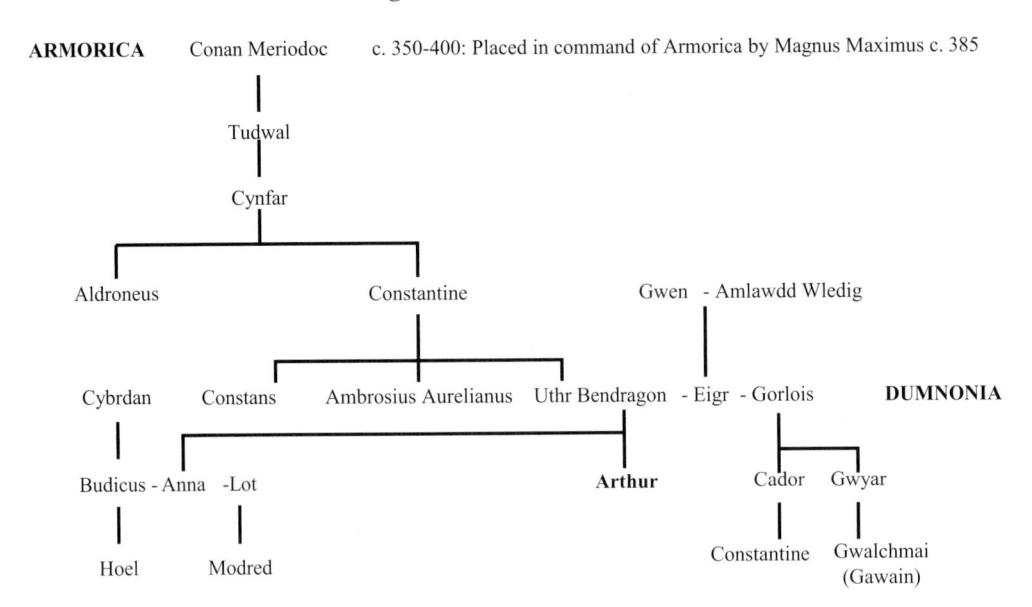

King Arthur: Man or Myth?

ARMORICA — Conan Meriodoc — c. 350-400: Placed in command of Armorica by Magnus Maximus c. 385
- Tudwal
  - Cynfar
    - Aldroneus
      - Cybrdan
        - Budicus — Anna — -Lot
          - Hoel
          - Modred
    - Constantine
      - Constans
      - Ambrosius Aurelianus
      - Uthr Bendragon — Eigr — Gorlois
        - **Arthur**
    - Gwen — Amlawdd Wledig

DUMNONIA
- Cador
  - Constantine
- Gwyar
  - Gwalchmai (Gawain)

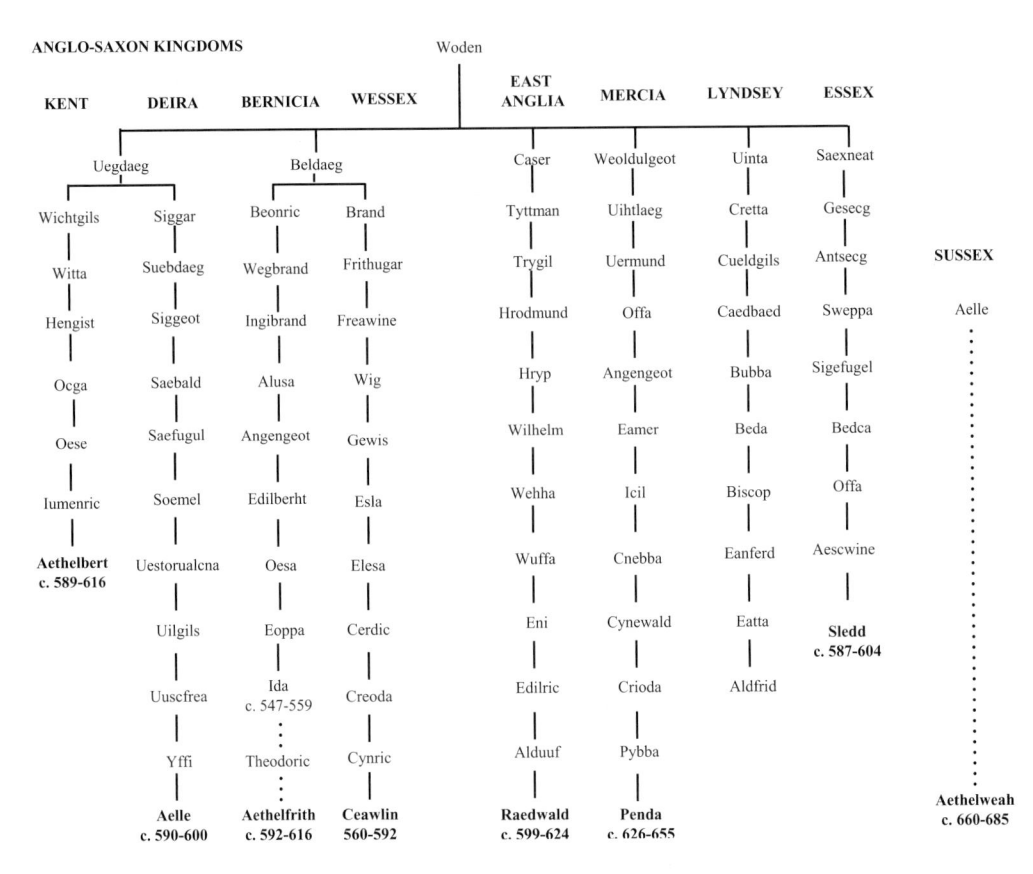

ANGLO-SAXON KINGDOMS

Woden

KENT	DEIRA	BERNICIA	WESSEX	EAST ANGLIA	MERCIA	LYNDSEY	ESSEX
Uegdaeg	Uegdaeg	Beldaeg	Beldaeg	Caser	Weoldulgeot	Uinta	Saexneat
Wichtgils	Siggar	Beonric	Brand	Tyttman	Uihtlaeg	Cretta	Gesecg
Witta	Suebdaeg	Wegbrand	Frithugar	Trygil	Uermund	Cueldgils	Antsecg
Hengist	Siggeot	Ingibrand	Freawine	Hrodmund	Offa	Caedbaed	Sweppa
Ocga	Saebald	Alusa	Wig	Hryp	Angengeot	Bubba	Sigefugel
Oese	Saefugul	Angengeot	Gewis	Wilhelm	Eamer	Beda	Bedca
Iumenric	Soemel	Edilberht	Esla	Wehha	Icil	Biscop	Offa
Aethelbert c. 589-616	Uestorualcna	Oesa	Elesa	Wuffa	Cnebba	Eanferd	Aescwine
	Uilgils	Eoppa	Cerdic	Eni	Cynewald	Eatta	**Sledd** c. 587-604
	Uuscfrea	Ida c. 547-559	Creoda	Edilric	Crioda	Aldfrid	
	Yffi	Theodoric	Cynric	Alduuf	Pybba		
	Aelle c. 590-600	**Aethelfrith** c. 592-616	**Ceawlin** 560-592	**Raedwald** c. 599-624	**Penda** c. 626-655		

SUSSEX
- Aelle
- Aethelweah c. 660-685

180

Genealogies and Kings

The kingdom of Elmet around the Leeds area was not conquered by Northumbria until 616. The rise of Mercia didn't occur until the seventh century. The West Saxons expanded from 550 onwards. What this means is that the situation at the time Arthur is supposed to have lived is similar, if not identical, to one Gildas describes. There is a partition. It is likely to involve the south east, at the very least Kent and the area covered by the Saxon Shore forts from Southampton to the Wash. London is already likely abandoned but surrounded by Saxon settlements, and as far inland as St Albans is cut off from the Britons. There are Angles all along the east coast from the wash to beyond Hadrian's wall. Yet Bernicia and Deira both have a Brythonic etymology. Ida is the first king of the Bernician's around 547 not before. It is not possible to know who was in control of Lincoln and York. All we know from Gildas is that around 540, Britain had a plethora of kings, at least five of whom deserve his condemnation. Britain also has it's Governors, in the plural, although what this means in terms of provincial structure can only be guessed at. At that time the kingdom of Powys stretched far into modern England. In fact, the bulk of modern England appears to have been still under British control. The genealogies we have today are from the surviving British kingdoms and the conquering Anglo-Saxon ones. Any records and king-lists from a small British kingdom around London, Lincoln or York around the time in which we are interested are lost to us.

Before we move onto the etymology of the name Arthur, there are some points to bear in mind:

- None of the early genealogies are contemporary or verifiable and none contain Arthur.
- Later legends, stories and genealogies place Arthur in an Armorican branch that marries into descendants of the earlier genealogies. These also cannot be verified and may have been later constructs to make the story believable.
- Taken at face value they place him between late fifth-century figures and mid- to late sixth-century figures, many of whom also can't be corroborated.
- Despite the many contradictions and lack of validity there is a level of consistency and coherence.
- An Arthur living between 490–540 would not be incompatible with the genealogies, saints' lives or later legends and stories.
- Anybody constructing a saint's life or story in the Middle Ages would have been well aware of all of the above.

Chapter 16

Arthur, the name

By the beginning of the fifth century Britain was largely a Christian province. Therefore the likelihood is that Arthur would have been a Christian, there is certainly no mention of any British leader not being Christian. Gildas denounces his five kings for various sins but paganism isn't among them. The name itself appears nowhere until his alleged time. Then at the end of the the sixth century we have a number of Arthurs in the royal pedigrees. They tend to be in two areas: southern Scotland or south west Wales, both heavily settled by Irish immigrants in the fifth century.

The first possible etymology is from the Latin Artorius meaning 'plowman'. This has been described as 'phonologically perfect'.[1] He is never referred to in this form, however, and is usually in the Brythonic form Arthur or Arthurus.[2] A correct Latin version would have been Arturus or the more classical Arcturus.[3] In fact 'Arturus' is found in the earliest Latin reference in the *Historia Brittonum*. Arcturus or Arthurus is a perfectly acceptable derivation from Artorius. However it also had significant meaning. The first half, 'Art', means bear and the second half, guardian. This would refer to a well-known star in the constellation of Bootes next to the constellation of Ursa Major – The Great Bear; hence 'Guardian of the Bear'. Any Romano-Briton asked what or who is Arturus would thus be likely to reply: 'the brightest star in Bootes, the Guardian of the Bear'.

Not everyone in Roman Britain would have spoken Latin. The first appearance of the name may occur in the supposed sixth-century poem *Y Gododdin*. There is a problem in that the ending, '-ur', is not common in Bythronic languages. However 'Arth' is commonly accepted as 'Bear', a rough, unmannerly or fierce person.[4] We are reminded of Gildas's description of Cuneglasus: 'You bear…ruler of many … you tawny butcher.'

Arthur, the name

The ending 'ur' may have come from 'gwr', meaning 'man', which would translate Arthur as 'Man of the Bear' or 'Bear-man'. However the '-wr' and '-ur' sounds are different and in Welsh poetry Arthur is always rhymed with -ur endings. So the Latin etymology appears more likely. Nevertheless, to both Roman and British ears, Arthur and Arturus would have the same meaning: Bear-man. Thus it could be a nickname, rather like a general acquiring the name Taurus, or Roman emperors adopting the name Ceasar or Augustus.

So on one hand we can dismiss any similar-sounding Welsh names such as Arthwys, as these come from a separate and well-documented root.[5] On the other hand we are confronted with the possibility it may have been a nickname. For example, the Emperor Caligula was actually named Gaius Caesar, but was nicknamed 'little boot' and the name stuck. Of course that's rather convenient. That means he could be anyone and many names have been put forward, although none with sufficient evidence such as a reference connecting the real name with the nickname. There is no consensus from academics about the etymology.

Some favour a native derivation,[6] although others see a Latin derivation from Artorius as more likely.[7] Later medieval works such as *Dialogue of Arthur and the Eagle* describe him as 'bear of men' and 'bear of the host'. A thirteenth-century copy of *Historia Brittonum* comments that Arthur in Latin translates as 'horrible bear'. He may have been named that at birth, acquired it as a nickname or been given it as kind of warrior name. There is a spate of Arthurs in the historical record for the late sixth and early seventh century: Arthur son of Aedan Mac Gabhrain of the Gaelic kingdom Dal Riada, killed in battle around 596; Artur ap Bicuir is recorded as killing an Ulster chieftain in 624; Arthur ap Pedr of Dyfed, grandson of Vortipor; an Irish Artur, grandfather of Faradach recorded in a law text of 697.[8] Some have suggested this is due to a historical Arthur a generation or more earlier making the name popular.

Let's consider the logic of that. First of all, Artorius was a perfectly common name throughout Roman times. Second, we have extensive examples of Celtic forms of Roman names. Third, these dates all seem far too late to be linked to any possible British Arthur fifty years either side of AD 500. Lastly, there are no British, or later Welsh examples as one would expect. These are all connected to Irish genealogies. We certainly do have various examples of Roman names such as Tacitus and Constantinus changing to Tegid and Custennin respectively. Or Gaius to

King Arthur: Man or Myth?

Kai. It's also important that we have no known further uses for 600 years until it was revived by the Norman romances.

There are theories linking Arthur to various gods. One example is Artio, a Gaulish bear goddess from Switzerland. Artaius, another Gaulish god, was linked to the Roman god Mercury but is considered to have been derived from the Gaulish 'artos', meaning bear. The Celtic god, Matunus, derives from the Celtic 'matu-', also meaning bear. There is no evidence to connect any of these with the Arthur of the *Historia* or any of the other later legends. There are similarities in Sarmatian and Alan tribal legends concerning swords, ladies in lakes and magical cups, but again there is no credible link. For example, one story has Sarmatians honouring a sword stuck in the ground. But there is no explanation of how this story evolved and travelled across several hundred years, with no evidence, to appear in the twelfth century. The simplest explanation is conveniently ignored: the first person to introduce the sword in the stone (actually an anvil on a stone) was Robert de Boron writing sometime around 1195–1210. He simply copied the story of St Galgano (1148–1181), who was canonised in 1185 and whose tomb did indeed contain a sword buried in rock. Interestingly, the sword can be viewed today and an analysis of the metal in 2001 found the sword is compatible with the era. Either that, or he made it up, but it's not our place to prove a negative or spend time disproving wild speculations.

The fact remains the Arthur of legend stems from Geoffrey of Monmouth's *History of the Kings of Britain* and later French romances. These in turn derive from a tradition that portray Arthur as living in Britain sometime either side of 500. The earliest of these references place him between the life of St Patrick and Ida of Northumbria. Whether he was fictitious or not, regardless of the intention or knowledge of the author of the *Historia*, that is when he is alleged to have lived. None of the legends place him in Roman Britain. There is an interesting Cornish legend that has him protecting Cornwall from the Vikings in the eighth century, but it's fair to say the bulk of the legends and all the earliest references place him in Britain at the end of the fifth century. Additionally, while there is an undoubted mythical and magical element, the core of the stories regard him as very human.

In summary, the name Arthur is a perfectly acceptable and common Roman name. The fact that it doesn't seem popular before or since suggests it wasn't commonly used by the Britons. Although the fact that

Arthur, the name

it was used by those with Irish connections is interesting. Having said all that, and I know this will be frustrating, it is also quite possible it was used as a type of Celtic nickname, bear-man. We can say many of the 'Arth-' type names in genealogies are in no way connected to or derived from Arthur. Thus, many of the theories proclaiming a favoured identification based on an 'Arth-' sounding name are flawed. There is no evidence the name is derived from a god or mythical figure.

The most likely explanation is that it is a Roman name. That doesn't mean he *was* Roman, or even Romano-British. Nor is it beyond the realms of possibility it was a Brythonic nickname. It doesn't mean he was historical, even if several centuries later people thought he was. Conversely, absence of evidence is not evidence of absence. If I were to speculate I would be torn between Ambrosius Aurelianus, placing a young Arturus in a position of command, and a Romano-British warrior either being called Arthurus or acquiring the nickname 'the Bear'. This makes the passage in Gildas so intriguing when he describes Cuneglasus as 'The bear'.

Chapter 17

Final Evidence

There are a variety of things we don't know. We don't know what the political and social situation was in Britain before the Romans left. We don't know for sure if there were four provinces or five, and we don't know if the northern provinces were overrun in Gildas's reports of marauding Irish and Picts. The fact the kingdoms of Rheged, Elmet, Gododdin and Strathclyde survived suggest the northern Britons remained a force. We don't know if the whole island spoke a Brythonic language or if there were widespread pockets of Germanic. The fact the Julius Caesar noted the Belgae tribe was present on both sides of the Channel suggests it is possible that languages other than Brythonic were present. The meaning of the phrase 'Saxon shore' is open to interpretation. Archaeological finds suggest Saxons were present much earlier than previously suspected, although it's always open to debate whether finds reflect changes in fashion or something more drastic. It does support the narrative that that Angles arrived in the middle of the fifth century and settled in the east of the island. Distinctive finds in Kent, Hampshire and Isle of Wight also support the idea that the Jutes were a distinctive group. It doesn't help that there's widespread misuse, even from Roman times, with labels such as Saxon.

Some sort of administrative structure may have continued after 410 and the visits by St Germanus in 429 and possibly in 437, or later, suggest some stability. The usually reliable *Gallic Chronicle* records a major power change in 440: 'Britain falls to the power of the Saxons.' Whether this relates to the revolt and subsequent partition recorded by Gildas is unclear. It could refer to an earlier political shift and the arrival of Hengist and subsequent revolt a separate incident. Alternatively, if they do concern the same circumstance, the dates are all slightly inaccurate, and the reference to Aetius, thrice consul, incorrect.

Final Evidence

However, the archaeological record does not support widespread destruction. In fact, a considerable amount of continuation in land use and occupation is evident. On the other hand, later, more reliable sources, do record conflict from the seventh century onwards and a steady expansion of what did become known as the Anglo-Saxon kingdoms. Looking back two or three centuries later these people did see themselves as different from the indigenous Romano-British population. The Law codes of Ine demonstrate this.

Thus we can summarise as follows: Roman Britain continued after 410. Something happened in the middle of the fifth century that shifted power to people described as Saxons. Whether these were immigrants, soldiers stationed in Britain, or part of the indigenous population is uncertain. There is then evidence of further Germanic immigration in the east of the island.

Gildas and Bede describe a process of revolt followed by a fight back by Ambrosius which culminates in the battle of Badon. This is followed by a couple of generations of peace. The consensus is that Gildas is writing in 540s and thus Badon is around 500. This is in no way certain. It's possible that the identification of Maglo with Maelgwn is wrong, the dates for Gildas's life are wrong and the interpretation of the passage concerning the '44 years' is also wrong.

So we are left with a Saxon revolt in 440 (*Gallic Chronicle*) and/or 450s (Bede, *Anglo-Saxon Chronicles*) followed by a period of warfare and an eventual fight-back by Ambrosius. It is not clear how long this period of warfare lasted but the victory of Mons Badonicus is certainly sometime between 450 and 550. In turn this is followed by a period of relative peace for two generations. The evidence from the *Anglo-Saxon Chronicles*, genealogies and literary sources begin to be more trustworthy towards the end of the sixth century. The beginnings of Anglo-Saxon kingdoms and further expansion appears to have began from 550 onwards.

Taking all the literary sources into account it is more likely that the battle was sometime between 470–520, and if we rely on Bede and the consensus about Gildas, some time between 490–500, although the *Welsh Annals* date it to 516. I suggest we keep the widest range and an open mind, because into this time period we must place Arthur. The first reference links him to two things: the battle of Badon and fighting the Saxons. Specifically after the death of Hengist in 488 (*Anglo-Saxon*

Chronicles) when Octha came from the north to rule the Kentishmen, but before the reign of Ida of Bernicia in around 547.

We can dismiss much of the legend attached to him. The story of Merlin was first attributed to Ambrosius in the *Historia Brittonum* and later attached to Myrddin Wylit to form a composite figure by Geoffrey of Monmouth. It may shock and disappoint the lay person, but it is likely that the Merlin figure in connection with Arthur is pure invention. The Round Table, Avalon, Camelot, Excalibur can also be explained as literary inventions or based on contemporary stories such as Charlemagne's round table and the sword of St Galgano. None of the later Welsh legends, Triads or saints' lives are in any way reliable, although the persistence of characters such as Guinevere, Uther and Mordred may be more credible than wizards and magic swords. Nothing Geoffrey of Monmouth wrote in 1136, or any other later literary source, can be taken seriously.

We are, therefore, left with a very vague picture with little evidence. A warrior, living sometime between 450 and 550, fighting with the kings of Britain against the Saxons. Possibly connected with Badon and a later Camlann, where he falls. The evidence we have left falls into four main categories:

1. One reference in a possible seventh-century poem comparing a warrior to Arthur.
2. The list of twelve battles in the *Historia Brittonum* written in the early ninth century.
3. Two references in the *Annales Cambriae* written in the mid-tenth century.
4. The existence of four persons called Arthur in genealogies at the end of the sixth century, suggesting the name became popular.

Some may claim the existence and persistence of a body of legends and myths enduring several hundred years does carry some weight. The fact that these legends exist and were believed means something. I have sympathy with this view, but it's difficult to value it as evidence when none of it can be verified and it's hundreds of years out of date. So we are left with the very real possibility that Arthur was a mythical character or literary device. If a historical character, then we are left to

Final Evidence

attempt to place him in the correct period. The saints' lives all point to the early sixth century in Wales and the South in particular, but none are contemporary or trustworthy.

Two main sources could be used to place a possible Arthur in a specific time. The first is the *Historia Brittonum*, stating Arthur fought after Hengist but before Ida. If we trust the other sources this means between 488 and 547, and yet these sources are no more reliable than the *Historia*. Given the contradictory statements within the document about the date of the coming of the Saxons, it is possible the entry for Arthur is misplaced as well and this might be important, given some of the possible identifications which are outside the time period. The second source is the *Annales Cambriae*, but the dates and entries are no more reliable either. In fact, the two entries concerning Arthur may have derived from the *Historia Brittonum* or have been added much later.

A common thread does emerge from the sources, however. The last legions leave Britain around 410, this is followed by a period of incursions and raids. Vortigern invites the Saxons who, a short time later, rebel. Ambrosius leads a fight-back that culminates in the battle of Badon, but some partition of the island has occurred. There then follows a period of stability and relative peace. Sometime between 550 and 600 the Anglo-Saxons start to expand once more. In the legends, when Arthur is placed into a timeframe, it is always after Ambrosius, in the context of fighting the Saxons and in being successful although later falling in a civil war. This timeline, Vortigern, Hengist, Ambrosius, Arthur, time of peace and fall, starts sometime after 410 and is certainly finished before 600. This puts Arthur sometime in between, but not too close to either of these two extremes.

This suggests three possible times in which to place him:

1. An early Arthur in the period 450–480. This would fall in line with Vortigern gaining power in 425 and the arrival of the Saxons in 428 as stated in one part of the *Historia Brittonum*. It would suggest a Saxon revolt in the late 430s and support the *Gallic Chronicle* entry for 440. This would place Ambrosius around 450 and presumably Badon sometime in the 460s or

470s. This would make Arthur a contemporary of Riothamus in 471. It would mean he was active at the same time as the Romano-Saxon wars of the 460s, the expansion of the Franks and Visigoths and the final fall of the Western Empire in 476. It would mean the dating and/or interpretation of Gildas is wrong and Bede's dates are all inaccurate. It would also dismiss the dates in the *Annales Cambriae* for Badon and Camlann. Additionally, Hengist arriving in the prime of his fighting life in 428 is unlikely to be still fighting battles in the 450s–70s, and later dying in 488 as recorded in the *Anglo-Saxon Chronicles*. It also doesn't explain the implied Saxon strength of Aelle in the *Anglo-Saxon Chronicles* from 477–91 and his description of Bretwalda by Bede.

2. A middle Arthur between 480–510. This is possibly the most popular and best fit based on the sources. This wouldn't necessarily dismiss an early Vortigern or Saxon arrival. A Vortigern gaining power in 425, might have received several groups of mercenaries and might still have been in power in 449 to welcome Hengist. This would agree with Bede and the *Anglo-Saxon Chronicles* for a revolt and battles in the 450s. This would place Ambrosius either side of the 470s and would fall into line with Bede's reference in the *Chronica Majora* regarding Ambrosius being active during the reign of Zeno (474–91). This would make Ambrosius a contemporary with Riothamus. A battle of Badon after 491 would explain the ending of references to Aelle in the *Anglo-Saxon Chronicles* and the gap of seventy years between the Bretwaldas, Aelle and Ceawlin, recorded by Bede. It would fall into line with archaeological evidence and the traditional dating for Bede, as well as the narrative of two generations of relative peace before the Anglo-Saxons start expanding again. It would make Arthur a contemporary of Clovis and the fall of the last Roman rump state, the kingdom of Soissons, in 486. Against this are the entries in the *Anglo-Saxon Chronicles* for the arrival of Cerdic in 495 (or 514 or even 532 depending on interpretation) and subsequent battles, which would contradict the narrative of two generations of peace. Also, it doesn't conform with the dates in the *Annales Cambriae* for Badon or Camlann.

Final Evidence

3. A later Arthur between 510–40. This is supported by the entries in the *Annales Cambriae* for Badon and Camlann and the date given for Arthur's death in the *History of the Kings of Britain* by Geoffrey of Monmouth. It is more in line with later stories which place him a generation before Myrddin Wylit and Taliesin and connect him with various Welsh saints, mainly in the first-half of the sixth century. It is not inconsistent with the *Historia Brittonum* and could be supported by the reverse emigration of Angles around 531 from Britain to Frankia during the Thuringian War. On the other hand it goes against the narrative and dates found in Gildas, Bede and the *Anglo-Saxon Chronicles*, although if Gildas has been misinterpreted and misdated, subsequent sources would have been affected.

Bearing all that in mind, a list of various suspects have been put forward by a range of different authors. One or two might fall outside the suggested time periods above.

Table 31

Figure	For	Against
Lucius Artorius Castus 140–197	Named Arthur. Fought battles in Britain and possibly Gaul.	Too early to be credible. No supporting sources in the well-documented centuries after. No evidence he fought against Saxons. Can't have fought at Badon.
Vortimer mid-fifth century	Correct time period. Fought against Saxons. Victorious in all his battles.	Only mentioned in one source. Portrayed as separate figure in earliest source that mentions both. Not called Arthur.
Ambrosius Aurelianus mid-fifth century	Correct time period. Fought against Saxons. Connected to Badon by Gildas.	Not called Arthur. Portrayed as separate figure by *Historia Brittonum* and later legends.

(continued)

Table 31: (Continued)

Figure	For	Against
Riothamus 460–70	Correct time period. Fought in Gaul. Name maybe a title – High King.	Not called Arthur. No record of presence in Britain.
Arthwys ap Mar mid-fifth century	Correct time period. 'Arth-' type name. Linked to northern kingdoms through genealogies.	Name not a derivative of Arthur. Genealogies not reliable. No evidence of battles or any other connection.
Owain Danwyn (white-tooth) late fifth century	Correct time period. King of Rhos. Father of Cynlas possibly referenced by Gildas with 'bear' imagery.	Not called Arthur. No evidence of battles or any other connection. Genealogies not reliable.
Cynlas early sixth century	Correct time period. king of Rhos. Possibly referenced by Gildas with 'bear' imagery.	Not called Arthur. No evidence of battles or any other connection.
Artuir ap Pedr circa 550–620?	Name a derivative of Arthur. Correct time period. King of Dyfed.	More likely to have lived end of sixth century. No evidence of battles or any other connection.
Artuir mac Aedan circa 560–96	Called Arthur. Historically attested figure. Fought many battles against Saxons. Many of the battles possibly linked to northern sites. Possibly fought at Dun Baetan in Ireland in 574.	End of sixth century and a little late for a historical Arthur. Localised battles ending in defeat. No record of contemporaries or later sources regarding him as the Arthur of legend.

	Son of a king.	
	Plethora of landmarks with Arthur connection.	
Athrwys ap Meurig circa 610–80	'Arth-' type name. King of Gwent	Outside likely time period. Most sources name him Atroys or similar. No evidence of battles or any other connection.

Some of these theories are very plausible on face value, but they can't all be Arthur. As we have seen, it doesn't have to be any of these. It could well be, in fact is more likely to be, someone not in any genealogies. To put it bluntly: we need a body. Some suggest he is just as likely to be a mythical figure historicised by the ninth century than he is to be a historical character.[1] One example would be Fionn in Gaelic literature.[2] One of his deeds was building the Giant's Causeway, yet he eventually was historicised in repelling Viking invaders. The processing of historicising legends was widespread in the Middle Ages hence the proliferation of foundation myths among the Romans, Franks, Anglo-Saxons and Britons. Other examples might be Robin Hood, William Tell and Sherlock Holmes. Supporting the theory of a mythical figure it is worth noting the following: much of the Welsh sources describe a legendary figure, often associated with magic. There's very little association with fighting Saxons or Badon. In an age before modern communications, the printing press and widespread literacy narratives lose their accuracy and reliability beyond about five generations. We must bare in mind that your grandfather might be able to relate reasonably accurately what *his* grandfather told him, but beyond that facts get distorted. We know how unreliable even eye-witness statements can be, or how conspiracy theories can form even days after an event. Thus some have suggested that beyond about 200 years we can no longer trust an account as contemporary.[3]

We do have the twelve battles in Nennius, the entries in the *Annales Cambriae* and the *Dream of Rhonabwy*, although the latter is set in the twelfth century and the earliest copy is from the fourteenth, so its validity is called into question. The *Annales Cambriae* was written in the tenth century and doesn't record against whom the Britons were fighting. In any event it is likely derived from the only early source that connects

Arthur with Badon and the Saxons, which is the ninth-century *Historia Brittonum*. The vast bulk of the Welsh myths and saints' lives portray a petty king or warrior often engaged in quests and supernatural events. It is possible that he was a mythical figure used in sagas and myths whose story evolved over 300 years. The figure and story then became historicised by the ninth century. All the subsequent Welsh legends stemmed from that before Geoffrey of Monmouth and the romance authors expanded it further.

There is an early Welsh poem, *Armes Prydein*, dated to the tenth century from the *Book of Taliesin*. It extols the Brythonic people to lead the Scots, Irish and Vikings to rise up and drive the Anglo-Saxons out. It mentions various Welsh heroes such as Cadwallon ap Cadfan and Cadwaladr ap Cadwallon, but not Arthur. There's very little indication that Arthur was seen as a major heroic Welsh figure prior to the twelfth century. Most of the early Welsh legends portray a fantastical mythological character.

Referring back to the *Historia Brittonum*, if, for argument's sake, we discount all the other evidence and just look at the sections between Vortigern and Ida, we can ask the following question: are there any figures in the text we know are fictional? Some, such as Vortimor, are not mentioned elsewhere, but I'm looking for definite falsehoods from the author. Although the foundation myth of Brutus and the later marvels of Britain lack credibility, there's nothing in those sections after Maximus that is a provable lie.

Something started the stories, and those stories were of such interest they persisted for several hundred years. While the story evolved, several key points remained. A warrior, perhaps a king, fighting successfully for the Britons. While swords, tables, grails and family tree may have been added or changed, his father, mother and wife appear to be consistent, and it must be remembered that Geoffrey of Monmouth's Arthur didn't appear out of nowhere. There was a fertile ground full of Arthurian myths which must have been present 600 years after he lived. Regardless of the later stories, the fact is the original persisted strongly, possibly through many changes, for 600 years. Given that, is it not more likely to be based on historical fact rather than some mythical figure?

The case for Arthur's existence might conclude as follows: we have a period of history between the Romans leaving at the start of the fifth century, and the emergence of Anglo-Saxon kingdoms towards the end of the sixth, for which we have little information. However, the sources

Final Evidence

seem to agree on a basic narrative. Roman Britain persisted for some time before a leader named Vortigern invited Germanic mercenaries to assist in repelling Irish and Pictish raids. There was a revolt and subsequent fight-back led by Ambrosius Aurelianus which culminated in the battle of Badon. There then followed a period of relative stability before the Anglo-Saxons expanded once more. Despite the lack of archaeological evidence for widespread warfare, the eventual emergence of those kingdoms appears to support this. In this mix we have Arthur. There is no reason to doubt his entry in that particular section of the *Historia Brittonum* any more than St Patrick or Ida, who are either side in the text. Likewise, there is no evidence that any of the entries in the *Annales Cambriae* are incorrect. The weight of other materials suggest there was a belief in the early Middle Ages, and beyond that Arthur was real.

There is a consistency in the narratives. His parents are always Uthr Pendragon and Eigr or Ygraine, his wife Gwenhwyfar. His sword Caledfwich, Latinised as Caliburn later, under French influence, changed to Calibur then Escalibur. We can see the evolution of the story across time. But the core remains and it is a story that has persisted down several centuries. The argument is not that the evidence is strong, nor does it rely on the 'no smoke without fire' argument. The position is, despite the evolution of the legend, there is a core, consistent, story. Arthur's story is not at all incompatible with the narrative in Bede or other sources. Academics have been unduly cautious in dismissing the evidence in the *Historia Brittonum* and *Annales Cambriae*. I would remind readers of the historical consensus concerning Troy. It was generally thought that Homer's *Iliad* was legend and Troy a myth, until the 1870s when Heinrich Schliemann uncovered the evidence.

The case to dismiss a historical Arthur as fictional might go like this: it is not for us to prove a negative. We are not required to prove for certain someone did not exist. The only requirement is to show there is not enough evidence, even on the balance of probabilities, and in doing so, the academic community has not been negligent or over-cautious in dismissing a historical Arthur. There are hundreds of fictional and unattested characters throughout historical sources. To ascertain if one has historical validity one must have evidence and that evidence must be of the appropriate standard. Lots of bad evidence is still bad evidence. Geoffrey of Monmouth is bad evidence. Worse than that, he is a thoroughly untrustworthy witness. All the so-called sources that come after him are tainted by his influence, but are poor in their own right as well as being far too distant in time to be considered. The Welsh legends also are too late to consider. The only evidence that could be considered has been found wanting.

To summarise the evidence we have:

The one line in *Y Gododdin*: Even if I grant it is a sixth-century entry, it doesn't follow that it refers to our Arthur. It could just as easily refer to a local Arthur. Even if it does refer to the Arthur of legend as understood by the populace in the early Middle Ages, it doesn't follow that he was not fictional. The apparent naming of three or four people as Arthur in the sixth century does not show that they were named after a historical character – it could easily be a coincidence. The numbers are so small it could be that records are just too poor for preceding years. It also doesn't mean they were named after a historical figure. Names are popularised today from films, celebrities, royalty and books. The only reason we consider someone like Artorius Castus is because of his name. If we had hundreds of Arthurs to chose from, he would likely be bottom of the list of suspects. It is similarly poor evidence to latch onto any figure with an 'Arth-' type name who lived any time near the period at which we are looking.

The argument about the weight of legendary material is simply the 'no smoke without fire' argument. It has no merit. We have hundreds of religious and mythical stories with a huge 'weight of material'. It doesn't follow all those stories are true; for that we need evidence. Which leaves me with the last two pieces of evidence. The *Annales Cambriae* was written 400 years after the supposed events and are not considered reliable by the academic community. They are simply not contemporary enough. It is likely the entries for Arthur derive from our last bit of evidence. The *Historia Brittonum* was written around 830, 300 years after the events. It contains a mass of contradictory dates and stories alongside mythical and magical entries. It is not considered at all valid or credible as a historical document, other than for what it shows about the time it was written. There is no reason to dismiss the magical references, but respect the battle list attributed to Arthur. If we had proper evidence, we wouldn't be looking at this at all. The only reason people spend so much time and effort on such poor evidence is because credible and valid sources do not exist. We have no credible evidence that is even within the 200-year period necessary for it to be considered – even at the far end of the definition of contemporary. Nothing within the memory of the oldest person living at the time, or even a grandparent of a grandparent, that could have been passed down.

We have rigorous historical methods and standards and it would be a great mistake to lower those standards. We have some contemporary evidence, both in Britain and on the Continent. It doesn't include an Arthur. If evidence identifying a historical figure presents itself, then it can be examined and possibly accepted. Until then we have no need of an Arthur and we shouldn't force historians to accept or invent one to satisfy our imagination.

Having covered those two arguments for and against in summary, we now have to ask ourselves the following: on the balance of probabilities, is there credible evidence for a historical Arthur? The evidence is sparse. One line in a possibly contemporary poem, together with an apparent popularisation of the name. A reference, albeit detailed, 300 years after the event and another 100 years later. Then a large body of legends and stories, what has been described as the 'no smoke without fire' argument. How much weight you give to each of these is for you to decide, I will lay out my theory in the discussion section next.

Discussion

Like many interested in the subject, I started hoping and wishing that such a figure existed, but perhaps willing to accept the evidence might not be there as yet. As I went through the sources I came to the disappointing conclusion that there is at least the possibility he did not exist and he was entirely a mythical figure. It's difficult to put a percentage on this, but the likelihood of Arthur being mythical or a real figure now seems a lot closer than I had previously hoped. Because of this, I found myself reluctantly moving my position from Arthur being a historical figure on the balance of probabilities, to one of there simply not being enough evidence to support this.

That, however, seems to me the easy way out, so let me remove that option and force myself to choose between a mythical or historical figure. There is a reasonable chance that either option is correct. I have to concede, I am biased; I want there to be an Arthur. I'm sure most people would say the same. Who would want him to be mythical? Who would give up the possibility of solving the mystery? But hopefully I can detach myself from my prejudices and base it on the evidence.

King Arthur: Man or Myth?

Regarding the possibility of a mythical figure, it has to be accepted there are countless examples throughout history of a mythical figure becoming historicised. There is plenty of evidence that even eye-witness accounts can be faulty and the prevalence of modern conspiracy theories, many of them contradictory, demonstrates that even in our own time a false narrative can gain traction. Within a few generations it can become distorted further and the truth forgotten. But it's a curious myth to develop, based as it is upon a very Roman-sounding name. In addition, one must consider the purpose of the *Historia Brittonum*, which was to inspire his contemporary ninth-century audience. It was written, I believe, with the expectation that the core story would be believed. We could say the same about the twelfth-century work of Geoffrey of Monmouth of course, which is riddled with falsehoods. There certainly was a great body of legends which had survived for the 600 years up to his time. Yet it may well be that 'history keeps peeking through the gaps'. But Geoffrey cannot be trusted. As a witness he would be dismissed for his unreliability and lack of credibility. If we are to be consistent and rigorous with evidence, we must also dismiss all the later legends, stories and French romances.

This means no Avalon, it's far too similar to other legends involving islands and nine maidens which existed separately to the Arthurian stories. It also means no Camelot, unless it's some corruption of Caerleon, which is recorded as Arthur's courts by Geoffrey of Monmouth. The Round Table is an obvious late addition and the simplest explanation is that it was stolen from Charlemagne's story. Arthur's sword was originally Caledfwlch and seems too similar to the Irish legendary sword Caladbolg. We can see the evolution from Caledfwlch to Caliburn, Calibur, Escalibur and so on. Its attributes are also similar to Charlemagne's sword, *Joyeuse*. The fact many of the additions arrive via Breton or Norman sources may be no coincidence.

There is no Lancelot, no lady in the lake, and most certainly no Holy Grail. Likewise the sword in the stone seems far too similar to the legend of St Galgano. I have a soft spot for the legend of the London Stone, where someone in authority touches the stone with his sword, but my liking of a legend doesn't make it true. Similarly, the idea of Arthur leading a cavalry unit is just guesswork. It may well be true, but there is no evidence. Perhaps he hated horses and was an infantryman throughout. Perhaps he hated swords and preferred a Frankish axe in

Final Evidence

battle. Nor can we speculate on Sarmatian cavalry or Eastern-European legends travelling thousands of miles and hundreds of years to appear in some veiled way with no clear evidence.

So what is left once we strip away the layers of the legend? We have a warrior; later legends call him a king or even emperor, although that goes too far. If king, it is a petty king, and he is one of many. He's most certainly Christian as is the society in which he lives. His parents are consistently named Uthr and Eigr or Igraine. His wife is Gwenhwyfar, and Mordred is possibly his cousin or nephew. It is worth mentioning in general terms about all the various theories put forward, many of which rely on the interpretation of genealogies. What seems clear is that none of the earliest genealogies mention Arthur or his parents and are all written hundreds of years after he is supposed to have lived. Later sources, in their attempt to add his family to existing lines, cannot be trusted. Nor can we interpret any 'Arth-' type name any way we like. Too many of the theories ride roughshod over the genealogies, locations and battle names to arrive at self-serving and highly suspect translations and interpretations. What we can say for sure is they can't all be right.

With that in mind I advise looking at two main sources for information. First, the original source material. This means good translations of Gildas, Bede, Nennius and the *Anglo-Saxon Chronicles*. Second, books, papers and research by respected academics. I looked at degree-level courses online to find out what text books were required and found academics like Dumville, Davies, Higham, Yorke and Bartrum invaluable. In addition, the references in these books and papers allow one to build up a library of credible sources. Prior to this I had read many of the theories and thought many were reasonable and plausible. After researching the sources and the experts, however, I reread them and found many to be lacking in credibility. In short, none of them are wholly convincing.

There are several geographical areas that appear to be of greater interest than others:

1. The South Wales region: Connected through the lives of the saints. St David's is named as one of his courts in the Triads. Caerleon is named as his palace by Geoffrey of Monmouth and may be the 'city of the legion' listed as one of his battles.
2. The North: Linked to northern genealogies as a great-great-grandson of Coel Hen. Linked to next generation through other characters,

King Arthur: Man or Myth?

Urien, Owain, Lot and Myrddin Wylit. At least one of the battles, Celidon Wood, is likely to have been in the north, but several others have been suggested. The northern military command led by the Dux Britanniarum was the strongest in the post-Roman provinces. Originally based at York and controlling Hadrian's Wall, it would likely be involved with any northern battles.
3. Lincoln: The most likely site of the four battles in the 'region of the Linnuis'. Could be defended from northern forces based at York.
4. Wroxeter area: The Roman city appears to be one of the few that shows signs of development into the sixth century. A major centre in the original kingdom of Powys, it is close to Baschurch, Caer Faddon, Buxton, Chester, the river Gamlan and many other sites suggested as possible battle identifications. It may have been the location of Cuneglasus, one of Gildas's five kings.
5. West country: Contains Amesbury, which has been suggested derives from Ambrosius, and later legends claim Guinevere retired to a convent. Close to Cadbury hill fort, Glastonbury and Bath, all associated with the later legends. Some of the saints' lives place him across the Severn or in Devon or Somerset.
6. Cornwall: Includes one of his courts at Kelliwig but also Tintagel and Camlann from Geoffrey of Monmouth.

From a military point of view and the likely identification of some of the battles, a northern commander based at York seems more logical. Yet many of the Welsh legends do seem to focus on South Wales and the West Country. The fact that the most likely battle sites appear to range fairly widely from the Caledonian Forest to Lincoln does not suggest a local petty ruler operating in one small area. What is clear is that there is no association with the south east. Outside of Geoffrey of Monmouth and later stories, cities such as London, Canterbury and Colchester do not feature at all.

If we decide that Arthur is historical, the next useful step is to decide if he falls in the time on which we are focused. If not, then we have to accept Nennius wildly misplaced him. Given the amount of historical knowledge it's unlikely such a figure could have gone unnoticed or misidentified either before 400 or after 600. The only likely candidate is Artur Mac Aedan of Dalriada. It is true that one could interpret all the twelve battles as being in the north, but we have to wonder why he became

Final Evidence

so famous as a British and later Welsh hero, and not as an Irish or later Scottish one. We also have a *Life of St Columba* who was a contemporary of Artur, although it was written a century later by Adomnan. Yet there is no connection made, either in this or any other source, that Artur was the Arthur of legend. So we are left with the period in which Nennius places him; that is after St Patrick but before Ida of Northumbria.

This brings us back to the three options left to us in the last chapter: an early Arthur 450–80; a middle Arthur 480–510; or a late Arthur 510–40. Each choice requires us to depart from some sources. It requires us to address certain questions:

- What does the *Gallic Chronicle* for 440 signify?
- How to interpret Gildas, especially his reference to Badon and forty-four years?
- How does Bede's date for the Saxon arrival square with the *Gallic Chronicle*?
- How to interpret the apparent double entry of Cerdic in the *Anglo-Saxon Chronicles*?

Let us first consider the political situation between Constantine III and circa 440 when the *Gallic Chronicle* records 'Britain falls to the power of the Saxons.' First, we can be fairly sure about what did not happen. We did not have a homogenous Romano-British society with no political, tribal, geographical or religious divides. Nor did we have one great mass of Anglo-Saxons, equally homogenous, who turned up en masse one day. We didn't have some fluctuating border moving back and forth with the fortunes of war.

We know there were political divisions at the start. Constantine left behind an administration, but the Britons rebelled against them and appealed straight to the emperor. Honorius's reply wasn't to the Vicarius or Provincial Governors, but to the civitates. So there was some tension between central control of the island, the provinces and civitates. We don't know if the provincial structure survived. Add to this tribal affinities; the fact that some tribal areas and civitates, such as Kent, survived even to this day, demonstrates there was continuity. However, it is unknown how much influence, if any, former tribal loyalties held. Then throw in religions tensions between the Pelagians and Orthodox Christians. There was also already a significant immigrant, and in particular, Saxon, population. Lastly, there was undoubtedly differing opinions regarding Rome and its influence. The letter-writers of 409 clearly felt connected to Rome, as did the appellants to Aetius a generation later. St Patrick referring to 'citizens', and Gildas referring to the 'last of the Romans', demonstrates the persistence of the link.

All these competing forces and agendas would not have lived in a vacuum of time and place, but would have shifted and changed across geography and time. For example, one can imagine trading ports and cities wishing to retain links with Rome and Gaul, while some tribal leaders flexed their muscles for independence. At the same time, some figures might have dreamed of following the footsteps of Constantine I, Maximus and Constantine III, uniting Britannia and declaring themselves emperor. Ethnic tensions may have risen, not just between Germanic immigrants and Romano-British, but between rival tribal areas. The religious divide on the Continent was often between Arian barbarians and Roman Orthodox Christians, although in Britain there are hints it also was between wealthy Pelagians and the more orthodox population. It's tempting to think the appellants to Honorius in 409 had destroyed the Provincial structure, so perhaps there were no Governors to exert control, and yet as late as 540 Gildas claims, 'Britain she has Governors, she has her watchmen'. From Gildas and Bede we hear there was a council of sorts, before approximately 450, to appeal to Aetius and hire mercenaries. Gildas certainly views the Romano-British as separate from the Saxons. He appeals to them as a whole, over the top of what he views as tyrant kings.

We have the makings of a complex and potentially dangerous political, racial, tribal and religious situation similar to many others throughout history, whether in the Balkans, Northern Ireland or Iraq. Yet the situation was calm enough to allow St Germanus to travel from Gaul in 429 and again years later. No kings are mentioned, but he meets a man of tribune rank. The people are Christian and on his second visit he's able to remove the offending heretics. Clearly there is some sort of structure. There appears to be an army still, if one believes the story of the Alleluia Victory over the Pictish and Saxon raid. The archaeological evidence suggests towns and cities started to diminish in the fifth century, and yet there is still continuity. Hill forts start to be rebuilt and used; the economy starts to suffer and coinage begins to disappear. Yet Gildas reports that cities are not populated as before rather than completely deserted, and

Final Evidence

some sites, such as Wroxeter, show expansion at this time. Here is where my first deviation from mainstream theory occurs. I think the second visit of St Germanus was in 437 rather than 447. I'm convinced by the evidence presented earlier, but also it just doesn't make sense if he visited after the incident that resulted in the *Gallic Chronicle* entry for 440. He would certainly have had something to say about that.

I think this is a very important date and it is another point on which I differ from past theories. Most people attempt to reconcile the 440 date with Bede's *Adventus Saxonum* of 449. In the great scheme of things nine years doesn't seem too great an obstacle to explain away. Yet when one looks at the sources of the *Chronicle* and Bede, the dates pull away from each other even more. It seems clear to me that this entry is accurate and the date, if anything, is before 440. What this means is a fundamental rethink of Gildas. Rather than the appeal being because of the Picts, it's more likely due to this event. All those competing forces present between 410 and 440 come to a head. Perhaps the Saxon Shore forts break away under a Saxon leader. Perhaps the South East civitates or Province does likewise. So the entry in the *Chronicle* and the events reported by Bede are recording two separate events. I would like to put forward three possible alternatives:

1. There is a Saxon and Pictish rebellion/incursion, more successful than the one encountered by St Germanus ten years previously. This results in the *Gallic Chronicle* reporting that Britain falls to the power of the Saxons and Gildas reports the Picts take land 'as far as the wall'. There is then an appeal to Aetius in 446. Subsequently, Angle and Jutish mercenaries are hired in 449 and it is this group who later rebel.
2. The narrative in Nennius is accurate in that mercenaries are invited around 428. He then goes on to describe further reinforcements, a marriage to a Saxon princess, being ceded Kent, the arrival of forty more ships, Vortimer's four battles and poisoning, the Saxons returning and being 'incorporated', the night of the long knives and the Saxons being ceded several districts. So the *Gallic Chronicle* and Bede's account could be describing two separate things within this. For example, the *Gallic Chronicle* could refer to a political change: Vortigern's marriage, Kent being handed over or Vortimer's death and subsequent return of Hengist. Bede on the other hand

could be referring to the return of the Saxons after Vortigern retakes the throne and their being 'incorporated'. The night of the long knives and taking over several districts in the South East could be the rebellion in Gildas.
3. The two dates do describe the same event, but the sources and timings are mistaken, meaning one, or both, sources are inaccurate.

I favour the first option, as we cannot completely trust Nennius. However, let us not forget that, other than the persistence of the legend over several hundred years, the *Historia Brittonum* is the only source that mentions Arthur within 300 years. So while I will conclude with an overall timeline, I will also attempt to create a timeline that best fits all the sources.

Once we accept that the *Gallic Chronicle* is a credible source, the next point in the sequence is the appeal to Aetius. There is no good reason to doubt it is Aetius, and the appeal is made when he is 'thrice consul'. On the balance of probabilities, we will accept the appeal took place some time after 446. The next point is the appeal for mercenaries. Gildas labels them Saxons but Bede is quite clear that their leaders, Hengist and Horsa, are the eventual rulers of Kent and they are Jutes. He placed their arrival within 'the time of Marcian and Valentinian', 449–55. While Bede relies on Gildas he has access to other sources and clearly nothing has caused him to deviate from Gildas. Additionally, any Germanic immigrants in the 'east of the island', or to the north east, near the wall, are more likely to have been Angles.

The *Anglo-Saxon Chronicle* now comes into play. It records battles in 455 and 456, one of them apparently identical to one of Vortimer's battles in Nennius. This could be the rebellion to which Gildas and Bede refer, thus the fight-back of Ambrosius occurs in the 460s. However, I would put forward an alternative, purely in an attempt to satisfy the *Historia Brittonum*. Vortimer is briefly successful but dies in the 450s. The Angles/Jutes return and are 'incorporated' (given official foederati status). Then there is the 'night of the long knives', where 300 British nobles are slain and the 'Saxons' are ceded Essex, Sussex, Middlesex and other districts. Could this be the rebellion? If so, then following the chronology it is more likely to be in the 460s. Interestingly, one of the entries in the *Anglo-Saxon Chronicle*

Final Evidence

for 465 records twelve Welsh chieftains being killed near Wipped's Creek. A flight of fancy I know, but perhaps the 300 nobles killed in Nennius is an exaggeration of the same event. Regardless, this puts the rebellion in the 460s, which makes Ambrosius more likely to start his fight-back in the 470–80s.

I am guilty of the same level of speculation of which I've accused others. However, if Bede is to be trusted, the Saxons arrived around 449 and Ambrosius was active 'in the time of Zeno', which means 474–91. When placing Arthur in the chronology it is rather academic what happened prior to Ambrosius if we can place him around 480, because Arthur is always after him in the narrative. The simplest answer to the riddle would be for Arturus Ambrosius Aurelianus to be the victor of Badon *and* the basis of the legend, in the same way Magnus Maximus became Macsen Wledig in Welsh legends. It wouldn't be the greatest surprise if evidence of that was discovered. However, the narrative is fairly consistent. Ambrosius is a separate person and Arthur comes after him. So let us move on to another controversial interpretation.

What did Gildas mean in his passage about Badon and forty-four years? If the mercenaries arrived between 449–55 and Ambrosius is active between 474–91, the start of his forty-four-year period could refer to either of these dates or to Badon, which he doesn't date. The end of this forty-four-year period could also mean either Badon or the time of Gildas writing. So when Gildas says forty-four years has passed, there are a number of interpretations:

1. The simplest is that he is writing forty-four years after Badon and at the time of Malicun (Maelgwn), 534–47. This means Badon was fought between 490–503.
2. Bede, writing 200 years later, with access to other sources plus perhaps a more recent copy of Gildas, interprets the text as forty-four years after the Adventus Saxonum, 449–55, placing Badon 493–99.
3. Badon occurred forty-four years after the first victory of Ambrosius, which Bede places in 474–91, leaving Badon 518–35.
4. Gildas is writing forty-four years after the first victory of Ambrosius, and Badon occurred at some point in between. However, given he states external wars have ended and a generation has passed since that

victory, this suggests Badon is closer to the time of Ambrosius than that of Maelgwn. Thus Ambrosius could have began his fightback as late as 490, Gildas could be writing in 534, and Badon could have occurred a generation before in 516, satisfying the *Annales Cambriae*.

It is unlikely to mean, as some have suggested, that he is writing a month after Badon and forty-four years after either Ambrosius or the arrival of the Saxons. This is because he makes it very clear that external wars have ceased and there's been a generation that has forgotten the horrors of that time. We are therefore left with two choices for the battle of Badon: a date in the 490s corresponding with Bede, or a date nearer to that in the *Annales Cambriae* entry for the year 516.

It is fair to say that most academics seem to favour the earlier date, but before we explore that further I want to focus on the genealogies; I want to reflect the fact that they simply don't stand up as credible evidence. Written centuries later for dubious purposes, it is impossible to know if they were written to 'fit' the timespan in the *Historia Brittonum*. Anyone writing a saint's life or a king's list in the twelfth century would try to attach their subject to a well-known figure of the time.

Our information is confined to a limited and non-contemporary number of sources: Harleian genealogies British library MS 3859 dated to the twelfth century; Northern genealogies (Bonedd Gwyr y Gogledd) dated to late thirteenth century; Genealogies from Jesus College (MS 20) compiled in late fourteenth century and includes a number of Welsh lineages especially those of South Wales; various saints' lives; various references in Welsh legends and Triads. If we put all this together we start to see an emerging picture, but are confronted with a problem straight away and it involves Cunedda.

Nennius refers to him as being 146 years before Maelgwn. Yet the genealogies have him as a great-grandfather. If Maelgwn reigns from 534–47 as suspected from the annals, we can estimate his birth to be around 500. If there's twenty-five years per generation, his father would have been born 475, grandfather in 450 and Cunedda in 425. It's very difficult to argue Cunedda moving to North Wales at fighting age in 388, and then three successive generations having children at the age of 40–50. The genealogy tables suggest Cunedda was born in the first quarter of the fifth century and moved to North Wales after the 'Adventus Saxonum' in 449. Or in other words, around the same time as Vortigern's mercenaries were hired or in response to the revolt. There is no evidence for any of this and people writing genealogy tables or saints' lives hundreds of years after the event would be trying to do exactly as we are doing here. However we can attempt to build a picture starting from before Cunedda.

The two main families are connected by marriage, with Cunedda marrying Coel Hen's daughter, Gwawl. If we label Magnus Maximus generation one, Coel Hen and Cunedda become generation three in approximately 400–50. His sons are generation four, 425–75. This is where it becomes interesting because Arthur, if he existed, should be in generation five or six to be fighting fit at Badon in either the 490s or 510s. Cunedda also had a daughter, Gwen, who married Amlawd Wledig. They in turn have a daughter, Eigr or Igraine, who marries Uthr Bendragon in generation five, 450–500. Which would place Uthr's supposed brother, Ambrosius, also in that time, allowing for him to be of fighting age 'in the time of Zeno', 474–91. What all this means is that Arthur is the same generation as Maelgwn and not the one before as many suppose. They are both great-grandsons of Cunedda. This doesn't mean they are the same age, they could easily be twenty-five years, or a whole generation, apart. Given that Cunedda had nine sons and at least one daughter, it's quite likely there is about twenty years from oldest to youngest.

Looking at Coel Hen's descendants, it shows Urien fighting against Bernicians in the 570s and various cousins, along with Peredur and Myrddin, fighting at Arfderydd in 573. We can thus work backwards from those figures to estimate when others lived. Within these two families we have a variety of saints and characters later connected to the Arthur story. Other families are separate from these including the kings of Dyfed, including Vortipor and Vortigern's family. The Brittany connection describes Ambrosius's father as being Constantius, brother of King Aldroneus, a fourth generation from Conan Meriadoc. If Meriadoc was connected to Magnus Maximus, this could indeed place Ambrosius in 'the time of Zeno'.

It does, however, mean Vortigern's floruit must have been long to allow for his sons to be fighting Hengist and Horsa in the 450s and for him to be deposed by Ambrosius in the 470s–80s. The stumbling block to this is the pillar of Eliseg which shows Vortigern married to Severa, daughter of Magnus Maximus, who died in 388. It is not impossible for Vortigern to be born in 390, marry Severa, obtain the crown in 425, have children of fighting age in 450 and still be in power aged 70 in the 460s. Far more likely Nennius is simply mistaken, there are two Vortigerns (high kings) or the pillar of Eliseg is mistaken.

Table 32: Genealogies compared

Generation with known example	House of Coel Hen	House of Cunedda	Kings of Brittany and Arthur	House of Vortigern	Anglo-Saxons and Jutes
1. c. 350–400 Magnus maximus c. 335–88			Conan Meriadoc		
2. c. 375–425 Constantine III d.411			Tudwal		
3. c. 400–50 St Germanus visit 429 & 437 Aetius 391–454	Coel Hen	Cunedda (marries Gwawl)	Cynfor	Severa + Vortigern	
4. c. 425–75	5 sons + Gwawl	9 sons + Gwen (marries Amlawdd Wledig)	Aldroneus and his brother Constantine	Vortimer, c. 420–50s Catigern, d. 456 Pascent	Hengist c. 430–88 and Horsa c. 430–56
5. c. 450–500	Grandsons	Eigr (Igraine marries Uthr). Owain Danwyn Cadwallon	Ambrosius, Uthr and Constans Budic II		Aesc Cerdic
6. c. 475–525	Athwrys ap Mor Athwrys ap Ceneu	Cynlas Goch (Cuneglasus) Maelgwn (reigned c. 534–47)	Arthur		Octa Cissa

Battle of Badon c. 490–520		St David (c. 500–89)　　Hoel St Illtud St Carannog Gwynllw Culhwch and Olwen Cadwr (cousin, son of Gorlois and Eigr)
7. c. 500–50	Peredur and Gwrgi (fought at Battle of Arfderydd 573) Gwallawg and Morcant (fought at Lindisfarne with Urien 570s)	St Cadoc (c. 497–580) St Paulinus Rhun ap Maelgwn Gildas
8. c. 525–75	Urien of Rheged c. 550–80 Gwenddoleu d.573 Myrddin	
9. 550–600	Owain (c. 570–97) and Rhun Rhydderch Hael	

There is a problem with this method. A person with ten children such as Cunedda could have a generation between the oldest and youngest child. So in our speculative floruit Cunedda's children could be born between 420 and 450. His grandchildren in turn could have been born between 440 and 490. In other words, it is quite possible to have grandchildren older than your youngest child. Thus different branches of the same family can cover a longer timespan. We can see this in Coel Hen's family descendants, who we know were alive at the end of the sixth century such as Owain and Rhun the sons of Urien of Rheged. Likewise Arthur, being of the same generation as Maelgwn, would not necessarily mean they were the same age.

Nor can the fact of any consensus or consistency be used as proof. Writers many hundreds of years later would be trying to construct genealogies that would be believed. An author of a saint's life in the Middle Ages would look at the genealogy tables and might wish to associate him with Arthur. He might well add that he was related in some way, and this in turn would be used in later stories and versions of family trees.

Having said all that, it does seem to fit together. From the saints' lives we have a picture of St Dubricius and St Illtud being senior to St Samson, St Gildas, St David, St Cadoc, St Carannog and Paul Aurelian. That's indeed what we find in the tables. Focusing on one branch of the Cunedda family, we have Glywys married to Gwawl, granddaughter of Cunedda. He has a number of sons: Gwynllyw, whom we met in the Life of St Cadoc receiving help from Arthur. Perphirius (literally 'clad in purple'), father of Paul Aurelian, possibly linked to the Aurelianus family; and St Pedrog listed in some legends as being a survivor of Camlan.

We start to build up a picture of Ambrosius Aurelianus being born around 450, just after a similarly named figure is Western Consul in 446, Quintus Aurelius Symmachus. In the *History of the Kings of Britain*, Vortigern takes charge as Ambrosius and Uthr are still very young. This then allows them to be of fighting age 'in the time of Zeno' 474–91. Interestingly, a second Quintus Aurelius Symmachus, son of the first, is Western Consul in 485 suggesting he is of the same generation as our Ambrosius. While Ambrosius and Uthr are growing up in Brittany, according to Geoffrey of Monmouth, Vortimer is fighting his battles in Kent only to be poisoned, Vortigern retakes the throne, the Angles rebel

Final Evidence

again in the 'night of the long knifes' killing 300 British nobles. Perhaps this is the 'storm' in which Gildas reports that his parents died.

This means Ambrosius's father cannot have been Constantine III, who died in 411. It means the Constantine cited by Geoffrey must have arrived in the 440s after the entry in the *Gallic Chronicle* and around the time of the appeal to Aetius. At that point Gildas states 'kings were anointed', and so one could reconcile these different narratives as follows: after the appeal to Aetius fails, a delegation to their Breton cousins in Armorica bears fruit and a Romano-Breton called Constantine comes across the channel and leads the British. The manner of his death differs with Gildas, claiming the parents of Ambrosius died in the Saxon revolt. Whatever the truth, an Ambrosius militarily active 'in the time of Zeno' 474–91 is likely to have been born to parents in the 440s. Which then allows time for a Vortigern figure to murder his successor and take control of a council before 450. None of this fits Geoffrey's tale of Constantine reigning for ten years and his son for three before being murdered. Length of reign aside, however, there is a consistency.

The fly in the ointment is St Germanus of Auxerre. It doesn't just mess with the timeline of Vortigern, but also with St Illtud who was supposed to be his disciple. If we pull the lines of Cunedda and Coel Hen back two generations, then we do indeed place Illtud a generation after St Germanus and Cunedda and Coel Hen in the same period as Magnus Maximus. But that pulls everyone else back, including those of whom we are fairly certain such as Urien and Maelgwn, as well as some saints. The only way to avoid this is by introducing the enigmatic St Garmon who was active in Wales in the 460s and died on the Isle of Man around 474. Then we go back to trying to have our cake and eat it by introducing two each of Vortigerns, Ambrosius Aurelianus and St Germanus like some Noah's Ark of Arthurian characters. Nevertheless, St Germanus Bishop of Man, or St Garmon, is said to have lived in the time of Gwrtheyrn or Vortigern.[4]

The suggested identifications of Arthur previously mentioned are just some of the more popular theories among a veritable army of Arthurs. They all share a number of characteristics. First, they all rely on an inordinate amount of assumptions about the accuracy of the sources they use. We have already seen that academics reject genealogies written centuries later and often for contemporary political reasons. Second, they are highly selective in which sources they use and which are rejected. There is a fair amount of semantics and leaps of linguistic logic, Anyone with an 'Arth-' type name, connected to bears in any way, or called Arthur, is latched upon. Aspects of the legend not present are dismissed or explained away. Those that are present are highlighted and held up as proof and counter evidence ignored. The last point they all share is that they are mutually exclusive. They all seem very reasonable when you read them with no knowledge of counter evidence. But when read together and in conjunction with the source material and academic research on that material, one quickly realises none of the theories are in any way close to proving anything. In fact some of them are extremely poor. The more credible theories still rely on scribal errors and leaps of logic.

Another major problem is the arrival of the West Saxons. The later expansion began after 552. This period is completely consistent with the narrative of two generations of stability after Badon. The reverse emigrated of Saxons in 531 to Frankia along with archaeological evidence also supports this. But with a Badon in the 490s silencing Aelle and preventing Octa in Kent expanding, what does the arrival of Cerdic in 495 mean? It presents two problems. The first is the entry for 508 and describes a heavy defeat for the British that hardly fits with a victorious Arthur and time of stability. The second is the apparent double entry. So we have their arrival in 495 and Cerdic 'conquering' the kingdom six years later. Then we have an almost identical entry for the West Saxons arriving in 514 and Cerdic 'succeeded to the kingdom' in 519. Both these dates are followed by a successful battle seven or eight years later in 508 and 527. It may be that the later dates are accurate and it is worth noting in that version that Cerdic inherits the kingdom of the West Saxons a year after Arthur fights at Badon or Camlann depending which timeline one follows. But this is hardly in line with Gildas talking of two generations of peace.

There are a couple of things that might be important here. First, Cerdic is a British name deriving from Ceretic. His father's name in the genealogy is Elesa, similar to Elasius met by St Germanus, described as 'chief of the region', although this is surely too early for a family connection. He is described as an 'ealdorman', which was the equivalent of dux in the Roman administration prevalent along the Saxon Shore both sides of the Channel. Second, most of the battles aren't recorded as victories at all and seem defensive in nature: Cerdic's Ford and Cerdic's Wood before the entry for 530 where they take the Isle of Wight. It reads like they are bottled up in what is now the New Forest and resort to turning south rather than inland. I can only make sense of it by taking the later date for Cerdic, arriving in 514, taking over the West Saxons around the Solent in 519 and being bottled up until after 552. There is some academic consensus that these dates are too early and it is more likely that Cerdic arrived in the 530s to fit in with the later Bretwalda Caewlin. This is all speculation, however, and the entry in the *Chronicles* for 508 or 527 remains a thorn in the side.

A major defeat of a British king, Natanleod, after Badon, doesn't fit with Gildas or Bede. However, Gildas does talk about civil wars, and there is the wording in the *Chronicle* to consider. In 494 they land at Cerdic's Shore with five ships. Then 'After six years [500] they conquered the West Saxons' kingdom.' This doesn't mean they were West Saxons themselves, or even that the area was West Saxon at the time. It is true that Stuf and Wihtgar are later identified as Saxons and Cerdic's nephews, but inter-marriage would not have been uncommon. Then later in 514, 'the West Saxons, Stuf and Wihtgar, came to Britain with 3 ships', also landing at Cerdic's Shore this time fighting the Britons and putting them to flight. In 519 Cerdic succeeds to the kingdom of the West Saxons. The two battles in 508 and 527 are not necessary duplicates. The 508 entry records Cerdic defeating a British king, Natanleod, together with 5,000 men. It doesn't say where this battle was, only the area controlled by Natanleod. The 527 entry mentions a battle at Cerdic's Wood, but does not record who wins. It is quite possible these are separate battles.

The assumption has been that these landings are the same event duplicated with one, or both, misdated. There is, however, an alternative explanation: Cerdic arrives in 494 and in six years they are the first to 'conquer the West Saxon land from the Britons', which archaeology suggests had more Jutish connections. There is no way of knowing the political situation at the time and given their British-sounding names it is not at all certain whose side they were on. In any event there is a battle in 508. It may well be that this is one of the civil wars for which the British are castigated by Gildas. The entry for 514 names Stuf and Wihtgar as leading the West Saxons and arriving, with a different number of ships. Cerdic then succeeds to their leadership in 519. These entries are not necessarily mutually exclusive. The later battles in the early sixth century seem confined to the original landing site and the Isle of Wight. Later battles from 550 onwards and other sources, however, suggest that the

West Saxons, or Gewisse, originated in the upper Thames valley, with the first West Saxon bishopric at Dorchester-on-Thames. The battles between 552 and 577 can be connected by a line north of the Chilterns and running south east between the south of Oxford and Salisbury, culminating in a battle in the west at Dyrham which captures Bath and Gloucester. The academic consensus is that the early landings of Cerdic and activity in Hampshire are highly suspect. Indeed Bede records these very same Jutish areas as being conquered by Caedwalla in 686.

If they are indeed misdated as many experts think, then why would Gildas not mention this new threat supposedly arriving in 532? If they came as stated in 495, how to explain battles between 508 and 530 also not discussed by Gildas. I think the answer to this lies in two places. First, the original name of the West Saxons were the Gewisse, meaning 'sure' or 'certain'. Second, the fact Gildas reports no external wars ending, but that civil wars were continuing. This would suggest that the Gewisse were in fact closely linked to a British power. The faint whispers of a connection with Vortigern in Nennius and Geoffrey of Monmouth and the prevalence of British named kings in the line. It is quite possible that Gildas didn't view them as anything other than Britons and it was only in Bede's time that they identified as West Saxons. What follows from this is the battles around the Hampshire and Isle of Wight areas could be against existing Jutish elements or part of a complex civil war.

One further point concerns fighting in Gaul and the story in Geoffrey of Monmouth about a Roman delegation demanding tribute. An Arthur active from 480s to 510 would have been contemporary with the rise of Clovis. Any request for help from Syagrius or Clovis in their war would have occurred before 486. Pressure from Frankish expansion on the borders with Armorica may have occurred after that date as did the purported treaty around 497 between Clovis and Brittany. Clovis was offered the Consulship by the Eastern Roman emperor, Anastasius I, after his victory over the Visigoths in 507. One could imagine a delegation, similar to that described in Geoffrey of Monmouth, coming from Gaul on behalf of Syagrius, Clovis or Anastasius. It is also possible a British leader, with links to Brittany, would have taken an interest (or even sides) in any Romano-Frankish war in 486 or border disputes after. Any military activity after 500 in Gaul seems unlikely. It is certainly the case that warfare between Bretons and Franks was present after the 550s, but there are a number of issues that would preclude this time:

Final Evidence

it's too late; there is well attested contemporary record from Gregory of Tours; it ends in defeat for the Bretons; it is during time of further expansion of Anglo-Saxon kingdoms in Britain that result in the loss of more land for the British. It has to be said, the only suggestion that Arthur fought outside Britain comes from Geoffrey of Monmouth and the Life of Saint Goeznovius. If, and it is a big if, there is some truth in this, then it's difficult to see any chance outside the latter-half of the fifth century.

I will attempt a timeline that best fits the evidence, pushes out the least amount, creates the least contradictions and need for multiple characters of the same name, or persons of unrealistic lifespans. First, it might be useful to list some of the hints from the sources so far:

- Two main families are portrayed as dominating the genealogies of the North and North Wales: The Coelings and the Cuneddas.
- Arthur's family stems from Brittany and this explains his absence from these genealogies. Uthr marries Cunedda's granddaughter.
- Ambrosius and Uthr arrive in Britain after the time of Vortimer (450s) and are active in the time of Zeno 474–91, suggesting Arthur was born in or after the 480s.
- Many of the saints are connected to either the Cuneddas or Brittany, but are active in South Wales. Their timelines appear to correspond to each other and Arthur if he was active in the first quarter of the sixth century.
- Later characters such as Ida, Urien, Myddrin and Peredur are linked to the second-half of the sixth century and are viewed as being in the next generation. Taliesin the bard was said to have known Arthur, Maelgwn and Urien, suggesting he was a young man in the 530s while Arthur still lived.
- In terms of location, the battles suggest more northerly or eastern locations whereas the saints' lives suggest South Wales and the West Country. The Triads, however, describe three courts in Cornwall, Wales and the North.

For the political situation one must look to a hundred years later for clues. There's no clear cut Britons vs Anglo-Saxons. The West Saxons fight the South Saxons and Kent. The Northumbrians fight the Mercians. Christian princes escape to pagan Picts while Christian

Britons ally with Pagan Saxons to attack Northumbria. Pagan Picts ally with Christian Britons to attack pagan Angles. It's just a series of competing petty kingdoms with shifting alliances where ethnicity, culture and religion are only three variables. Having said that, Gildas does view the island as being partitioned. He at least sees a clear divide at the time of writing but also hints at many petty kingdoms emerging after Ambrosius and the battle of Badon. What this might mean is Ambrosius attempted to restore the earlier provincial structure of sorts. With Ambrosius leader of one part and Aelle as self-styled 'Bretwalda' of other areas. This wouldn't necessarily mean a clear divide between Romano-British and Anglo-Saxons or Christians and Pagans. A likely scenario would be western/northern areas and eastern/southern areas, but with conflict within them and fluid political situation.

The fact that Bernecia and Deira both have British etymologies may be important. Berneich, as described in the *Historia Brittonum,* and Derw which may mean stem from people of the Derwent. It is impossible to know whether these were British or Angle controlled areas in 500. It is almost certain the south east was affected by Gildas's 'partition of the island'. By Arthur's time London appears to have been abandoned and St Albans cut off. It is not at all certain who the Gewisse were and on whose side they fought. Elmet, around Leeds, is certainly still British, but York and Lincoln we can only guess. If we take Geoffrey at face value, then they were lost but retaken. We must remember it is very likely that a large Romano-British population remained in Saxon controlled areas. Likewise, significant numbers of Saxon and Angle settlers would have lived in British controlled areas. We can not assume a member of Cantii, for example, would have supported a British leader from the west. Likewise an Angle warband settled near Hadrian's wall may have been quite willing to be hired by a British king to fight Saxon settlers elsewhere.

Nevertheless, while it was likely a complex and fluid situation there were clearly some, like Gildas, who saw the situation in ethnic or cultural terms. Thus a line of partition may well have designated some areas as clearly different politically and culturally. It is likely Arthur's military activity occurred, at least at times, near this line of partition. We can only speculate where this boundary was, but it is likely within a broad corridor from the eastern end of Hadrian's wall down to the Solent.

Final Evidence

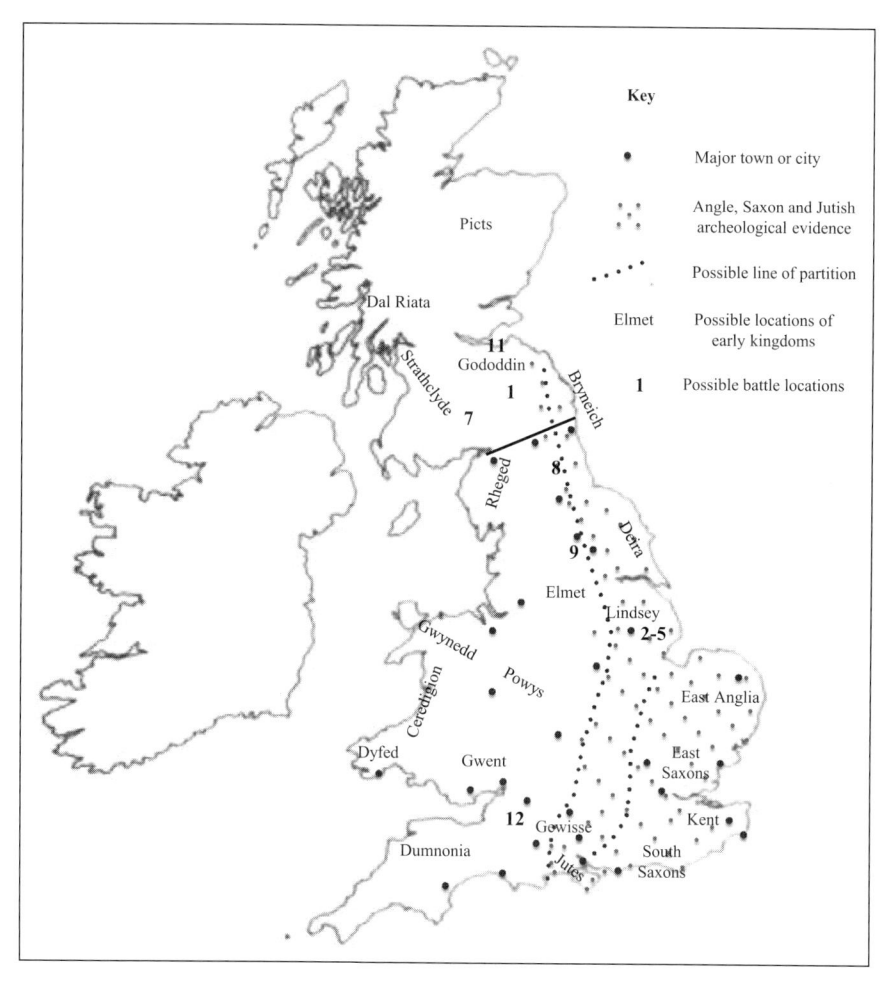

Britain circa AD 500.

It's worth reminding ourselves what we know and what we can be reasonably confident about. Even some of these few facts are debatable as we can't be sure about much between the time of Constantine in 411 and the arrival of Augustine to Kent, the kingdom of Aethelbert in 597:

Table 33: Likely timeline

407	Constantine III leaves Britain for Gaul.
409	Britain rebels against Constantine's administration and appeals to Honorius.
410	Honorius advises civitates to look to themselves.

(continued)

Table 33: (Continued)

411	Constantine III killed.
429	St Germanus visits.
437, 444 or 447	St Germanus second visit.
440 or 441	*Gallic Chronicle*: Britain falls to the power of the Saxons.
446–54	Groans of the Britons: Appeal to Aetius, 'thrice consul'.
449–56	Bede records the coming of the Saxons led by Hengist and Horsa.
474–91	Bede places Ambrosius Aurelianus in the time of Zeno.
490–500	Bede places the Battle of Badon forty-four years after the Saxon arrival. Gildas appears to place it forty-four years prior to his writing.
534–47	Reign of Maelgwn and time of Gildas writing.
550–600	Emergence of known historical figures and reliable sources.
597	St Augustine's mission to Aethelbert of Kent.

The consensus of academics is that Badon is around 500, regardless of which interpretation of Gildas's forty-four years one uses. This would place Arthur c. 480–520 and on balance it's the time I prefer; the 'middle Arthur' option from our earlier evidence. It's also quite possible to create a timeline favouring the 'early Arthur' if one views Bede as inaccurate, Gildas as misdated and all the Welsh legends and saints' lives as invalid. Geoffrey of Monmouth's Constantine, however, is clearly not Constantine III, given the alleged family tree and his place in the chronology. Thus it is at least possible, if not probable, to associate this with Gildas reporting 'kings were appointed' after the appeal to Aetius around 446. It follows from this that Ambrosius would be born in the 450s allowing for him being of military age 'in the time of Zeno'. Interestingly, expert opinion does indeed place the Federate treaty, rebellion and subsequent fight-back much later, with the latter occurring as late as 490.[5]

The 'best fit', then, requires a 'late Arthur' that falls into line with genealogical and hagiographical sources, but also a less conventional interpretation of the 'forty-four years' and the battle of Badon. The table below therefore attempts to satisfy all the sources and address all the apparent contradictions while leaving the least out. Next to each year I have attempted to match the corresponding entry from the *Gallic Chronicle*, Gildas, Bede, Nennius, *Annales Cambriae*, *Anglo-Saxon Chronicles* and Geoffrey of Monmouth.

Final Evidence

Table 34: All the sources side by side

388	Magnus Maximus killed.
398	Roman response by General Stilicho.
	Gildas: first assault of Scots and Picts, legion sent and destroyed them.
	Bede: Assault of Irish and Picts, legion sent and destroyed them.
	Geoffrey of Monmouth: Picts and Huns attack while Maximus in Gaul, two legions sent.
407	Constantine III takes troops to Gaul.
408	Second assault of barbarians recorded in Gildas and Bede. Romans respond and leave for last time leaving plans for weapons and defence.
	Geoffrey of Monmouth: Scots, Norwegians and Danes attack. Romans defeat them.
409	Britain rebels against Constantine's administration and appeals to Honorius.
410	Honorius advises civitates to look to themselves.
411	Constantine III killed.
425	Nennius: Vortigern takes power
	Pillar of Eliseg: 'Brittu son of Vortigern who was married to Severa daughter of Maximus'.
429	St Germanus of Auxerre first visit.
437	St Germanus of Auxerre second visit.
440	*Gallic Chronicle*: Britain falls to the power of the Saxons.
	Gildas and Bede: third assault, Scots and Picts seized whole of north up to wall. Towns and wall abandoned, British massacre. Enemy assaults, internal disorders over whole region.
	Geoffrey of Monmouth: Scots, Picts, Norwegian, Danes and others seize land up to wall. Cities and wall abandoned.
446–54	Gildas and Bede: Groans of the Britons: Appeal to Aetius, 'thrice consul'.
	Anglo-Saxon Chronicle: Dates appeal to 443.
	Gildas: British victory over enemies. Time of plenty. kings anointed. Disease and plague.
	Bede: Famine. Victory over Irish and Picts. Abundance. Plague.

(continued)

Table 34: (Continued)

	Geoffrey of Monmouth: Constantine arrives from Brittany, crowned king, achieves first victory. Has three sons: Constans, Aurelius Ambrosius, Utherpendragon. Genealogical sources: Cunedda sent to North Wales from Manau Gododdin with sons to expel Irish.
449–56	Gwrtheyrn Gortheneu (Vortigern) leads council. Gildas: Rumour of attack, council led by 'Proud Tyrant' appeals for help from Saxons. Bede: Vortigern invites Angles and Saxons due to rumours of attack. *Anglo-Saxon Chronicles*: Angles invited by Vortigern Geoffrey of Monmouth: Vortigern invents rumour of attack to gain power over Constans, (Constantine now dead). Constans is murdered and Vortigern crowned. Ambrosius and Uthr still in their cradle escaped to King Budicius of Brittany. Genealogical sources: Grandchildren of Cunedda start being born including Eigr (Igraine) c. 460.
449–56	Gildas: first Saxons arrive in three keels or warships Bede: Angles and Saxons in three warships led by Hengist and Horsa. Nennius: Hengist and Horsa in three keels. *Anglo-Saxon Chronicles*: three ships land at Ebba's Creek in South East. Geoffrey of Monmouth: three keels land in Kent led by Hengist and Horsa. Gildas: Larger company arrive. Bede: after first victory against Picts, larger force arrive. Nennius: Asked for original supplies, further sixteen keels arrive, one with Hengist's daughter. *Anglo-Saxon Chronicles*: More troops from Angeln sent for. Hengist and Horsa named. Geoffrey of Monmouth: After victory against Picts Hengist given land in Lindsey (Lincoln). Eighteen more ships arrive and Hengist's daughter Renwein. Gildas: after a 'long time' Saxons asked for more supplies.

Final Evidence

	Bede: Saxons asked for more supplies, threatened to break treaty.
	Nennius: Saxons asked for original supplies.
	Nennius: Vortigern marries Hengist's daughter and Hengist is given Kent. Octha and Ebissa with forty ships given land in north near the wall.
	Geoffrey of Monmouth: Vortigern marries Hengist's daughter and Hengist is given Kent. Octa and Ebissa with 300 ships given land in north near the wall.
	Archaeological evidence: increasing Angle and Jutish immigration into Eastern areas.
455	Nennius: Vortimer fought four battles against them, Horsa and Catigern killed.
	Geoffrey of Monmouth: Vortimer made king and fights four battles, Horsa and Katigern killed.
	Anglo-Saxon Chronicle: 455 Battle at Agelesford (Aylesford?), Horsa killed.
	456 Hengist and son Aesc defeat Britons at Crayford and they flee to London abandoning Kent.
c. 460	Nennius: Vortimer dies. Vortigern regains crown. Hengist returns.
	Geoffrey of Monmouth: Vortimer poisoned. Vortigern restored, Hengist returns with 300,000 men.
460s	St Garmon or St Germanus of Man active in Wales later mistaken for St Germanus of Auxerre.
c. 465	Gildas: Saxon rebellion over 'whole island … all major towns laid low'.
	Bede: Saxon revolt from 'east to western sea'.
	Nennius: Night of long knives. 300 nobles killed. Vortigern captured. Saxons take Essex, Sussex, Middlesex.
	Geoffrey of Monmouth: Night of long knives, 460 nobles killed, Saxons ceded London, York, Lincoln and Winchester.
	Anglo-Saxon Chronicle: 465 Hengist fought at Wipped's Creek, twelve Welsh Chieftains killed.
	Gildas and Bede describe increased emigration from Britain.
	St Garmon active in Britain. Story of Vortigern and St Germanus confused with St Germanus of Auxerre.

(continued)

Table 34: (Continued)

474–91	Gildas: Ambrosius Aurelianus fights back, wins first victory c. 480s. Parents had been killed in troubles (c. 450–60s) and grandchildren alive at time of writing (c. 540). Bede: Ambrosius Aurelianus fights back 'in the time of Zeno' 474–91 (*Chronica Majora*). *Anglo-Saxon Chronicles*: 473 Hengist and Aesc victory. Arrival of Aelle and South Saxons and victories recorded for 477, 485, 491. Geoffrey of Monmouth: Ambrosius defeats Vortigern first then Hengist. Gildas laments 'partition of the island' since that time. Bede describes Aelle as the first 'Bretwalda' or Britain Ruler perhaps of the Anglo-Saxon areas only.
488	*Anglo-Saxon Chronicles*: Hengist dies Aesc succeeds. Nennius: On Hengist's death his son Octha came from the north to the kingdom of Kentishmen.
490s	Geoffrey of Monmouth: Uthr succeeds Ambrosius, marries Eigr, who already has a son, Cadwr, from first marriage so likely now in 30s. A comet in 497 gives his epithet 'Pendragon'. Genealogical sources: Great-grandchildren of Cunedda start being born: St Illtud, Gwynllw, Culwch, Olwen, St Caraannog, Cadwr, St David, Maelgwn, Arthur.
493	Nennius: St Patrick dies aged 120. Irish annals: St Patrick dies.
495–514	*Anglo-Saxon Chronicles*: 495 Cerdic and Cynric land five ships at Cerdic Shore fought battle. 501 Port and sons, Bieda and Maelga, land two ships at Portsmouth, kill nobleman. 508 Cerdic and Cynric defeat Natanleod and 5,000 at Battle near Charford, Netley. 514 West Saxons Stuf and Wihtgar (nephews of Cerdic) land three ships at Cerdic's Shore.
500–50	Genealogies: generation after Arthur – birth of grandchildren of Ambrosius, denounced by Gildas. St Cadoc and Paul Aurelian c. 500, Rhun ap Maelgwn c. 525
512	*Anglo-Saxon Chronicles*: Aesc dies. Octa succeeds him in Kent.

Final Evidence

	Nennius: **Then Arthur fought against them: twelve battles.**
	(After St Patrick dies and Octha comes to Kent.)
516	**Battle of Badon**: *Annales Cambriae*. Arthur and Britons the victors.
	Gildas and Bede: siege of Badon Hill, last but not least victory.
	Geoffrey of Monmouth: Saxons led by Colgrin and Balduff besiege Bath and are killed. Cheldric escapes (none of these are present in any genealogies or legends).
	Genealogies place Aesc or Octha in Kent, Aelle or Cissa with South Saxons.
	ASC: West Saxons Stuf and Wihtgar and Cerdic, Cynric or possibly Creoda.
	Nennius names Octha as Arthur's opponent generally.
	Welsh legends name Osla.
519	*Anglo-Saxon Chronicles*: Cerdic and Cynric succeed to kingdom of West Saxons.
	527: Battle at Cerdic's Ford.
	530: Take Isle of Wight.
	534: Cerdic dies, Cynric rules. Isle of Wight given to Stuf and Wihtgar.
Badon to time of De Excidio	Gildas and Bede: External wars stopped but not civil ones. Generation 'kept to their stations' and remembered, but they died. Age has succeeded ignorant of the storm.
	One generation of twenty-five years: 516 + 25 = 541.
520–30s	Genealogies: Urien, Taliesin, Myrddin Wylit born.
	Saints Dubricious, Illtud, Gildas, David, Cadog, Carannog, Padarn all active in South Wales.
531	Saxon emigrants from Britain used by Franks in Thurungian war and given land.
537	*Annale Cambriae*: **Battle of Camlann. Arthur and Mordred fall**
	Geoffrey of Monmouth: dates Camlann to 542
534–47	Reign of Maelgwn.
c. 534	Gildas writes 'De Excidio et Conquestu Britanniae' forty-four years after the first victory of Ambrosius. A generation after Badon (twenty years) and in the time of the grandchildren of Ambrosius.
547	Maelgwn dies

(continued)

Table 34: (Continued)

550	West Saxons expand territory in South. Angle kings emerge in Bernicia, Deira and East Anglia.
550–600	Emergence of known historical figures and reliable sources.
570	*Annales Cambriae*: Gildas dies.
573	*Annales Cambriae*: Battle of Arfderydd where 'Myrddin Wylit went mad'.
597	St Augustine's mission to Aethelbert of Kent.
c. 600	Possible original source of *Y Gododdin* with first reference: 'he was no Arthur'.
731	Bede writes *An Ecclesiastical History of the English People* using Gildas but also other sources.
c. 830	*Historia Brittonum* written possibly by Nennius. First definite reference to Arthur and connection to Badon.
c. 954	*Annales Cambriae* written at St David's, Dyfed. First recorded date for Badon and first reference to Camlann.
Tenth to fourteenth century	Welsh legends and poems start to be recorded. A more mythical Arthur portrayed. Uthr, Eigr, Mordred and Guinevere connected to early legends.
	Genealogical records start to be written down but don't refer to Arthur's family until after Geoffrey of Monmouth in twelfth century.
Eleventh century	Lives of saints start to include Arthur.
1136	Geoffrey of Monmouth writes *History of the Kings of Britain*. Introduces Merlin, lays out traditional family tree.
Twelfth century	Vulgate and post Vulgate romances.
	Introduction of concepts now connected to legend: Round table, sword in stone, Avalon, Camelot, Lady in Lake, Lancelot, Morgan Le Fey, Holy Grail.
1485	Le Morte D'Arthur written by Thomas Mallory. Legend evolves into modern times.

The table would not pass any test of historical evidence, but it does create a best-fit of all the sources.

So in conclusion: it is quite possible Arthur didn't exist. There is certainly no current evidence to prove the case. Much of the evidence used to support his existence is just not credible. The line from *Y Gododdin*

Final Evidence

provides no more proof than a few people called Arthur lived in the fifth and sixth centuries. We are thus left with two main arguments. The entry in the *Historia Brittonum* over 300 years later; and the fact the legend persisted over hundreds of years. The last of these is the 'no smoke without fire' argument which, aside from being technically inaccurate, can easily be shown to be not the case in other legends. So we are left with the whole edifice possibly resting on Nennius, or whoever was the original author. Do you believe it is likely someone writing in the early ninth century would have placed a fictional character into the narrative? Or is it possible a fictional character could become historicised within the intervening 300 years?

My guess, and it is a guess, is that there was an original figure who lived between 450–550. It is possible he lived outside this time and was misdated by Nennius. However there are no likely candidates and no evidence to support this, therefore I would say it is very unlikely. We are thus left with our three possibilities: an early, middle, or late Arthur. An early Arthur would follow from the timeline suggested by the *Gallic Chronicle*, but would mean Gildas and Bede are mistaken. A middle Arthur would fall into line with Gildas and Bede and also a rough consensus of modern historians around a date for Badon of c. 500. A later Arthur would tie in with with the *Annales Cambriae* and saints' lives.

In order to create a credible timeline that provides a 'best fit' of the sources, I've made some judgements about the evidence which I hope the reader doesn't find unreasonable:

- The audience of the *Historia Brittonum* were aware of a historical Arthur.
- The *Gallic Chronicle* entry for 440 is to be trusted.
- The Adventus Saxonum described by Bede and Gildas is a separate event from 440 and occurred in 449–56.
- St Germanus of Man has been mistaken for St Germanus of Auxerre leading to the misdating of Vortigern by Nennius.
- Gwrtheyrn Gortheneu or Vortigern's floruit is 440s–470
- The dating of Ambrosius militarily active in 474–91 by Bede is to be trusted.
- The chronology of *Historia Brittonum* places Arthur after Hengist and St Patrick around 490 but before Ida around 547.
- The dating of Gildas, De Excidio and Badon are roughly correct although open to interpretation but place Badon at least one generation before Maelgwn's reign.

While I found this a useful exercise, on balance I would go for a middle Arthur; born before 480, coming of fighting age in the mid 490s. Fighting 'at that time' or just after the *Historia Brittonum* records the deaths of Hengist and St Patrick, which elsewhere are unreliably recorded for 488 and 493 respectively. Conveniently placing Badon 493–500, forty-four years both after Bede's Adventus Saxonum and before Gildas writing his tract during the reign of Maelgwn 534–47. The 'last but not the least' victory. If his reign extended up to the 520s, this would have enabled him to interact with many of the saints associated with him.

Arthur has a Roman name because he likely comes from a Romano-British/Armorican/Gaulish father, although with a British mother. He is not to be found in Welsh genealogies because he doesn't belong there, at least in none of the paternal lines or king's lists. If he was, his presence would have been lauded and used for political reasons. It is very telling that Ambrosius Aurelianus, someone who we can be confident is real, is not in the genealogies either. A Romano-British fight-back would likely have involved the remnants of the remaining military forces. With the south east already fallen 'to the power of the saxons', the last command was the northern forces and it is reasonable to suggest a military or administrative command for Ambrosius, and later Arthur, rather than a royal one. I thus find it unlikely that any of the figures identified from the genealogies are our man. The original legend retains Uthr, Eigr and Medrawt and Gwenhwyfar, but doesn't rely on any of this. Even if all these characters and legends were early embellishments it still wouldn't necessarily throw out the Arthur in the *Historia Brittonum*. However, many of the concepts associated with the legend are certainly later additions and we must imagine our warrior without Excalibur, Camelot, Avalon, Lancelot or Merlin.

The battles have a distinctly northern flavour with Lincoln, Northumberland and southern Scotland likely locations. Badon seems an outlier but I would retain its association with Bath for two reasons. First, in the 'Wonders of Britain' section of the *Historia Brittonum*, Nennius refers to Baths of Badon. Second, I think it is telling that it's later Anglo-Saxon name is Badanceaster. If, as is suspected, the Belgae used some form of proto-Friesian language, the Gewisse were Germanic mercenaries, or Saxon mercenaries were already prevalent in the south then it may well be the name Badon was in common usage long before it fell to the West Saxons after Gildas. A Romano-British military command based at York and covering up to Hadrian's wall would be a likely scenario. Especially with London, the Saxon Shore command and the south east lost. Perhaps also active in South Wales through family ties and saints' lives and a court at Caerleon. Thus with a court in the north and links to Cornwall, he wasn't just a localised petty ruler.

I hope I have demonstrated the 'when', and at the very least, who he was not. One cannot simply pluck an 'Arth-' type name from the genealogies, or construct a theory by selectively picking sources we like and dismissing other more inconvenient ones. I hope I have also clarified the issues for the layperson and separated the wheat from the chaff. We can dismiss at least the fanciful theories and later embellishments. If Arthur did exist, he is the Arthur of the *Historia Brittonum*, which means he fought the Saxons in twelve battles in the time of Octha around 490–520.

It is possible, of course, that somewhere in Britain, buried in the earth, are coins bearing the inscription 'Ambrosius Rex' or perhaps 'Uthr Bendragon'. Or a letter from Sidonius Appollinaris to Arcturus, or vice-versa, lying untouched in an old manuscript. A letter from the Pope hidden in some vault. An engraving on a tablet, 'Artorius, Dux Brittoniarum' thrown into a pit. Perhaps a tomb will be uncovered with an engraved cross that can be dated to the early sixth century. Maybe a stone, embedded in an old church or castle, its face hidden from view. The Latin or Ogham inscription will read 'Arthur, dux bellorum, fought here and won in the year of Christ…'

References and Bibliography

Adoman of Iona, *Life of St Columba.* (Penguin, London, 1995).

Ammianus Marcellinus, (translated by Hamilton, Walter), *The Later Roman Empire AD 354–378.* (Penguin Books, London, 1986).

Ardrey, A., *Finding Arthur,* (Overlook Press, New York, 2013).

Arnold, C.J., *An Archaeology of the Early Anglo-Saxon Kingdoms,* (Routledge, London, 2000).

Ashe, Geoffrey, *The Discovery of King Arthur,* (The History Press, Stroud, 2010).

Ashe, Geoffrey, *The Landscape of King Arthur,* (Anchor Press Doubleday, London, 1985).

Ashley, Mike, *The Mammoth Book of King Arthur,* (Constable and Robinson Ltd, London 2005).

Baring-Gould, Sabine, *The Lives of British Saints Volumes 1-4,* (Forgotten Books, London, 2012).

Bartrum, Peter, *A Welsh Classical Dictionary,* (National Library of Wales, 1993).

Beard, D., *Astronomical references in the Anglo-Saxon Chronicles,* (Journal of the British Astronomical Association, Vol. 115, No. 5, p.261, 2005).

Bede, *The Ecclesiastical History of the English People,* (Oxford University Press, Oxford, 1994).

Breeze, Andrew, *The Name of King Arthur,* (Mediaevistic, Internationale Zeitschrift für interdisziplinäre Mittelalterforschung, Peter Laing. 2015).

Bromwich, Jarman and Roberts, *The Arthur of the Welsh,* (University of Wales Press, Cardiff 1995).

Bromwich, Rachel, *The Triads of the Island of Britain (4th Edition),* (University of Wales Press, Cardiff, 2014).

Bury, John, *The Life of St Patrick and His Place in History,* (Dover Publications, London, 1998).

References and Bibliography

Chadwick et al, *Studies in Early British History,* (Cambridge University Press, Cambridge 1959).
Charles-Edwards, T.M., *Wales and the Britons 350-1064*, (Oxford University Press, Oxford, 2014).
Clemoes, Peter, *Anglo-Saxon England Volume 5,* (Cambridge University Press, Cambridge 1976).
Cusack, Mary Francis, *History of Ireland from AD 400 to 1800,* (Senate, London 1995).
Cunliffe, Barry, *Britain Begins,* (Oxford University Press, Oxford, 2013).
Dark, K, R., *Civitas to Kingdom; British Political Continuity 300-800,* (Leicester University Press, London, 1994).
Dark, Ken, *Britain and the End of the Roman Empire,* (Tempus Publishing Ltd, Stroud, 2000).
Dumville, David, *Saint Patrick,* (Boydell Press, Woodbridge, 1999).
Gantz, Jeffrey, *The Mabinogion,* (Penguin Books, London, 1976).
Geoffrey of Monmouth, *The Life of Merlin, Vita Merlini,* (Read a classic, USA 2011)
Gilbert, Wilson and Brackett, *The Holy Kingdom*, (Bantam Press, London, 1998).
Goldsworthy, Adrian, *The Fall of the West,* (Phoenix, London, 2010).
Griffen, T., *Names from the Dawn of British Legend,* (Llanerch, Dyfed, 1994).
Halsall, Guy, *Worlds of Arthur,* (Oxford University Press, Oxford, 2014).
Higham, N.J., *King Arthur Myth-Making and History,* (Routledge, Abingdon, 2009).
Higham, N.J., Rome, *Britain and the Anglo-Saxons,* (Seaby, London, 1992).
Higham, N. and Ryan, R., *The Anglo-Saxon World,* (Yale University Press, New Haven, 2015).
Hobbs, R. & Jackson, R., *Roman Britain,* (The British Museum Press, London, 2015).
Jarman, A., *Aneirin, Y Gododdin,* (Gomer Press, Ceredigion, 1990).
Jordanes (translated by Charles Mierow), *The Origin and Deeds of the Goths,* (Dodo Press, Princetown 1908).
Keegan, Simon, *Pennine Dragon,* (Newhaven Publishing, 2016).
Lapidge, Michael and Dumville, David: *Gildas, New Approaches,* (Boydell Press, Woodbridge, 1984).

Laycock, Stuart, *Britannia The Failed State,* (The History Press, Stroud, 2011).

Low, D.M., *Gibbon's The Decline and Fall of the Roman Empire,* (Chatto and Windus, London, 1981).

Matthews, John, *Taliesin, The Last Celtic Shaman,* (Inner Traditions, Vermont, 2002).

Moffat Alistair, *The British: A Genetic Journey,* (Birlinn, Edinburgh, 2013).

Morris, J., *Arthurian Period Sources Volume 3 Persons: Ecclesiastics and Laypeople,* (Phillimore, Chichester, 1995).

Morris, J., *Arthurian Period Sources Volume 7 Gildas,* (Phillimore, Chichester, 1978).

Morris, J., *Arthurian Period Sources Volume 8 Nennius,* (Phillimore, Chichester, 1980).

Naismith, Rory, *Citadel of the Saxons,* (I.B. Tauris and Co. London, 2019).

O Croinin, Daibhi, *Early Medieval Ireland 400-1200 second Edition,* (Routledge, London, 2017).

Oppenheimer, Stephen, *The Origins of the British,* (Robinson, London, 2007).

Padel, O.J., *Arthur in Medieval Welsh literature,* (University of Wales Press, Cardiff, 2013).

Pearson, Andrew, *The Roman Shore Forts,* (The History Press, Stroud, 2010).

Pennar, Merion, *The Black Book of Carmarthen,* (Llanerch Enterprises, 1989).

Phillips, Graham, *The Lost Tomb of King Arthur, Bear and Company,* (Rochester, Vermont, 2016).

Procopius (Williamson, G & Sarris, P., trans.), *The Secret History,* (Penguin Books, London, 2007).

Thomas, Charles, *Christianity in Romand Britain to AD 500,* (Batsford, London 1981).

Salway, Peter, *A History of Roman Britain,* (Oxford University Press, Oxford, 2001).

Sisam, Kenneth, *Anglo-Saxon Royal Genealogies,* The British Academy, london, 1953.

Stenton, Frank, *Anglo-Saxon England,* Oxford University Press, Oxford, 1989.

References and Bibliography

Swanton, Michael, *The Anglo-Saxon Chronicles,* (Phoenix Press, London, 2000).

Sykes, Brian, *Blood of the Isles,* (Corgi Books, London, 2006).

Thornton, D., *Kings, Chronicles and Genealogies: Studies in the Political History of Early Medieval Ireland and Wales,* (Linacre College, Oxford, 2003).

Thorpe Lewis (trans.), *Gerald of Wales,* (Penguin Books, London, 1988).

Thorpe Lewis (trans.), *Gregory of Tours The History of the Franks,* (Penguin Books, London 1977).

Thorpe Lewis (trans.), *Geoffrey of Monmouth, The History of the Kings of Britain,* (Penguin Books, London, 1966).

Wacher, John, *The Towns of Roman Britain,* (BCA, London, 1995).

Wallace-Hadrill, J.M., *The Barbarian West 400–1000,* (Blackwell, Oxford, 1999).

Wallace-Hadrill, J.M., *The Long-Haired kings,* (Methuen & Co, London, 1962).

Webster, L & Brown, M, *The Transformation of the Roman World* AD *400-900,* (British Museum Press, London, 1997).

Webb, Simon, *Life in Roman London,* (The History Press, Stroud, 2011).

Wilson, Roger J.A., *A Guide to the Roman Remains in Britain,* (Constable & Company, London, 1980).

Yorke, Barbara, *Kings and the Kingdoms of Early Anglo-Saxon England,* (Routledge, London, 2013).

Zosimus (trans.), *Zosimus Historicus,* (Green and Chaplin, London, 1814)

www.vortigernstudies.org.uk

Endnotes

Chapter 1: Roman Britain
1. Wilson, 1980: 271
2. Goldsworthy, 2010: 340
3. Salway, 2001: 230
4. Storr, 2016: 56
5. Goldsworthy, 2010: 341
6. Goldsworthy, 2010: 337
7. Guy de la Bedoyere, 2001: 239
8. Charles-Edwards 2014: 31
9. Salway, 2001: 277
10. Goldsworthy, 2010: 344
11. Thomas, 1981: 198
12. Goldsworthy, 2010: 338, 345
13. Charles Thomas, 1981: 274

Chapter 2: The End of the West
1. Wallace-Hadrill, 1999: 26
2. Wallace-Hadrill, 1961:2
3. Wallace-Hadrill, 1999: 22
4. Wallace-Hadrill, 1961: 29
5. Stenton, 1989: 12
6. Wallace-Hadrill, 1999: 66

Chapter 3: Contemporary Sources
1. http://www.vortigernstudies.org.uk/artsou/artsou.htm
2. Wood in Dumville and Lapwood, 1984: 8
3. Wood in Dumville and Lapwood, 1984: 16
4. O Croinin, 2017: 47

5. Dumville, 1999
6. O Croinin, 2017: 46
7. Bury, 1998: 192
8. Bury, 1998: 193

Chapter 4: Gildas, going to hell in a handcart
1. Lapidge and Dumville, 1984: 59
2. Lapidge and Dumville, 1984: 52
3. Morris, 1978: 28
4. Halsall, 2014: 55
5. Morris, 1978: 19
6. Lapidge and Dumville, 1984: 104
7. Lapidge and Dumville, 1984: 47
8. Lapidge and Dumville, 1984: 50
9. Lapidge and Dumville, 1984: 67
10. Charles-Edwards, 2014: 57
11. Lapidge and Dumville, 1984: 53
12. Lapidge and Dumville, 1984: 59

Chapter 6: The *Historia Brittonum*
1. Charles-Edwards 2014: 438
2. Higham, 2009:119
3. Ashley, 2005:178
4. Higham, 2009: 145
5. Bromwich, 1995:2
6. Higham, 2009:148
7. Padel, 2013:3
8. Bromwich, 1995: 18 and Higham, 2009: 133
9. Bromwich, 1995: 21
10. Higham, 2009: 120 & 123
11. Higham, 2009: 130
12. Higham, 2009: 135
13. Higham, 2009: 119-120
14. Higham, 2009: 141

Chapter 7: The Welsh Annals
1. Higham, 2009: 194
2. Higham, 2009: 209

3. Padel, 2013: 9
4. Bromwich, 1991:26-7
5. Higham, 2009: 209
6. Higham, 2009:195
7. Higham, 2009: 217

Chapter 8: The Anglo-Saxons

1. Swanton, 2000: xviii
2. Swanton, 2000: xiv
3. Stenton, 1989: 17
4. Beard, 2005: 263
5. Yorke, 2013: 131
6. Yorke, 2013: 132

Chapter 9: Archaeology and Other Evidence

1. Arnold, 2000: 23
2. Stenton, 1989: 1
3. Stenton, 1989: 6
4. Stenton, 1989: 19
5. Higham and Ryan, 2015: 78
6. Stenton, 1989: 23
7. Higham and Ryan, 2015: 59
8. Oppenheimer 2007: 307
9. Oppenheimer 2007: 331
10. Oppenheimer 2007: 380
11. Oppenheimer 2007: 358
12. Oppenheimer 2007: 361
13. Oppenheimer 2007:382
14. Higham, 1992: 74
15. Arnold, 2000: 29
16. Higham and Ryan, 2015: 111
17. Higham and Ryan, 2015: 42
18. Higham and Ryan, 2015: 104
19. Higham, 1992:8
20. Higham, 1992:79-80
21. Arnold, 2000: 20 & 21
22. Higham, 1992:9

23. Moffatt, 2013: 177
24. Sykes, 2006: 325 & 338
25. Higham and Ryan, 2015: 91
26. Moffatt, 2013: 182
27. Higham and Ryan, 2015: 91
28. Higham and Ryan, 2015: 107
29. Higham, 1992: 208
30. Higham and Ryan, 2015: 98
31. Naismith, 2019: 52
32. Naismith, 2019: 49
33. Higham, 1992:8
34. Higham, 1992:1
35. Webb, 2011: 132
36. Naismith, 2019: 42
37. Naismith, 2019: 43
38. Webb, 2011: 132

Chapter 11: Saints' Lives

1. Ashe, 1985: 103
2. Padel, 2013: 30
3. Padel, 2013: 35
4. Baring-Gould, 1911: 60

Chapter 12: *The History of the Kings of Britain* by Geoffrey of Monmouth

1. Padel, 2013: 10
2. Higham, 1992:2
3. Lewis, 1966: 17 & 19

Chapter 13: French Romances and Welsh Legends

1. Green, 2009: 101
2. Bartrum, 1993: 28

Chapter 14: The Brittany Connection

1. Charles-Edwards, 2014: 59
2. Charles-Edwards, 2014: 70-71
3. Charles-Edwards, 2014: 71

4. Bromwich, 1991: 251
5. Higham, 2009: 216
6. Bromwich, 1991: 262

Chapter 15: Genealogies and Kings

1. Green, 2009: 20
2. Lapidge and Dumville, 1984:55
3. Charles-Edwards, 2014: 364
4. Green, 2009: 20
5. Higham, 2009: 25
6. 1988, 55
7. Dumville 1988: 59
8. Davies 1982: 203
9. Davies 1982: 207
10. Charles-Edwards, 2014: 364
11. Higham, 2009: 217
12. Chadwick, 1959: 31
13. Yorke, 2013: 75
14. Yorke, 2013: 77
15. Yorke, 2013: 26
16. Yorke, 2013: 27
17. Yorke, 2013: 32
18. Sisam, 1953: 328
19. Sisam, 1953: 346
20. Clemoes, 1976: 30
21. Yorke: 2013
22. Bartrum, 1993: 29
23. Thornton, 2003: 27
24. Thornton, 2003: 30
25. Charles-Edwards, 2014: 250
26. Bartrum, 1993: 31

Chapter 16: Arthur, the name

1. Higham, 2009: 74
2. Green, 2009: 26
3. Griffin, 1994: 82
4. Griffin, 1994: 85
5. Green, 2009: 30

Endnotes

6. Green, 2009: 27
7. Higham, 2009: 80
8. Breeze, 2015: 24

Chapter 17: Final Evidence

1. Green, 2009: 13
2. Green, 2009: 16
3. Dark, 2000: 229
4. Baring-Gould Volume 3, 1907: 64
5. Dumville, 1988: 83

List of Maps

1. Tribal areas 1st century — 2
2. Roman Provinces of Britain — 8
3. Military commands — 9
4. Saxon Shore Forts — 10
5. Riothamus — 18
6. North western Gaul in the late fifth century — 19
7. 'Barbarians seize up to the wall', scenarios — 36
8. Partition of the island — 41
9. Possible locations of Gildas's kings — 44
10. Bede: Saxons, Angles and Jutes — 52
11. Locations in *Historia Brittonum* — 59
12. Possible battle locations — 63
13. Foundation stories in the Anglo-Saxon Chronicles — 78
14. Location of battles in the Anglo-Saxon Chronicles — 81
15. Fifth century archaeological evidence — 83
16. Post Roman Britain — 86
17. The Tribal Hidage — 90
18. Timelines, possible sequence of events — 101
19. Barbarian revolt, comparison of sources — 116
20. Arthurian locations in Welsh legends — 145
21. Arthurian landmarks — 146
22. Britain circa 500 AD — 217

List of Tables

1.	Roman Britain: rebel Emperors and revolts	6
2.	Barbarian raids 4th to 5th century	11
3.	Contemporary sources	21
4.	Gallic Chronicle entries	25
5.	Gildas, chapter contents	38
6.	Gildas's tyrant kings	42
7.	Bede, chapter contents	48
8.	*Historia Brittonum*, dates for the arrival of the Saxons	55
9.	*Historia Brittonum*, chapter contents	56
10.	Arthur's 12 battles	61
11.	*Annales Cambriae* entries	69
12.	Anglo-Saxon Chronicle entries, early fifth century	74
13.	Anglo-Saxon Chronicle entries, Hengist and Horsa	76
14.	Anglo-Saxon Chronicle entries, Aelle	76
15.	Anglo-Saxon Chronicle entries, Cerdic and Cynric and West Saxons	77
16.	The Tribal Hidage	89
17.	Timelines, comparison of sources	96
18.	Arthur in the Saints' lives	107
19.	Saints connected to aspects of the legend	109
20.	The French Romances	129
21.	Welsh legends	131
22.	Arthurian themes	136
23.	Arthur's family	143
24.	Details from Welsh legends	148
25.	Timelines of 5th and 6th century Britain and Gaul	155
26.	Genealogies of Welsh kingdoms	165
27.	Genealogy of kings of Kent	169
28.	Early Anglo-Saxon genealogies	172

29.	Early Welsh genealogies	174
30.	Northern British genealogies	175
31.	The usual suspects	191
32.	Genealogies compared	208
33.	Likely timeline	217
34.	Timeline, the sources side by side	219

Genealogy Tables

1.	Genealogy of Arthur	144
2.	Arthur's connection with Welsh kings and saints	178
3.	The Old North	179
4.	The Breton connection	180
5.	Anglo-Saxon kingdoms	180

Index

Adventus Saxonum, 37-8, 40, 55, 71, 167, 205-206, 225-6
Aegidius, xii, 17, 37, 151
Aelle, 76, 78-9, 81-2, 93, 151, 168, 171, 174, 190, 212, 216
Aetius, xi, xii, 16-7, 37-8, 40-3, 49, 51, 84, 94-100, 115, 151, 186, 202-4, 211
Agned, battle of, 60
Aldroneus, 158, 207
Ambrosius Aurelianus, xi, xiii, 16, 31, 32, 40, 43-5, 50-2, 54, 56, 58, 65-7, 70, 76, 80, 91-2, 94-5, 100, 102, 104, 111, 114-5, 117, 120, 122, 142, 144, 158, 161, 164, 167, 185, 187-190, 195, 200, 204-207, 210-1, 215-6, 218, 225-7
Amhar *see* Amr
Amlawdd Wledig, 144, 177
Ammianus Marcellinus, 5
Amr, 67
Aneirin viii, 131
Anglo-Saxon Chronicles, xiv, 34, 38, 45, 55, 58, 60, 74-81, 91, 94-5, 100, 151, 164, 167-9, 171, 187-8, 190-1, 199, 201, 213, 218
Anna, Arthur's sister, 118, 158

Annales Cambriae, ix, xiv, 40, 43, 51, 69-72, 78, 94-5, 100-102, 110-12, 114, 117, 120, 142, 146-9, 159, 188-191, 193, 195-6, 206, 218, 225
Anthemius, Western Emperor, 17-8, 150
Antonine Wall, 4, 7, 35
Aqua Sulis *see* Bath
Arfderydd, 64, 70, 117, 159, 207
Artur Mac Aedan, 64-5, 147, 183, 200-201
Atrebates, 1
Attila the Hun, xii, 17
Aurelius Caninus, 43, 120
Avalon, 119, 124-6, 142, 149, 188, 198, 226

Badon, viii, ix, xi, xiii, xiv, 30-33, 38, 40-1, 43, 45-6, 50-51, 60-61, 64-5, 69-72, 79-80, 94-5, 100-102, 111-12, 115, 118-9, 123, 145, 161, 171, 174, 187-191, 193, 195, 201, 205-207, 212-3, 216, 218, 225-226
Bacaudae, 15
Baschurch, 200
Bassas, battle of, 60

see also Baschurch
Bath, 45-46, 71, 79-80, 118, 200, 214, 226
Bede, xi, xiv, 11, 13, 24-6, 31-2, 38, 43, 45-6, 47-52, 55, 58, 64-6, 68, 71-2, 75-6, 79-81, 82-4, 87, 90-3, 94-5, 100-101, 111-6, 120, 122, 151, 161-2, 167-8, 171, 176, 187, 190-1, 195, 199, 201-206, 213-4, 218, 225-6
Bedwyr, 104-105, 149
Bedivere, see Bedwyr
Belgae, 1, 46, 84, 186, 226
Bernicia, 64, 66, 71, 92-3, 117, 147, 167-8, 174, 181, 188, 207
Bonedd Y Saint, 159, 206
Breguoin see Agned
Bretwalda, 81, 93, 171, 190, 213, 216
Brigantes, 1
Budicus, 158
Builth, 67

Cai, 104-105, 149
Ceawlin, 78, 82, 171, 190, 213
Cador *see* Cadwy
Cadwy, 106-107, 118
Caerleon, 7, 33, 113, 198-9, 227
Caledfwlch, 198
Caliburn, 119, 195, 198
Camboglanna, 4
Camelon, 4
Camelot, ix, 4, 142, 149, 188, 198, 226
Camlann, ix, 40, 71-2, 111-12, 115, 119-20, 145, 150, 188, 190-1, 200, 210, 212

see also Gamlan, River
Camulodunum, 1-3
see also Colchester
Catevellauni, 1
Catigern, 58, 100
Caledonian Forest, 64, 70, 200
Celestine, Pope, 28
Celidonis, battle of, 64, 70, 118, 200
Celliwig *see* Kelliwig
Celyddon Forest *see* Celidonis
Cerdic, 73, 78-80, 83, 88, 151, 168, 171, 174, 190, 201, 212-4
Chelric, 119
Chester, 7, 33, 64, 70, 200
Childeric, xii, 105, 151
Chretien de Troyes, ix, 143, 154
City of the Legions, 33, 117
Claudius, 1, 3, 114
Claudus Claudianus, 21
Clovis I, xii, xiii, 13, 19, 118, 151-7, 190, 214
Coel Hen, 159, 177, 199, 207, 210-11, 215
Coelings *see* Coel Hen
Colchester, 7, 34, 200
see also Camulodunum
Conomer, 105, 152-3, 157
Constantine see Cuneglasus
Constantine III, x, xi, 5, 15-6, 24, 34-6, 40, 43, 115, 144, 150
Constantius of Lyon, 26, 28, 30, 47, 111
Comes Britanniarum, 8
Comet, 117, 119
Coroticus, 28-30
Culhwch and Olwen, 67, 174

Index

Cunedda, 111, 144, 158-60, 165-6, 174, 177, 206-207, 210-11, 215
Cuneglasus, 43, 182, 185, 200

Dalriada, 64, 85, 147, 200
Dal Riata *see* Dalriada
Deira, 89, 147, 167-8, 181, 216
Deisi, 166
Dream of Rhonabwy, 174, 193
Douglas, River *see* Dubglas
Dubglas, battle of, 60, 118
Dux Britanniarum, 7, 8, 59, 200
Dyfed, 69, 106, 159-60, 162, 166, 177, 183, 207

Eigr *see* Ygraine
Eliseg, pillar of, 162, 207
Eleutherius, Pope, 13
Elmet, 92, 147, 160, 174, 176, 181, 186, 216
Euric, King of the Goths, 17, 150
Excalibur, ix, 114, 119, 142, 149, 188, 226
see Caliburn, Sword in the stone,

Gallic Chronicle, xi, xiv, 10, 16, 24-7, 35, 37-8, 40, 51, 55, 75, 84, 87, 92, 94-5, 100-101, 116, 186-7, 189, 201, 203-4, 211, 218, 225
Gamlan, River, 200
Gawain, 118, 149
Geoffrey of Monmouth, viii, ix, xii, xiv, 13, 16, 19, 31, 43, 54, 72, 80, 100, 103-4, 108, 113-127, 128, 130-1, 142-4, 146-151, 153-4, 156, 158, 164, 174, 184, 188, 191, 194-5, 198-200, 211, 214-6, 218
Gerald of Wales, 45, 106, 124-6
Gewisse, 80-1, 90, 164, 214, 216, 226
Gildas, x, xi, xiii, xiv, 11, 13, 16, 20, 24, 26, 31-46, 47, 50-1, 54, 56, 58, 65-6, 71-3, 79-81, 81, 83-4, 87, 92, 94-5, 100, 102, 111, 114-6, 120, 122, 142, 144, 160-2, 164, 171, 174, 176, 181-2, 185-7, 190-1, 199-206, 210-14, 216, 218, 225-6
Life of Saint Gildas, 105-106, 125, 157
partition, 33-5, 41, 92, 102, 181, 186, 189, 216
Glastonbury, 106, 124-126, 200
Glein, battle of 60, 64, 170
Glycerus, Roman Emperor, 119
Glywysing, 177
Gododdin viii, 53, 131, 145, 147, 149, 160, 182, 186, 196, 224
Grail ix, 119, 125, 142-3, 149, 194, 198
Gregory of Tours 17-8, 20, 47, 150-153, 171, 215
Gregory, Pope, 13, 153
Guinnion, battle of 60, 70-1, 119
Guinevere see Gwenhwyfar
Guithelinus, 115, 158
Gwenhwyfar 106, 118, 124-5, 143, 149, 188, 200 195, 199, 226
Gwent, 176-7
Gwynedd, 43, 46, 53, 65, 69, 85, 107, 120, 158-60, 176

243

Hadrian's Wall 4, 7, 11-3, 33-35, 37, 64, 92, 95, 181, 200, 216, 227
Harleian Genealogies 120, 159-160, 162, 164, 166, 174, 206
Hengist and Horsa 52, 58, 60, 64-5, 67, 73, 75, 78-9, 81, 86, 91, 95, 100, 115, 117, 151, 160, 167-170, 177, 186-7, 189-190, 203-4, 207, 226
Henry of Huntingdon 123, 155
Historia *Brittonum* viii, xv, 25, 46, 53-68, 69-73, 75-6, 81, 94-5, 100-101, 104, 111-2, 114, 142, 149, 154, 158-161, 163, 165, 167, 176, 182-4, 188-9, 191, 194-6, 198, 204, 206, 216, 225-7
Historia Regnum Britanniae (History of the Kings of Britain), *see Geoffrey of Monmouth*
Honorius, x, xi, 15, 24, 34, 36, 114, 201-202

Iceni, x, 1-2
Ida 65-7, 78, 92, 167-8, 181, 184, 188-9, 194-5, 201, 205, 215, 225
Igraine *see* Ygraine
Ine, law code of, 88, 187

Jordanes 17-8, 20, 151
Julius Caesar 1, 3, 74, 114, 186

Kelliwig, 200

Lady in the Lake, 198
Lancelot, ix, 119, 149, 198, 226
Leo, Roman Emperor, 119, 122

Leo, Pope, 119
Liber Pontificalis, 13
Lincoln, 7, 33-4, 64, 86, 93, 115-6, 118, 160, 170, 181, 200, 216, 226
Lincolnshire *see* Lincoln
Lindsey, 47, 60, 85, 115, 160, 170,
see also Lincoln
Linnuis, 64, 160, 170, 200
see also Lincoln
Llandaff Charters, 176-7
Lucius Artorius Castus, 12-4
London, 1, 3-4, 7, 10, 24, 26, 33-4, 47, 76, 91-92, 113, 115-6, 121, 158, 181, 198, 200, 216, 227
Loth, 118, 158, 200
Lot see Loth
Lucius, King, 13

Mabinogion, 131, 154
Magnus Maximus, 5, 35, 40, 54, 114, 118, 150, 154, 158-9, 162-3, 166, 177, 194, 202, 205, 207, 211
Maelgwn, 43-44, 50, 94, 107, 111, 120, 144, 158, 160, 166, 174, 176, 187, 205-7, 210-11, 215, 226
Maglocunnus see Maelgwn
Medraut, ix, 70, 72, 118-9, 124, 158, 188, 199, 226
Medrawt see Medraut
Merlin, 64, 70, 80, 114, 116-7, 125, 142, 149, 154-5, 159, 188, 191, 200, 207, 226
Modred, see Medraut
Mordred, *see* Medraut
Myrddin Wylit, see Merlin

Index

Nennius, s*ee Historia Brittonum*
Notitia Dignitatum, 8, 161

Octa, see Octha
Octha, 58, 60, 76, 95, 115, 117-8, 160, 168-170, 174, 188, 212, 227
Odoacer, xii, 16-7, 19
Orosius, 47
Osla 'big-knife', *see* Octha

Palladius, 28, 75
Pelagian heresy, xi, 26-28, 201-202
Pen Rhionydd, 144
Percival, 149
Powys, 34, 56, 65, 93, 159, 162-4, 181, 200
Procopius, 82, 84, 151-2
Prosper of Aquitaine, 26

Ranulf Higden, 121
Renwein 115
Riothamus xiii, 17-20, 100, 118, 120, 150-2, 157, 190
Riotimus *see* Riothamus
Roman de Brut see Wace
Round table viii, ix, 114, 119, 128, 142, 144, 149, 188, 198

Saints Aaron and Julius, 33
Saint Alban, 33
Saint Albans, 1, 17, 26, 33-4, 91-2, 118, 181, 216
Saint Aurelian, 110, 157, 210
Saint Cadoc, 104-105, 111, 126, 210
Saint Carannog, 106, 111, 210

Saint Carantoc, see saint Carannog
Saint David, 110-11, 210
Saint David's, 69, 199
Saint Dubricius, 110-11, 117-8, 176, 210
Saint Efflam, 107
Saint Galgano, 144, 184, 188, 198
Saint Garmon, 111, 211
Saint Germanus, xi, 17, 20, 26-28, 30, 34, 37-8, 47, 56, 58, 67, 74, 94, 100, 107, 111, 115, 161, 163-4, 186, 202-203, 211-12, 225
Saint Goeznovius, 104, 156, 215
Saint Illtud, 110-111, 210-11
Saint Padarn 107, 111
Saint Patrick 13, 20, 28, 30, 35, 59-60, 66-7, 73, 75, 106, 125, 184, 195, 201-202, 225-6
Saint Samson 105, 107, 110-11, 117, 210
Saint Teilo 176
Sarmatians vi, 5, 11-12, 184, 199
Saxon Shore, 186, 212, 227
Count of, 7, 10, 25
forts, 7, 9-10, 46, 84, 181, 203
Stilicho 15-6, 35
Sword in the Stone, 114, 128, 142, 144, 149, 184, 198
Syagrius, xii, 17, 151-2, 154, 214

Tacitus, 3, 84, 183
Taliesin, viii, 131, 191, 194, 215
Thirteen Treasures of the Island of Britain, 107
Triads of Britain, 131, 144, 188, 198-9, 206, 215
Tribal Hidage, 80, 89-91

245

Tribuit, battle of 60
Tristan and Iseult 129, 157
Tryfrwyd *see Tribuit*
Twych Trwyth 67

Urien of Rheged, 53, 71, 93, 159, 176, 200, 207, 210-11, 215
Uther 16, 43, 115, 117-9, 143-4, 149, 158-9, 177, 188, 195, 199, 207, 210, 215, 226-7

Verulamium, *see* Saint Albans
Viroconium, *see* Wroxeter
Vortigern, xi, 28, 45, 50, 52, 54-5, 58, 65-7, 70, 75, 79-80, 91, 94-5, 100, 104, 115-7, 120, 122, 158-160, 163-4, 166-7, 177, 189-90, 194, 203-204, 206-207, 210-11, 214, 225

Vortimer, 58, 66, 75, 95, 100, 115, 118, 163, 167, 203-204, 210, 215
Vortipor, 43-4, 120, 160, 162, 176-7, 183, 207

Wace ix, 154
William of Malmesbury 122, 125
William of Newburgh 121
Winchester, 73, 84, 116, 119
Wroxeter, 91, 200, 203

Ygraine 118, 137, 149, 159, 177, 195, 199, 207, 226
York, 5, 7, 12, 33-4, 116-8, 176, 181, 200, 216, 227

Zeno, Eastern Emperor 51, 76, 111, 120, 190, 205, 207, 210-11, 215, 218